56th Annual Meeting of the Association for Computational Linguistics (ACL 2018)

System Demonstrations

Melbourne, Australia
15 – 20 July 2018

ISBN: 978-1-5108-6708-6

ACL 2018

The 56th Annual Meeting of the Association for Computational Linguistics

Proceedings of System Demonstrations

July 15 - July 20, 2018
Melbourne, Australia

Introduction

Welcome to the proceedings of the system demonstrations session. This volume contains the papers of the system demonstrations presented at the 56th Annual Meeting of the Association for Computational Linguistics on July 15-20, 2018 in Melbourne, Australia.

The ACL 2018 demonstrations track invites submissions ranging from early research prototypes to mature production-ready systems. We received 79 submissions this year, of which 24 were selected for inclusion in the program (acceptance rate of 30%) after review by three members of the program committee.

We would like to thank the members of the program committee for their timely help in reviewing the submissions. A subset of the program committee members also helped us in selecting the best demo paper. The candidate papers were selected by the demo chairs based on the feedback received by reviewers. These are the papers nominated for the best demo paper:

- **CRUISE: Cold-Start New Skill Development via Iterative Utterance Generation** by Yilin Shen, Avik Ray, Abhishek Patel and Hongxia Jin

- **Out-of-the-box Universal Romanization Tool** by Ulf Hermjakob, Jonathan May and Kevin Knight

- **Platforms for Non-Speakers Annotating Names in Any Language** by Ying Lin, Cash Costello, Boliang Zhang, Di Lu, Heng Ji, James Mayfield and Paul McNamee

- **YEDDA: A lightweight Collaborative Text Span Annotation Tool** by Jie Yang, Yue Zhang, Linwei Li and Xingxuan Li

The winner of the best demo paper will be announced at ACL 2018. We would like to thank the best demo paper committee for their dedicated work in this task. Lastly, we thank the many authors that submitted their work to the demonstrations track.

Demonstrations papers will be presented during the three day conference along side the poster sessions.

Best,
Fei Liu and Thamar Solorio
ACL 2018 Demonstration Track Chairs

Demonstration Chairs:

Fei Liu, Univeristy of Central Florida
Thamar Solorio, University of Houston

Program Committee:

Marianna Apidianaki
John Arevalo
Alberto Barrón-Cedeño
Laurent Besacier
Yonatan Bisk
Eduardo Blanco
Chris Brockett
Vittorio Castelli
Arun Chaganty
Kai-Wei Chang
Angel Chang
Chen Chen
Christian Chiarcos
Hai Leong Chieu
Eunsol Choi
Christos Christodoulopoulos
Stephen Clark
Vincent Claveau
Anne Cocos
Bonaventura Coppola
Danilo Croce
Marina Danilevsky
Daniël de Kok
Vera Demberg
Jesse Dodge
Doug Downey
Carsten Eickhoff
Tomaž Erjavec
Yansong Feng
Annemarie Friedrich
Dimitris Galanis
Michael Gamon
Marcos Garcia
Tao Ge
Filip Ginter
Pawan Goyal
Sonal Gupta
Ben Hachey
Dilek Hakkani-Tur
Xianpei Han
Ales Horak
Shajith Ikbal

Mamoru Komachi

Valia Kordoni

Jayant Krishnamurthy

Carolin Lawrence

John Lee

Alessandro Lenci

Kang Liu

Nikola Ljubešić

Adrian Pastor López Monroy

Wei Lu

Nitin Madnani

Suraj Maharjan

Wolfgang Maier

Suresh Manandhar

Benjamin Marie

Stella Markantonatou

Pascual Martínez-Gómez

Yelena Mejova

Ivan Vladimir Meza Ruiz

Makoto Miwa

Taesun Moon

Roser Morante

Alessandro Moschitti

Philippe Muller

Preslav Nakov

Borja Navarro-Colorado

Vincent Ng

Hiroshi Noji

Pierre Nugues

Naoaki Okazaki

Constantin Orasan

Yannick Parmentier

Verónica Pérez-Rosas

Mohammad Taher Pilehvar

Stelios Piperidis

Maja Popović

John Prager

Prokopis Prokopidis

Alessandro Raganato

Altaf Rahman

Carlos Ramisch

German Rigau

Angus Roberts

Saurav Sahay

Satoshi Sekine

Michel Simard

Sameer Singh

Sunayana Sitaram

Vivek Srikumar

Irina Temnikova

Juan-Manuel Torres-Moreno

Andrea Varga
David Vilares
Svitlana Volkova
Ivan Vulić
V.G.Vinod Vydiswaran
Byron Wallace
William Yang Wang
Rui Wang
Huazheng Wang
Guillaume Wisniewski
Qingyun Wu
Kun Xu
tae yano
Hai Zhao
Jun Zhao
Guangyou Zhou
Imed Zitouni
Pierre Zweigenbaum

Best Demo Paper Selection Committee:

Michael Gamon
Vivek Srikumar
Benjamin Marie
Alessandro Raganato

Table of Contents

Conference Program

July 16th, 2018

12:30PM–14:00PM Demo Poster Session 1

Platforms for Non-speakers Annotating Names in Any Language
Ying Lin, Cash Costello, Boliang Zhang, Di Lu, Heng Ji, James Mayfield and Paul McNamee

NovelPerspective: Identifying Point of View Characters
Lyndon White, Roberto Togneri, Wei Liu and Mohammed Bennamoun

Out-of-the-box Universal Romanization Tool uroman
Ulf Hermjakob, Jonathan May and Kevin Knight

HarriGT: A Tool for Linking News to Science
James Ravenscroft, Amanda Clare and Maria Liakata

Jack the Reader – A Machine Reading Framework
Dirk Weissenborn, Pasquale Minervini, Isabelle Augenstein, Johannes Welbl, Tim Rocktäschel, Matko Bosnjak, Jeff Mitchell, Thomas Demeester, Tim Dettmers, Pontus Stenetorp and Sebastian Riedel

YEDDA: A Lightweight Collaborative Text Span Annotation Tool
Jie Yang, Yue Zhang, Linwei Li and Xingxuan Li

NextGen AML: Distributed Deep Learning based Language Technologies to Augment Anti Money Laundering Investigation
Jingguang Han, Utsab Barman, Jeremiah Hayes, Jinhua Du, Edward Burgin and Dadong Wan

NLP Web Services for Resource-Scarce Languages
Martin Puttkammer, Roald Eiselen, Justin Hocking and Frederik Koen

12:30PM–14:00PM Demo Poster Session 2

DCFEE: A Document-level Chinese Financial Event Extraction System based on Automatically Labeled Training Data
Hang Yang, Yubo Chen, Kang Liu, Yang Xiao and Jun Zhao

Sentence Suggestion of Japanese Functional Expressions for Chinese-speaking Learners
Jun Liu, Hiroyuki Shindo and Yuji Matsumoto

Translating a Language You Don't Know In the Chinese Room
Ulf Hermjakob, Jonathan May, Michael Pust and Kevin Knight

SANTO: A Web-based Annotation Tool for Ontology-driven Slot Filling
Matthias Hartung, Hendrik ter Horst, Frank Grimm, Tim Diekmann, Roman Klinger and Philipp Cimiano

NCRF++: An Open-source Neural Sequence Labeling Toolkit
Jie Yang and Yue Zhang

TALEN: Tool for Annotation of Low-resource ENtities
Stephen Mayhew and Dan Roth

A Web-scale system for scientific knowledge exploration
Zhihong Shen, Hao Ma and Kuansan Wang

ScoutBot: A Dialogue System for Collaborative Navigation
Stephanie M. Lukin, Felix Gervits, Cory Hayes, Pooja Moolchandani, Anton Leuski, John Rogers, Carlos Sanchez Amaro, Matthew Marge, Clare Voss and David Traum

12:30PM–14:00PM Demo Poster Session 3

The SUMMA Platform: A Scalable Infrastructure for Multi-lingual Multi-media Monitoring
Ulrich Germann, Renars Liepins, Guntis Barzdins, Didzis Gosko, Sebastião Miranda and David Nogueira

CRUISE: Cold-Start New Skill Development via Iterative Utterance Generation
Yilin Shen, Avik Ray, Abhishek Patel and Hongxia Jin

Praaline: An Open-Source System for Managing, Annotating, Visualising and Analysing Speech Corpora
George Christodoulides

Marian: Fast Neural Machine Translation in C++
Marcin Junczys-Dowmunt, Roman Grundkiewicz, Tomasz Dwojak, Hieu Hoang, Kenneth Heafield, Tom Neckermann, Frank Seide, Ulrich Germann, Alham Fikri Aji, Nikolay Bogoychev, André F. T. Martins and Alexandra Birch

DeepPavlov: Open-Source Library for Dialogue Systems
Mikhail Burtsev, Alexander Seliverstov, Rafael Airapetyan, Mikhail Arkhipov, Dilyara Baymurzina, Nickolay Bushkov, Olga Gureenkova, Taras Khakhulin, Yuri Kuratov, Denis Kuznetsov, Alexey Litinsky, Varvara Logacheva, Alexey Lymar, Valentin Malykh, Maxim Petrov, Vadim Polulyakh, Leonid Pugachev, Alexey Sorokin, Maria Vikhreva and Marat Zaynutdinov

RETURNN as a Generic Flexible Neural Toolkit with Application to Translation and Speech Recognition
Albert Zeyer, Tamer Alkhouli and Hermann Ney

A Flexible, Efficient and Accurate Framework for Community Question Answering Pipelines
Salvatore Romeo, Giovanni Da San Martino, Alberto Barrón-Cedeño and Alessandro Moschitti

Moon IME: Neural-based Chinese Pinyin Aided Input Method with Customizable Association
Yafang Huang, Zuchao Li, Zhuosheng Zhang and Hai Zhao

Platforms for Non-Speakers Annotating Names in Any Language

Ying Lin,[1] Cash Costello,[2] Boliang Zhang,[1] Di Lu,[1]
Heng Ji,[1] James Mayfield,[2] Paul McNamee[2]
[1] Rensselaer Polytechnic Institute
{liny9,zhangb8,lud2,jih}@rpi.edu
[2] Johns Hopkins University
{ccostel2,mayfield,mcnamee}@jhu.edu

Abstract

We demonstrate two annotation platforms that allow an English speaker to annotate names for any language without knowing the language. These platforms provided high-quality *"silver standard"* annotations for low-resource language name taggers (Zhang et al., 2017) that achieved state-of-the-art performance on two surprise languages (Oromo and Tigrinya) at LoreHLT2017[1] and ten languages at TAC-KBP EDL2017 (Ji et al., 2017). We discuss strengths and limitations and compare other methods of creating silver- and gold-standard annotations using native speakers. We will make our tools publicly available for research use.

1 Introduction

Although researchers have been working on unsupervised and semi-supervised approaches to alleviate the demand for training data, most state-of-the-art models for name tagging, especially neural network-based models (Pan et al., 2017; Zhang et al., 2017) still rely on a large amount of training data to achieve good performance. When applied to low-resource languages, these models suffer from data sparsity. Traditionally, native speakers of a language have been asked to annotate a corpus in that language. This approach is uneconomical for several reasons. First, for some languages

with extremely low resources, it's not easy to access native speakers for annotation. For example, Chechen is only spoken by 1.4 million people and Rejiang is spoken by 200,000 people. Second, it is costly in both time and money to write an annotation guideline for a low-resource language and to train native speakers (who are usually not linguists) to learn the guidelines and qualify for annotation tasks. Third, we observed poor annotation quality and low inter-annotator agreement among newly trained native speakers in spite of high language proficiency. For example, under DARPA LORELEI,[2] the performance of two native Uighur speakers on name tagging was only 69% and 73% F_1-score respectively.

Previous efforts to generate "silver-standard" annotations used Web search (An et al., 2003), parallel data(Wang and Manning, 2014), Wikipedia markups (Nothman et al., 2013; Tsai et al., 2016; Pan et al., 2017), and crowdsourcing (Finin et al., 2010). Annotations produced by these methods are usually noisy and specific to a particular writing style (e.g., Wikipedia articles), yielding unsatisfactory results and poor portability.

It is even more expensive to teach English-speaking annotators new languages. But can we annotate names in a language we don't know? Let's examine a Somali sentence:

> *"Sida uu saxaafadda u sheegay Dr **Jaamac Warsame Cali** oo fadhigiisu yahay magaalada **Baardheere** hadda waxaa shuban caloolaha la yaalla xarumaha caafimaadka 15-cunug oo lagu arkay fuuq bax joogto ah, wuxuu xusay dhakhtarku in ay wadaan dadaallo ay wax kaga qabanayaan xaaladdan"*

Without knowing anything about Somali, an English speaker can guess that "*Jaamac Warsame Cali*" is a person name because it's capitalized, the

We thank Kevin Blissett and Tongtao Zhang from RPI for their contributions to the annotations used for the experiments. This material is based upon work supported by the Defense Advanced Research Projects Agency (DARPA) under Contracts No. HR0011-15-C-0115 and No. HR0011-16-C-0102. The views, opinions and/or findings expressed are those of the authors and should not be interpreted as representing the official views or policies of the Department of Defense or the U.S. Government.

[1] https://www.nist.gov/itl/iad/mig/lorehlt-evaluations

[2] https://www.darpa.mil/program/low-resource-languages-for-emergent-incidents

Proceedings of the 56th Annual Meeting of the Association for Computational Linguistics-System Demonstrations, pages 1–6
Melbourne, Australia, July 15 - 20, 2018. ©2018 Association for Computational Linguistics

word on its left, "*Dr,*" is similar to "*Dr.*" in English, and its spelling looks similar to the English "*Jamac Warsame Ali.*" Similarly, we can identify "*Baardheere*" as a location name if we know that "*magaalada*" in English is "*town*" from a common word dictionary, and its spelling is similar to the English name "*Bardhere.*"

What about languages that are not written in Roman (Latin) script? Fortunately language universal romanization (Hermjakob et al., 2018) or transliteration[3] tools are available for most living languages. For example, the following is a Tigrinya sentence and its romanized form:

"ናይዚ እዋን'ዚ ፕረዝደንት ዓብደልፈታሕ አል-ሲሲ ነቲ ናይ 2011 ዓ.ም.ፈ ተቃውሞ ብምንኣድ እቲ ተቃውሚ ሓዳስ ግብጺ ዘምጸእ'ዩ ኢሎም ::"

"*naayezi 'ewaane'zi perazedanete **'aabedale-fataahhe 'ale-sisi** nati naaye 2011 'aa.me.fa taqaawemo bemene'aade 'eti taqaawemi hhaadaase gebetsi zametsa'a 'yulome .*"

An English speaker can guess that "ዓብደልፈታሕ አል-ሲሲ." is a person name because its romanized form "*aabedalefataahhe 'ale-sisi*" sounds similar to the English name "*Abdel-Fattah el-Sissi,*" and the romanized form of the word on its left, "ፕረዝደንት," (*perazedanete*) sounds similar to the English word "*president.*"

Moreover, annotators (may) acquire language-specific patterns and rules gradually during annotation; e.g., a capitalized word preceded by "*magaalaa*" is likely to be a city name in Oromo, such as "*magaalaa Adaamaa*" (Adama city). Synchronizing such knowledge among annotators both improves annotation quality and boosts productivity.

The Information Sciences Institute (ISI) developed a "*Chinese Room*" interface[4] to allow a non-native speaker to translate foreign language text into English, based on a small set of parallel sentences that include overlapped words. Inspired by this, RPI and JHU developed two collaborative annotation platforms that exploit linguistic intuitions and resources to allow non-native speakers to perform name tagging efficiently and effectively.

2 Desiderata

We see the following requirements as being most important to allow a non-speaker to annotate a language, independent of interface. None of these requirements is necessary, but the more that are satisfied, the easier it will be for the annotator to produce accurate annotations:

Word recognition. Presentation of text in a familiar alphabet makes it easier to see similarities and differences between text segments, to learn aspects of the target language morphology, and to remember sequences previously seen.

Word pronunciation. Because named entities often are transliterated into another language, access to the sound of the words is particularly important for annotating names. Sounds can be exposed either through a formal expression language such as IPA,[5] or by transliteration into the appropriate letters of the annotator's native language.

Word and sentence meaning. The better the annotator understands the full meaning of the text being annotated, the easier it will be both to identify which named entities are likely to be mentioned in the text and what the boundaries of those mentions are. Meaning can be conveyed in a variety of ways: dictionary lookup to provide fixed meanings for individual words and phrases; description of the position of a word or phrase in a semantic space (e.g., Brown clusters or embedding space) to define words that are not found in a dictionary; and full sentence translation.

Word context. Understanding how a word is used in a given instance can benefit greatly from understanding how that word is used broadly, either across the document being annotated, or across a larger corpus of monolingual text. For example, knowing that a word frequently appears adjacent to a known person name suggests it might be a surname, even if the adjacent word in the current context is not known to be a name.

World knowledge. Knowledge of some of the entities, relations, and events referred to in the text allows the annotator to form a stronger model of what the text as a whole might be saying (e.g., a document about disease outbreak is likely to include organizations like Red Cross), leading to better judgments about components of the text.

History. Annotations previously applied to a use of a word form a strong prior on how a new instance of the word should be tagged. While some of this knowledge is held by the annotator, it is difficult to maintain such knowledge over time. Programmatic support for capturing prior conclusions (linguistic patterns, word translations, possible annotations for a mention along with their frequency) and making them available to the annotator is essential for large collaborative annotation efforts.

---

[3]https://github.com/andyhu/transliteration
[4]https://www.isi.edu/ ulf/croom/ChineseRoomEditor.html

[5]https://en.wikipedia.org/wiki/IPA

Adjudication. Disagreements among annotators can indicate cases that require closer examination. An adjudication interface is beneficial to enhance precision (see Section 4).

The next section discusses how we embody these requirements in two annotation platforms.

3 Annotation Platforms

We developed two annotation tools to explore the range of ways the desiderata might be fulfilled: ELISA and Dragonfly. After describing these interfaces, Figure 1 shows how they fulfill the desiderata outlined in Table 2.

3.1 ELISA

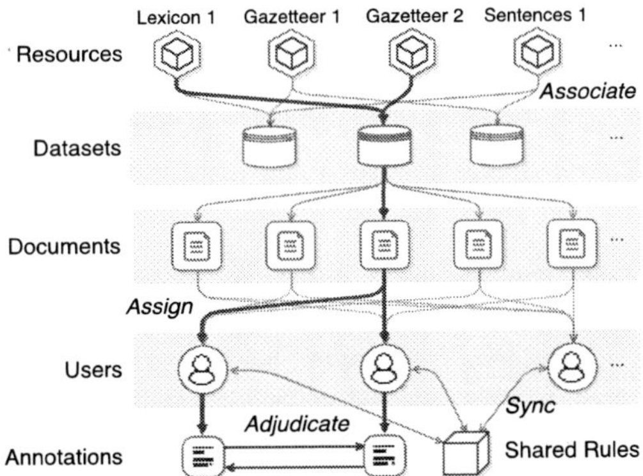

Figure 1: ELISA IE Annotation Architecture.

The ELISA IE annotation platform was developed at Rensselaer Polytechnic Institute.[6] Figure 1 depicts ELISA's overall architecture. Figure 2 demonstrates the main annotation interface, which consists of:

Annotation Panel. For each sentence in a document, we show the text in the original language, its English translation if available, and automatic romanization results generated with a language-universal transliteration library.[7] To label a name mention, the annotator clicks its first and last tokens, then chooses the desired entity type in the annotation panel. If the selected text span has been labeled before, previous annotations are displayed at the bottom of the panel for reference. Annotated mentions are styled differently according to type.

Resource Lookup Panel. This panel is used to browse/search the associated resources. Right clicking a token in the document will show its full definition in lexicons and bilingual example sentences containing that token. A floating pop-up displaying romanization and simple definition appears instantly when hovering over a token.

Rule Editor. Annotators may discover useful hueristics to identify and classify names, such as personal designators and suffixes indicative of locations. They can encode such clues as *rules* in the rule editor. Once created, each rule is rendered as a strikethrough line in the text and is shared among annotators. For example (Figure 1, if an annotator marks *"agency"* as an organization, all annotators will see a triangular sign below each occurrence of this word.

Adjudication Interface. If multiple users process the same document we can consolidate their annotations through an adjudication interface (Figure 3). This interface is similar to the annotation interface, except that competing annotations are displayed as blocks below the text. Clicking a block will accept the associated annotation. The adjudicator can accept annotations from either annotator or accept the agreed cases at once by clicking one of the three interface buttons. Then, the adjudicator need only focus on disputed cases, which are highlighted with a red background.

3.2 Dragonfly

Dragonfly, developed at the Johns Hopkins University Applied Physics Laboratory, takes a more word-centric approach to annotation. Each sentence to be annotated is laid out in a row, each column of which shows a word augmented with a variety of information about that word.

Figure 4 shows a screenshot of a portion of the Dragonfly tool being used to annotate text written in the Kannada language. The top entry in each column is the Kannada word. Next is a Romanization of the word (Hermjakob et al., 2018). The third entry is one or more dictionary translations, if available. The fourth entry is a set of dictionary translations of other words in the word's Brown cluster. (Brown et al., 1992) While these tend to be less accurate than translations of the word, they can give a strong signal that a word falls into a particular category. For example, a Brown cluster containing translations such as *"Paris," "Rome"* and *"Vienna"* is likely to refer to a city, even if no translation exists to indicate which city. Finally, if automated labels for the sentence have been generated, e.g., by a trained name tagger, those labels

---

[6]See examples at http://nlp.cs.rpi.edu/demo/elisa_annotation.html.

[7]https://github.com/andyhu/transliteration

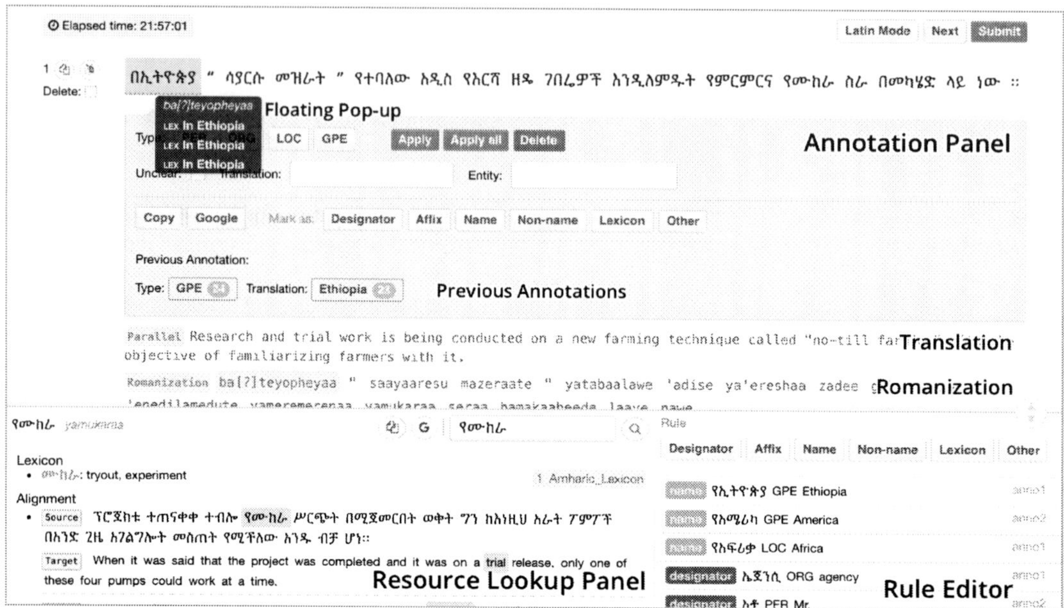

Figure 2: ELISA IE Annotation Interface in use annotating a Tigrinya document.

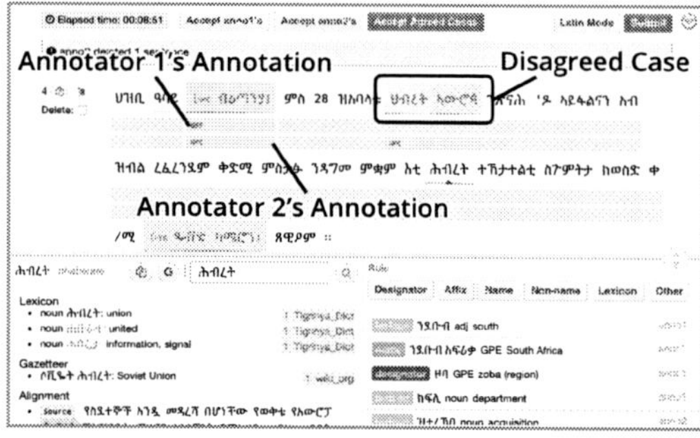

Figure 3: ELISA IE Adjudication Interface in use annotating a Tigrinya document.

are displayed at the bottom of the column.

In addition to word-specific information, Dragonfly can present sentence-level information. In Figure 4, an automatic English translation of the sentence is shown above the words of the sentence (in this example, from Google Translate). Translations might also be available when annotating a parallel document collection. Other sentence-level information that might prove useful in this slot includes a topic model description, or a bilingual embedding of the entire sentence.

Figure 4 shows a short sentence that has been annotated with two name mentions. The first word of the sentence (Romanization "*uttara*") has translations of "*due north*," "*northward*," "*north*,"

etc. The second word has no direct translations or Brown cluster entries. However, its Romanization, "*koriyaavannu*," begins with a sequence that suggests the word 'Korea' with a morphological ending. Even without the presence of the phrase "*North Korea*" in the MT output, an annotator likely has enough information to draw the conclusion that the GPE "*North Korea*" is mentioned here. The presence of the phrase "*North Korea*" in the machine translation output confirms this choice.

The sentence also contains a word whose Romanization is "*ttramp*." This is a harder call. There is no translation, and the Brown cluster translations do not help. Knowledge of world events, examination of other sentences in the document, the translation of the following word, and the MT output together suggest that this is a mention of "*Donald Trump*;" it can thus be annotated as a person.

4   Experiments

We asked ten non-speakers to annotate names using our annotation platforms on documents in various low-resource languages released by the DARPA LORELEI program and the NIST TAC-KBP2017 EDL Pilot (Ji et al., 2017). The genres of these documents include newswire, discussion forum and tweets. Using non-speaker annotations as "*silver-standard*" training data, we trained

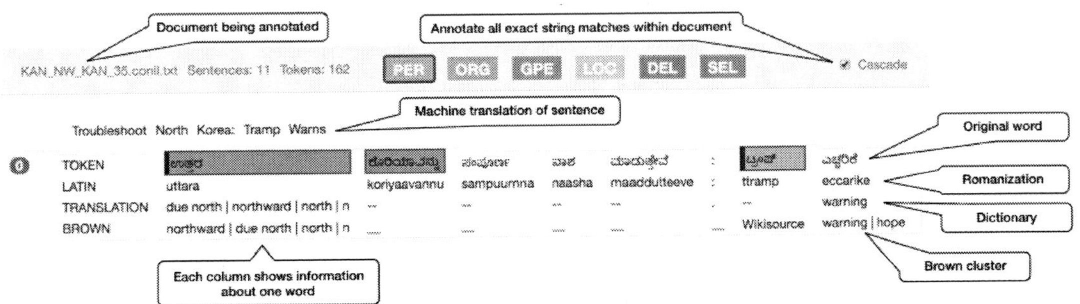

Figure 4: The Dragonfly tool in use annotating a Kannada document.

	ELISA	Dragonfly
Recognition & pronunciation	universal transliteration	uroman
Meanings	Resource Lookup Panel; pop-ups; Annotation Panel	Dictionary; Brown clusters; sentence translation
Word context	Resource Lookup Panel	Concordance
World knowledge	External	External
History	Previous annotations; Rule Editor	Cascade; pop-ups
Adjudication	Adjudication interface	None

Table 1: How Platforms Fulfill Desiderata

name taggers based on a bi-directional long short-term memory (LSTM) network with a Conditional Random Fields (CRFs) layer (Lample et al., 2016). The lexicons loaded into the ELISA IE annotation platform were acquired from Panlex,[8] Geonames[9] and Wiktionary.[10] Dragonfly used bilingual lexicons by (Rolston and Kirchhoff, 2016).

4.1 Overall Performance

The agreement between non-speaker annotations from the ELISA annotation platform and gold standard annotations from LDC native speakers on the same documents is between 72% and 85% for various languages. The ELISA platform enables us to develop cross-lingual entity discovery and linking systems which achieved state-of-the-art performance at both NIST LoreHLT2017[11] and ten languages at TAC-KBP EDL2017 evaluations (Ji et al., 2017).

	Albanian	Kannada	Nepali	Polish	Swahili
#sents	1,652	535	959	1,933	1,714
#tokens	41,785	8,158	16,036	26,924	42,715
#dict entries	96,911	9,931	10,048	644,232	216,323
#names	2,683	900	1,413	1,356	2,769
F_1(%)	75.9	58.4	65.0	55.7	74.2

Table 2: Data Statistics and Performance on KBP2017 EDL Pilot

Four annotators used two platforms (two each) to annotate 50 VOA news documents for each of the five languages listed in Table 2. Their annotations were then adjudicated through the ELISA adjudication interface. The process took about one week. For each language we used 40 documents for training and 10 documents for test in the TAC-KBP2017 EDL Pilot. In Table 2 we see that the languages with more annotated names (i.e., Albanian and Swahili) achieved higher performance.

4.2 Silver Standard Creation

We compare our method with Wikipedia based silver standard annotations (Pan et al., 2017) on Oromo and Tigrinya, two low-resource languages in the LoreHLT2017 evaluation. Table 3 shows the data statistics. We can see that with the ELISA annotation platform we were able to acquire many more topically-relevant training sentences and thus achieved much higher performance.

Data	Oromo	Tigrinya
ELISA Annotated Training	4,717	6,174
Wikipedia Markup Derived Training	631	152
Gold Standard Unsequestered	2,957	2,201

Table 3: # Sentences in Oromo and Tigrinya Data.

[8]https://panlex.org/
[9]http://www.geonames.org/
[10]https://www.wiktionary.org/
[11]https://www.nist.gov/itl/iad/mig/lorehlt-evaluations

Method	Oromo	Tigrinya
ELISA Annotated	**68.2**	**71.3**
Wikipedia Markup	6.2	2.7

Table 4: Comparison of Silver Standard Creation Methods (F-score %).

4.3 Comparison with Native Speaker Annotations

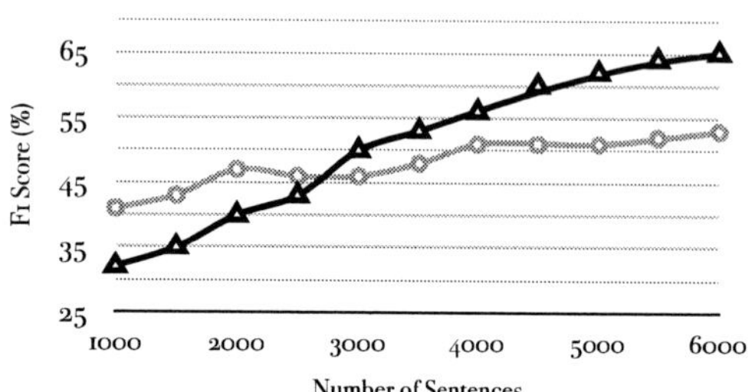

Figure 5: Russian Name Tagging Performance Using Native-speaker and Non-speaker Annotations.

Figure 5 compares the performance of Russian name taggers trained from Gold Standard by LDC native speakers and Silver Standard by non-speakers through our annotation platforms, testing on 1,952 sentences with ground truth annotated by LDC native speakers. Our annotation platforms got off to a good start and offered higher performance than annotations from native speakers, because non-speakers quickly capture common names, which can be synthesized as effective features and patterns for our name tagger. However, after all low-hanging fruit was picked, it became difficult for non-speakers to discover many uncommon names due to the limited coverage of lexicon and romanization; thus the performance of the name tagger converged quickly and hits an upper-bound. For example, the most frequently missed names by non-speakers include organization abbreviations and uncommon person names.

4.4 Impact of Adjudication

Table 5 shows that the adjudication process significantly improved precision because annotators were able to fix annotation errors after extensive discussions on disputed cases and also gradually learned annotation rules and linguistic patterns. Most missing errors remained unfixed during the adjudication so the recall was not improved.

Language	Adjudication	P (%)	R (%)	F (%)
Oromo	Before	68.6	61.3	64.7
	After	**76.2**	**61.8**	**68.2**
Tigrinya	Before	67.3	67.1	67.2
	After	**76.4**	66.8	**71.3**

Table 5: Impact of Annotation Adjudication

References

J. An, S. Lee, and G. G. Lee. 2003. Automatic acquisition of named entity tagged corpus from world wide web. In *ACL*.

P. F. Brown, P. V. deSouza, R. L. Mercer, V. J. D. Pietra, and J. C. Lai. 1992. Class-based n-gram models of natural language. *COLING* .

T. Finin, W. Murnane, A. Karandikar, N. Keller, J. Martineau, and M. Dredze. 2010. Annotating named entities in twitter data with crowdsourcing. In *NAACL HLT 2010 Workshop*.

U. Hermjakob, J. May, and K. Knight. 2018. Out-of-the-box universal romanization tool uroman. In *PRoc. ACL2018 Demo Track*.

H. Ji, X. Pan, B. Zhang, J. Nothman, J. Mayfield, P. McNamee, and C. Costello. 2017. Overview of TAC-KBP2017 13 languages entity discovery and linking. In *TAC*.

G. Lample, M. Ballesteros, K. Kawakami, S. Subramanian, and C. Dyer. 2016. Neural architectures for named entity recognition. In *NAACL HLT*.

J. Nothman, N. Ringland, W. Radford, T. Murphy, and J. R Curran. 2013. Learning multilingual named entity recognition from wikipedia. *Artificial Intelligence* 194:151–175.

X. Pan, B. Zhang, J. May, J. Nothman, K. Knight, and H. Ji. 2017. Cross-lingual name tagging and linking for 282 languages. In *ACL*.

Leanne Rolston and Katrin Kirchhoff. 2016. Collection of bilingual data for lexicon transfer learning. In *UWEE Technical Report*.

C. Tsai, S. Mayhew, and D. Roth. 2016. Cross-lingual named entity recognition via wikification. In *CoNLL*.

M. Wang and C. Manning. 2014. Cross-lingual projected expectation regularization for weakly supervised learning. *Transactions of the Association of Computational Linguistics* 2:55–66.

B. Zhang, X. Pan, Y. Lin, T. Zhang, K. Blissett, S. Kazemi, S. Whitehead, L. Huang, and H. Ji. 2017. RPI BLENDER TAC-KBP2017 13 languages EDL system. In *TAC*.

NovelPerspective: Identifying Point of View Characters

Lyndon White, Roberto Togneri, Wei Liu, and **Mohammed Bennamoun**
`lyndon.white@research.uwa.edu.au, roberto.togneri@uwa.edu.au,`
`wei.liu@uwa.edu.au,` and `mohammed.bennamoun@uwa.edu.au`
The University of Western Australia.
35 Stirling Highway, Crawley, Western Australia

Abstract

We present NovelPerspective: a tool to allow consumers to subset their digital literature, based on point of view (POV) character. Many novels have multiple main characters each with their own storyline running in parallel. A well-known example is George R. R. Martin's novel: "A Game of Thrones", and others from that series. Our tool detects the main character that each section is from the POV of, and allows the user to generate a new ebook with only those sections. This gives consumers new options in how they consume their media; allowing them to pursue the storylines sequentially, or skip chapters about characters they find boring. We present two heuristic-based baselines, and two machine learning based methods for the detection of the main character.

1 Introduction

Often each section of a novel is written from the perspective of a different main character. The characters each take turns in the spot-light, with their own parallel storylines being unfolded by the author. As readers, we have often desired to read just one storyline at a time, particularly when reading the book a second-time. In this paper, we present a tool, NovelPerspective, to give the consumer this choice.

Our tool allows the consumer to select which characters of the book they are interested in, and to generate a new ebook file containing just the sections from that character's point of view (POV). The critical part of this system is the detection of the POV character. This is not an insurmountable task, building upon the well established field of named entity recognition. However to our knowledge there is no software to do this. Such a tool would have been useless, in decades past when booked were distributed only on paper. But today, the surge in popularity of ebooks has opened a new niche for consumer narrative processing. Methods are being created to extract social relationships between characters (Elson et al., 2010; Wohlgenannt et al., 2016); to align scenes in movies with those from books (Zhu et al., 2015); and to otherwise augment the literature consumption experience. Tools such as the one presented here, give the reader new freedoms in controlling how they consume their media.

Having a large cast of characters, in particular POV characters, is a hallmark of the epic fantasy genre. Well known examples include: George R.R. Martin's "A Song of Ice and Fire", Robert Jordan's "Wheel of Time", Brandon Sanderson's "Cosmere" universe, and Steven Erikson's "Malazan Book of the Fallen", amongst thousands of others. Generally, these books are written in *limited* third-person POV; that is to say the reader has little or no more knowledge of the situation described than the main character does.

We focus here on novels written in the *limited* third-person POV. In these stories, the main character is, for our purposes, the POV character. Limited third-person POV is written in the third-person, that is to say the character is referred to by name, but with the observations limited to being from the perspective of that character. This is in-contrast to the *omniscient* third-person POV, where events are described by an external narrator. Limited third-person POV is extremely popular in modern fiction. It preserves the advantages of first-person, in allowing the reader to observe inside the head of the character, while also allowing the flexibility to the perspective of another character (Booth, 1961). This allows for multiple concurrent storylines around different characters.

Proceedings of the 56th Annual Meeting of the Association for Computational Linguistics-System Demonstrations, pages 7–12
Melbourne, Australia, July 15 - 20, 2018. ©2018 Association for Computational Linguistics

Our tool helps users un-entwine such storylines, giving the option to process them sequentially.

The utility of dividing a book in this way varies with the book in question. Some books will cease to make sense when the core storyline crosses over different characters. Other novels, particularly in epic fantasy genre, have parallel storylines which only rarely intersect. While we are unable to find a formal study on this, anecdotally many readers speak of:

- "Skipping the chapters about the boring characters."

- "Only reading the *real* main character's sections."

- "Reading ahead, past the side-stories, to get on with the *main* plot."

Particularly if they have read the story before, and thus do not risk confusion. Such opinions are a matter of the consumer's personal taste. The NovelPerspective tool gives the reader the option to customise the book in this way, according to their personal preference.

We note that sub-setting the novel once does not prevent the reader from going back and reading the intervening chapters if it ceases to make sense, or from sub-setting again to get the chapters for another character whose path intersects with the storyline they are currently reading. We can personally attest for some books reading the chapters one character at a time is indeed possible, and pleasant: the first author of this paper read George R.R. Martin's "A Song of Ice and Fire" series in exactly this fashion.

The primary difficulty in segmenting ebooks this way is attributing each section to its POV character. That is to say detecting who is the point of view character. Very few books indicate this clearly, and the reader is expected to infer it during reading. This is easy for most humans, but automating it is a challenge. To solve this, the core of our tool is its character classification system. We investigated several options which the main text of this paper will discuss.

2 Character Classification Systems

The full NovelPerspective pipeline is shown in Figure 1. The core character classification step (step 3), is detailed in Figure 2. In this step the raw text is first enriched with parts of speech, and named entity tags. We do not perform co-reference resolution, working only with direct entity mentions. From this, features are extracted for each named entity. These feature vectors are used to score the entities for the most-likely POV character. The highest scoring character is returned by the system. The different systems presented modify the **Feature Extraction** and **Character Scoring** steps. A broadly similar idea, for detecting the focus location of news articles, was presented by (Imani et al., 2017).

2.1 Baseline systems

To the best of our knowledge no systems have been developed for this task before. As such, we have developed two deterministic baseline character classifiers. These are both potentially useful to the end-user in our deployed system (Section 5), and used to gauge the performance of the more complicated systems in the evaluations presented in Section 4.

It should be noted that the baseline systems, while not using machine learning for the character classification steps, do make extensive use of machine learning-based systems during the pre-processing stages.

2.1.1 "First Mentioned" Entity

An obvious way to determine the main character of the section is to select the first named entity. We use this to define the "First Mentioned" baseline In this system, the **Feature Extraction** step is simply retrieving the position of the first use of each name; and the **Character Scoring** step assigns each a score such that earlier is higher. This works for many examples: *"One dark and stormy night, Bill heard a knock at the door."*; however it fails for many others: *" 'Is that Tom?' called out Bill, after hearing a knock."*. Sometimes a section may go several paragraphs describing events before it even mentions the character who is perceiving them. This is a varying element of style.

2.1.2 "Most Mentioned" Entity

A more robust method to determine the main character, is to use the occurrence counts. We call this the "Most Mentioned" baseline. The **Feature Extraction** step is to count how often the name is used. The **Character Scoring** step assigns each a score based what proportional of all names used were for this entity. This works well for many books. The more important a character

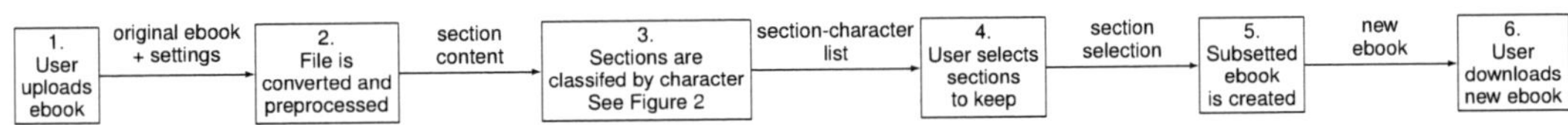

Figure 1: The full NovelPerspective pipeline. Note that step 5 uses the original ebook to subset.

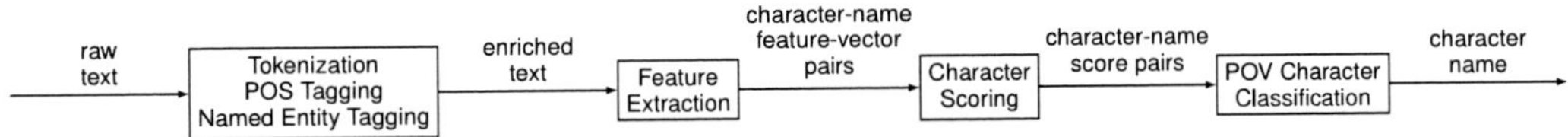

Figure 2: The general structure of the character classification systems. This repeated for each section of the book during step 3 of the full pipeline shown in Figure 1.

is, the more often their name occurs. However, it is fooled, for example, by book chapters that are about the POV character's relationship with a secondary character. In such cases the secondary character may be mentioned more often.

2.2 Machine learning systems

One can see the determination of the main character as a multi-class classification problem. From the set of all named entities in the section, classify that section as to which one is the main character. Unlike typical multi-class classification problems the set of possible classes varies per section being classified. Further, even the total set of possible named characters, i.e. classes, varies from book to book. An information extraction approach is required which can handle these varying classes. As such, a machine learning model for this task can not incorporate direct knowledge of the classes (i.e. character names).

We reconsider the problem as a series of binary predictions. The task is to predict if a given named entity is the point of view character. For each possible character (i.e. each named-entity that occurs), a feature vector is extracted (see Section 2.2.1). This feature vector is the input to a binary classifier, which determines the probability that it represents the main character. The **Character Scoring** step is thus the running of the binary classifier: the score is the output probability normalised over all the named entities.

2.2.1 Feature Extraction for ML

We investigated two feature sets as inputs for our machine learning-based solution. They correspond to different **Feature Extraction** steps in Figure 2. A hand-engineered feature set, that we call the "Classical" feature set; and a more modern "Word Embedding" feature set. Both feature sets give information about how the each named entity token was used in the text.

The "Classical" feature set uses features that are well established in NLP related tasks. The features can be described as *positional features*, like in the First Mentioned baseline; *occurrence count features*, like in the *Most Mentioned* baseline and *adjacent POS counts*, to give usage context. The *positional features* are the index (in the token counts) of the first and last occurrence of the named entity. The *occurrence count features* are simply the number of occurrences of the named entity, supplemented with its rank on that count compared to the others. The *adjacent POS counts* are the occurrence counts of each of the 46 POS tags on the word prior to the named entity, and on the word after. We theorised that this POS information would be informative, as it seemed reasonable that the POV character would be described as doing more things, so co-occurring with more verbs. This gives 100 base features. To allow for text length invariance we also provide each of the base features expressed as a portion of its maximum possible value (e.g. for a given POS tag occurring before a named entity, the potion of times this tag occurred). This gives a total of 200 features.

The "Word Embedding" feature set uses Fast-Text word vectors (Bojanowski et al., 2017). We use the pretrained 300 dimensional embeddings trained on English Wikipedia [1]. We concatenate the 300 dimensional word embedding for the word immediately prior to, and immediately after each occurrence of a named entity; and take the element-wise mean of this concatenated vector over all occurrences of the entity. Such averages of word embeddings have been shown to be a useful

---

[1] https://fasttext.cc/docs/en/pretrained-vectors.html

feature in many tasks (White et al., 2015; Mikolov et al., 2013). This has a total of 600 features.

2.2.2 Classifier

The binary classifier, that predicts if a named entity is the main character, is the key part of the **Character Scoring** step for the machine learning systems. From each text in the training dataset we generated a training example for every named entity that occurred. All but one of these was a negative example. We then trained it as per normal for a binary classifier. The score for a character is the classifier's predicted probability of its feature vector being for the main character.

Our approach of using a binary classifier to rate each possible class, may seem similar to the one-vs-rest approach for multi-class classification. However, there is an important difference. Our system only uses a single binary classifier; not one classifier per class, as the classes in our case vary with every item to be classified. The fundamental problem is information extraction, and the classifier is a tool for the scoring which is the correct information to report.

With the classical feature set we use logistic regression, with the features being preprocessed with 0-1 scaling. During preliminary testing we found that many classifiers had similar high degree of success, and so chose the simplest. With the word embedding feature set we used a radial bias support vector machine, with standardisation during preprocessing, as has been commonly used with word embeddings on other tasks.

3 Experimental Setup

3.1 Datasets

We make use of three series of books selected from our own personal collections. The first four books of George R. R. Martin's "A Song of Ice and Fire" series (hereafter referred to as ASOIAF); The two books of Leigh Bardugo's "Six of Crows" duology (hereafter referred to as SOC); and the first 9 volumes of Robert Jordan's "Wheel of Time" series (hereafter referred to as WOT). In Section 4 we consider the use of each as a training and testing dataset. In the online demonstration (Section 5), we deploy models trained on the combined total of all the datasets.

To use a book for the training and evaluation of our system, we require a ground truth for each section's POV character. ASOIAF and SOC provide

Dataset	Chapters	POV Characters
ASOIAF	256	15
SOC	91	9
WOT	432	52
combined	779	76

Table 1: The number of chapters and point of view characters for each dataset.

ground truth for the main character in the chapter names. Every chapter only uses the POV of that named character. WOT's ground truth comes from an index created by readers.[2] We do not have any datasets with labelled sub-chapter sections, though the tool does support such works.

The total counts of chapters and characters in the datasets, after preprocessing, is shown in Table 1. Preprocessing consisted of discarding chapters for which the POV character was not identified (e.g. prologues); and of removing the character names from the chapter titles as required.

3.2 Evaluation Details

In the evaluation, the systems are given the body text and asked to predict the character names. During evaluation, we sum the scores of the characters alternative aliases/nick-names used in the books. For example merging `Ned` into `Eddard` in ASOIAF. This roughly corresponds to the case that a normal user can enter multiple aliases into our application when selecting sections to keep. We do not use these aliases during training, though that is an option that could be investigated in a future work.

3.3 Implementation

The full source code is available on GitHub. [3] Scikit-Learn (Pedregosa et al., 2011) is used for the machine learning and evaluations, and NLTK (Bird and Loper, 2004) is used for textual preprocessing. The text is tokenised, and tagged with POS and named entities using NLTK's default methods. Specifically, these are the Punkt sentence tokenizer, the regex-based improved Tree-Bank word tokenizer, greedy averaged perceptron POS tagger, and the max-entropy binary named entity chunker. The use of a binary, rather than

---

[2] http://wot.wikia.com/wiki/List_of_Point_of_View_Characters

[3] https://github.com/oxinabox/NovelPerspective/

Test Set	Method	Train Set	Acc
ASOIAF	First Mentioned	—	0.250
ASOIAF	Most Mentioned	—	0.914
ASOIAF	ML Classical Features	SOC	0.953
ASOIAF	ML Classical Features	WOT	**0.984**
ASOIAF	ML Classical Features	WOT+SOC	0.977
ASOIAF	ML Word Emb. Features	SOC	0.863
ASOIAF	ML Word Emb. Features	WOT	0.977
ASOIAF	ML Word Emb. Features	WOT+SOC	0.973
SOC	First Mentioned	—	0.429
SOC	Most Mentioned	—	0.791
SOC	ML Classical Features	WOT	0.923
SOC	ML Classical Features	ASOIAF	0.923
SOC	ML Classical Features	WOT+ASOIAF	0.934
SOC	ML Word Emb. Features	WOT	0.934
SOC	ML Word Emb. Features	ASOIAF	**0.945**
SOC	ML Word Emb. Features	WOT+ASOIAF	**0.945**
WOT	First Mentioned	—	0.044
WOT	Most Mentioned	—	0.660
WOT	ML Classical Features	SOC	0.701
WOT	ML Classical Features	ASOIAF	**0.745**
WOT	ML Classical Features	ASOIAF+SOC	0.736
WOT	ML Word Emb. Features	SOC	0.551
WOT	ML Word Emb. Features	ASOIAF	0.699
WOT	ML Word Emb. Features	ASOIAF+SOC	0.681

Table 2: The results of the character classifier systems. The best results are **bolded**.

a multi-class, named entity chunker is significant. Fantasy novels often use "exotic" names for characters, we found that this often resulted in character named entities being misclassified as organisations or places. Note that this is particularly disadvantageous to the First Mentioned baseline, as any kind of named entity will steal the place. Nevertheless, it is required to ensure that all character names are a possibility to be selected.

4 Results and Discussion

Our evaluation results are shown in Table 2 for all methods. This includes the two baseline methods, and the machine learning methods with the different feature sets. We evaluate the machine learning methods using each dataset as a test set, and using each of the other two and their combination as the training set.

The First Mentioned baseline is very weak. The Most Mentioned baseline is much stronger. In almost all cases machine learning methods outperform both baselines. The results of the machine learning method on the ASOIAF and SOC are very strong. The results for WOT are weaker, though they are still accurate enough to be useful when combined with manual checking.

It is surprising that using the combination of

Test Set	Method	Train Set	Acc
ASOIAF	ML Classical Features	ASOIAF	0.980
ASOIAF	ML Word Emb. Features	ASOIAF	0.988
SOC	ML Classical Features	SOC	0.945
SOC	ML Word Emb. Features	SOC	0.956
WOT	ML Classical Features	WOT	0.785
WOT	ML Word Emb. Features	WOT	0.794

Table 3: The training set accuracy of the machine learning character classifier systems.

two training sets does not always out-perform each on their own. For many methods training on just one dataset resulted in better results. We believe that the difference between the top result for a method and the result using the combined training sets is too small to be meaningful. It can, perhaps, be attributed to a coincidental small similarity in writing style of one of the training books to the testing book. To maximise the generalisability of the NovelPerspective prototype (see Section 5), we deploy models trained on all three datasets combined.

Almost all the machine learning models resulted in similarly high accuracy. The exception to this is word embedding features based model trained on SOC, which for both ASOIAF and WOT test sets performed much worse. We attribute the poor performance of these models to the small amount of training data. SOC has only 91 chapters to generate its training cases from, and the word embedding feature set has 600 dimensions. It is thus very easily to over-fit which causes these poor results.

Table 3 shows the training set accuracy of each machine learning model. This is a rough upper bound for the possible performance of these models on each test set, as imposed by the classifier and the feature set. The WOT bound is much lower than the other two texts. This likely relates to WOT being written in a style that closer to the line between third-person *omniscient*, than the more clear third-person *limited* POV of the other texts. We believe longer range features are required to improve the results for WOT. However, as this achieves such high accuracy for the other texts, further features would not improve accuracy significantly, without additional more difficult training data (and may cause over-fitting).

The results do not show a clear advantage to either machine learning feature set. Both the classical features and the word embeddings work well.

Though, it seems that the classical feature are more robust; both with smaller training sets (like SOC), and with more difficult test sets (like WOT).

5 Demonstration System

The demonstration system is deployed online at `https://white.ucc.asn.au/tools/np`. A video demonstrating its use can be found at `https://youtu.be/iu41pUF4wTY`. This web-app, made using the CherryPy framework,[4] allows the user to apply any of the model discussed to their own novels.

The web-app functions as shown in Figure 1. The user uploads an ebook, and selects one of the character classification systems that we have discussed above. They are then presented with a page displaying a list of sections, with the predicted main character(/s) paired with an excerpt from the beginning of the section. The user can adjust to show the top-k most-likely characters on this screen, to allow for additional recall.

The user can select sections to retain. They can use a regular expression to match the character names(/s) they are interested in. The sections with matching predicted character names will be selected. As none of the models is perfect, some mistakes are likely. The user can manually correct the selection before downloading the book.

6 Conclusion

We have presented a tool to allow consumers to restructure their ebooks around the characters they find most interesting. The system must discover the named entities that are present in each section of the book, and then classify each section as to which character's point of view the section is narrated from. For named entity detection we make use of standard tools. However, the classification is non-trivial. In this design we implemented several systems. Simply selecting the most commonly named character proved successful as a baseline approach. To improve upon this, we developed several machine learning based approaches which perform very well. While none of the classifiers are perfect, they achieve high enough accuracy to be useful.

A future version of our application will allow the users to submit corrections, giving us more training data. However, storing this information poses copyright issues that are yet to be resolved.

---

[4]`http://cherrypy.org/`

Acknowledgements This research was partially funded by Australian Research Council grants DP150102405 and LP110100050.

References

Bird, S. and Loper, E. (2004). Nltk: the natural language toolkit. In *Proceedings of the ACL 2004 on Interactive poster and demonstration sessions*, page 31. Association for Computational Linguistics.

Bojanowski, P., Grave, E., Joulin, A., and Mikolov, T. (2017). Enriching word vectors with subword information. *Transactions of the Association for Computational Linguistics*, 5:135–146.

Booth, W. C. (1961). *The rhetoric of fiction*. University of Chicago Press.

Elson, D. K., Dames, N., and McKeown, K. R. (2010). Extracting social networks from literary fiction. In *Proceedings of the 48th Annual Meeting of the Association for Computational Linguistics*, ACL '10, pages 138–147, Stroudsburg, PA, USA. Association for Computational Linguistics.

Imani, M. B., Chandra, S., Ma, S., Khan, L., and Thuraisingham, B. (2017). Focus location extraction from political news reports with bias correction. In *2017 IEEE International Conference on Big Data (Big Data)*, pages 1956–1964.

Mikolov, T., Sutskever, I., Chen, K., Corrado, G. S., and Dean, J. (2013). Distributed representations of words and phrases and their compositionality. In *Advances in Neural Information Processing Systems*, pages 3111–3119.

Pedregosa, F., Varoquaux, G., Gramfort, A., Michel, V., Thirion, B., Grisel, O., Blondel, M., Prettenhofer, P., Weiss, R., Dubourg, V., Vanderplas, J., Passos, A., Cournapeau, D., Brucher, M., Perrot, M., and Duchesnay, E. (2011). Scikit-learn: Machine learning in Python. *Journal of Machine Learning Research*, 12:2825–2830.

White, L., Togneri, R., Liu, W., and Bennamoun, M. (2015). How well sentence embeddings capture meaning. In *Proceedings of the 20th Australasian Document Computing Symposium*, ADCS '15, pages 9:1–9:8. ACM.

Wohlgenannt, G., Chernyak, E., and Ilvovsky, D. (2016). Extracting social networks from literary text with word embedding tools. In *Proceedings of the Workshop on Language Technology Resources and Tools for Digital Humanities (LT4DH)*, pages 18–25.

Zhu, Y., Kiros, R., Zemel, R., Salakhutdinov, R., Urtasun, R., Torralba, A., and Fidler, S. (2015). Aligning books and movies: Towards story-like visual explanations by watching movies and reading books. In *Proceedings of the IEEE international conference on computer vision*, pages 19–27.

Out-of-the-box Universal Romanization Tool *uroman*

Ulf Hermjakob, Jonathan May, Kevin Knight
Information Sciences Institute, University of Southern California
{ulf, jonmay, knight}@isi.edu

Abstract

We present *uroman*, a tool for converting text in myriads of languages and scripts such as Chinese, Arabic and Cyrillic into a common Latin-script representation. The tool relies on Unicode data and other tables, and handles nearly all character sets, including some that are quite obscure such as Tibetan and Tifinagh. *uroman* converts digital numbers in various scripts to Western Arabic numerals. Romanization enables the application of string-similarity metrics to texts from different scripts without the need and complexity of an intermediate phonetic representation. The tool is freely and publicly available as a Perl script suitable for inclusion in data processing pipelines and as an interactive demo web page.

1 Introduction

String similarity is a useful feature in many natural language processing tasks. In machine translation, it can be used to improve the alignment of bitexts, and for low-resource languages with a related language of larger resources, it can help to decode out-of-vocabulary words. For example, suppose we have to translate *degustazione del vino* without any occurrence of *degustazione* in any training corpora, but we do know that in a related language *dégustation de vin* means *wine tasting*, we can use string similarity to infer the meaning of *degustazione*.

String similarity metrics typically assume that the strings are in the same script, but many cross-lingual tasks such as machine translation often involve multiple scripts. If we can romanize text from a non-Latin script to Latin, standard string similarity metrics can be applied, including edit distance-based metrics (Levenshtein, 1966; Winkler, 1990) and phonetic-based metrics such as Metaphone (Philips, 2000).

Hindi, for example, is written in the Devanagari script and Urdu in the Arabic script, so any words between those two languages will superficially appear to be very different, even though the two languages are closely related. After romanization, however, the similarities become apparent, as can be seen in Table 1:

	Hindi	Urdu	English
Original	नेपाल	نیپال	Nepal
Romanization	nepaal	nipal	Nepal

Table 1: Example of Hindi and Urdu romanization

Foreign scripts also present a massive cognitive barrier to humans who are not familiar with them. We devised a utility that allows people to translate text from languages they don't know, using the same information available to a machine translation system (Hermjakob et al., 2018). We found that when we asked native English speakers to use this utility to translate text from languages such as Uyghur or Bengali to English, they strongly preferred working on the romanized version of the source language compared to its original form and indeed found using the native, unfamiliar script to be a nearly impossible task.

1.1 Scope of Romanization

Romanization maps characters or groups of characters in one script to a character or group of characters in the Latin script (ASCII) with the goal to approximate the pronunciation of the original text and to map cognates in various languages to similar words in the Latin script, typically without the

Proceedings of the 56th Annual Meeting of the Association for Computational Linguistics-System Demonstrations, pages 13–18
Melbourne, Australia, July 15 - 20, 2018. ©2018 Association for Computational Linguistics

	Original	Romanization
Amharic	በርሊን የጃረማኔ ዋናዉ ካተማ ነዉ።	bareline yajaremane waanaa katamaa nawe.
Arabic	المملكة العربية السعودية	almmlka al'rbya als'wdya
Greek	Γερούν Ντάισελμπλουμ	Geroun Daiselbloum
Hebrew	עזרת תורה בירושלים	'zrt tvrh vyrvshlym
Japanese	アメリカ	amerika
Korean	세계에서 6번째로 면적이 넓은 나라이다.	segyeeseo 6beonjjaero myeonjeogi neolbeun naraida.
Mandarin	北卡罗来纳	beikaluolaina
Nepali	तिब्बती भाषामा यसको नाम चोमोलुङ्गमा हो ।	tibbatii bhaassaamaa yasako naam comolunggamaa ho .
Tamil	இதன் தலைநகராகச் சென்னை உள்ளது.	itan talainakaraakac cennai ullatu.
Tibetan	ལྷ་ས་གྲོང་ཁྱེར	lha·sa·grong·khyer

Table 2: Romanization examples for 10 scripts

use of any large-scale lexical resources. As a secondary goal, romanization standards tend to prefer reversible mappings. For example, as standalone vowels, the Greek letters ι (iota) and υ (upsilon) are romanized to *i* and *y* respectively, even though they have the same pronunciation in Modern Greek.

uroman generally follows such preference, but *uroman* is not always fully reversible. For example, since *uroman* maps letters to ASCII characters, the romanized text does not contain any diacritics, so the French word *ou* ("or") and its homophone *où* ("where") both map to romanized *ou*.

uroman provides the option to map to a plain string or to a lattice of romanized text, which allows the system to output alternative romanizations. This is particularly useful for source languages that use the same character for significantly different sounds. The Hebrew letter *Pe* for example can stand for both *p* and *f*. Lattices are output in JSON format.

Note that romanization does not necessarily capture the exact pronunciation, which varies across time and space (due to language change and dialects) and can be subject to a number of processes of phonetic assimilation. It also is not a translation of names and cognates to English (or any other target language). See Table 3 for examples for Greek.

A romanizer is not a full transliterator. For example, this tool does not vowelize text that lacks explicit vowelization such as normally

Modern Greek	Κρήτη	γεωλογία	μπανάνα
Pronunciation	Kriti	yeoloyia	banana
Romanization	Krete	geologia	banana
English	Crete	geology	banana
German	Kreta	Geologie	Banane

Table 3: Examples of Greek romanization

occurring text in Arabic and Hebrew (i.e., without diacritics/points); see Table 4.

	Normal text	With diacritics
Arabic	واشنطن	وَاشِنْطُن
Romanization	washntn	waashintun
English	Washington	Washington

Table 4: Romanization with and without diacritics

1.2 Features

uroman has the following features:

1. Input: UTF8-encoded text and an optional ISO-639-3 language code

2. Output: Romanized text (default) or lattice of romanization alternatives in JSON format

3. Nearly universal romanization[1]

4. N-to-m mapping for groups of characters that are non-decomposable with respect to romanization

5. Context-sensitive and source language-specific romanization rules

---

[1]See Section 4 for a few limitations.

6. Romanization includes (digital) numbers

7. Romanization includes punctuation

8. Preserves capitalization

9. Freely and publicly available

Romanization tools have long existed for specific individual languages such as the Kakasi[2] kanji-to-kana/romaji converter for Japanese, but to the best of our knowledge, we present the first publicly available (near) universal romanizer that handles n-to-m character mappings. Many romanization examples are shown in Table 2 and examples of n-to-m character mapping rules are shown in Table 7.

2 System Description

2.1 Unicode Data

As its basis, *uroman* uses the character descriptions of the Unicode table.[3] For the characters of most scripts, the Unicode table contains descriptions such as *CYRILLIC SMALL LETTER SHORT U* or *CYRILLIC CAPITAL LETTER TE WITH MIDDLE HOOK*. Using a few heuristics, *uroman* identifies the phonetic token in that description, i.e. *U* and *TE* for the examples above. The heuristics use a list of anchor keywords such as *letter* and *syllable* as well as a number of modifier patterns that can be discarded. Given the phonetic token of the Unicode description, *uroman* then uses a second set of heuristics to predict the romanization for these phonetic tokens, i.e. *u* and *t*. For example, if the phonetic token is one of more consonants followed by one or more vowels, the predicted romanization is the leading sequence of consonants, e.g. SHA $\rightarrow$ *sh*.

2.2 Additional Tables

However, these heuristics often fail. An example of a particularly spectacular failure is SCHWA $\rightarrow$ *schw* instead of the desired *e*. Additionally, there are sequences of characters with non-compositional romanization. For example, the standard romanization for the Greek sequence omikron+upsilon, (ου) is the Latin *ou* rather than the character-by-character romanization *oy*.

As a remedy, we manually created additional correction tables that map sequences of one or more characters to the desired romanization, with

currently 1,088 entries. The entries in these tables can be restricted by conditions, for example to specific languages or to the beginning of a word, and can express alternative romanizations. This data table is a core contribution of the tool.

uroman additionally includes a few special heuristics cast in code, such as for the vowelizations of a number of Indian languages and Tibetan, dealing with diacritics, and a few language-specific idiosyncrasies such as the Japanese sokuon and Thai consonant-vowel swaps.

Building these *uroman* resources has been greatly facilitated by information drawn from Wikipedia,[4] Richard Ishida's script notes,[5] and ALA-LC Romanization Tables.[6]

2.3 Characters without Unicode Description

The Unicode table does not include character descriptions for all scripts.

For Chinese characters, we use a Mandarin pinyin table for romanization.

For Korean, we use a short standard Hangul romanization algorithm.[7]

For Egyptian hieroglyphs, we added single-sound phonetic characters and numbers to *uroman*'s additional tables.

2.4 Numbers

uroman also romanizes numbers in digital form.

For some scripts, number characters map one-to-one to Western Arabic numerals 0-9, e.g. for Bengali, Eastern Arabic and Hindi.

For other scripts, such as Amharic, Chinese, and Egyptian hieroglyphics, written numbers are structurally different, e.g. the Amharic number character sequence $10 \cdot 9 \cdot 100 \cdot 90 \cdot 8 = 1998$ and the Chinese number character sequence $2 \cdot 10 \cdot 5 \cdot 10000 \cdot 6 \cdot 1000 = 256000$. *uroman* includes a special number module to accomplish this latter type of mapping. Examples are shown in Table 5.

Note that for phonetically spelled-out numbers such as Greek οχτώ, *uroman* romanizes to the spelled-out Latin *okto* rather than the digital *8*.

---

[2]http://kakasi.namazu.org
[3]ftp://ftp.unicode.org/Public/UNIDATA/UnicodeData.txt

[4]https://en.wikipedia.org
[5]https://r12a.github.io/scripts/featurelist
[6]https://www.loc.gov/catdir/cpso/roman.html
[7]http://gernot-katzers-spice-pages.com/var/korean_hangul_unicode.html

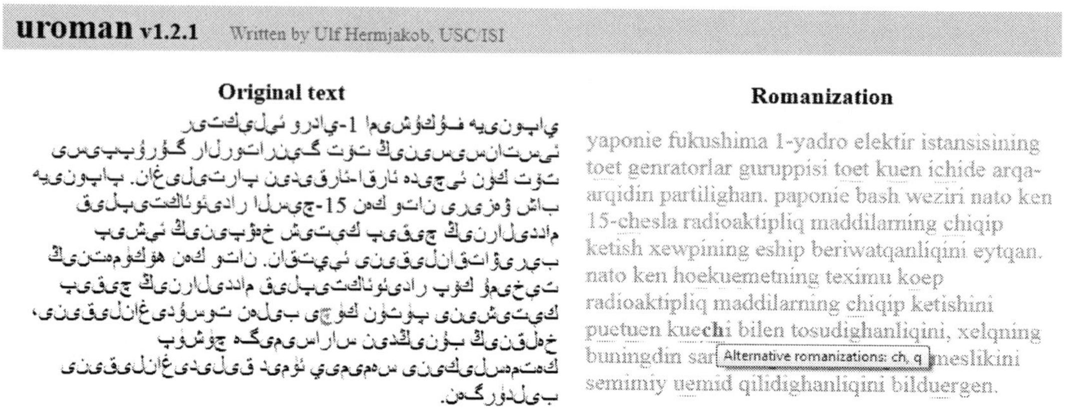

Original text   **Romanization**

يابونىيه فۇلكۇشىما 1-يادرو ئېلىكتىر
نىستانسىسىنىڭ تۆت گېنىراتورلار گۇرۇپپىسى
تۆت كۈن ئىچىدە ئارقا-ئارقىدىن پارتىلىغان. پاپونىيه
باش ۋەزىرى ناتو كەن 15-چېسلا رادىوئاكتىپلىق
مادّىلارنىڭ چىقىپ كېتىش خەۋپىنىڭ ئېشىپ
بېرىۋاتقانلىقىنى ئېيتقان. ناتو كەن ھۆكۈمەتنىڭ
تېخىمۇ كۆپ رادىوئاكتىپلىق مادّىلارنىڭ چىقىپ
كېتىشىنى پۈتۈن كۈچى بىلەن توسۇدىغانلىقىنى،
خەلقنىڭ بۇنىڭدىن سارا سىمىمىگە دە چوشرۇپ
كەتمەسلىكىنى سېمىمىي ئۈمىد قىلىدىغانلىقىنى
بىلدۈرگەن.

yaponie fukushima 1-yadro elektir istansisining
toet genratorlar guruppisi toet kuen ichide arqa-
arqidin partilighan. paponie bash weziri nato ken
15-chesla radioaktipliq maddilarning chiqip
ketish xewpining eship beriwatqanliqini eytqan.
nato ken hoekuemetning teximu koep
radioaktipliq maddilarning chiqip ketishini
puetuen kuechi bilen tosudighanliqini, xelqning
buningdin sar[Alternative romanizations: ch, q]meslikini
semimiy uemid qilidighanliqini bilduergen.

Figure 1: Screenshot of Uyghur romanization on demo site at bit.ly/uroman

	Original	Romanization
Amharic	፲፱፻፺፰	1998
Bengali	১৯৪৯	1949
Chinese	二十五万六千	256000
	25.6万	256000

Table 5: Romanization/Arabization of numbers

2.5 Romanization of Latin Text

Some Latin script-based languages have words for which spelling and pronunciation differ substantially, e.g. the English name *Knight* (IPA: /naɪt/) and French *Bordeaux* (/bɔʁ.do/), which complicates string similarity matching if the corresponding spelling of the word in the non-Latin script is based on pronunciation.

uroman therefore offers alternative romanizations for words such as *Knight* and *Bordeaux* (see Table 6 for an example of the former), but, as a policy *uroman* always preserves the original Latin spelling, minus any diacritics, as the top romanization alternative.

	Japanese	English
Original	ナイト	Knight
Top romanization	naito	Knight
An alternative rom.	nait	Nait
Alternative lattice	nai(to|t)	(Kn|N)(ight|ait)

Table 6: Romanization with alternatives

Table 7 includes examples of the Romanization rules in *uroman*, including n-to-m mappings.

2.6 Caching

uroman caches token romanizations for speed.

```
::s μπ ::t b ::use-only-at-start-of-word
::s μπ ::t mb ::t-alt b, mp
::s چ ::t ch ::t-alt q ::lcode uig
::s ئو ::t o ::lcode uig
::s ち ょ ::t cho
::s フ ェ ::t fe
::s eaux ::t eaux ::t-alt o ::example Bordeaux
::s gh ::t gh ::t-alt f, "" ::ex. laugh, daughter
```

Table 7: Romanization rules with two examples each for Greek, Uyghur, Japanese, and English, with a variety of n-to-m mappings.
(::s = source; ::t = target; ::lcode = language code)

3 Download and Demo Sites

uroman v1.2 is publicly available for download at bit.ly/isi-nlp-software. The fully self-sufficient software package includes the implementation of *uroman* in Perl with all necessary data tables. The software is easy to install (gunzip and tar), without any need for compilation or any other software (other than Perl).

Typical call (for plain text output):

```
uroman.pl --lc uig < STDIN > STDOUT
```

where *–lc uig* specifies the (optional) language code (e.g. Uyghur).

There is also an interactive demo site at bit.ly/uroman. Users may enter text in the language and script of their choice, optionally specify a language code, and then have *uroman* romanize the text.

Additionally, the demo page includes sample texts in 290 languages in a wide variety of scripts. Texts in 21 sample languages are available on the demo start page and more are accessible as *ran-*

dom texts. After picking the first random text, additional random texts will be available from three corpora to choose from (small, large, and Wikipedia articles about the US). Users can then restrict the randomness in a special option field. For example, `--l` will exclude texts in Latin+ scripts. For further information about possible restrictions, hover over the word *restriction* (a dotted underline indicates that additional info will be shown when a user hovers over it).

The romanization of the output at the demo site is mouse sensitive. Hovering over characters of either the original or romanized text, the page will highlight corresponding characters. See Figure 1 for an example. Hovering over the original text will also display additional information such as the Unicode name and any numeric value. To support this interactive demo site, the *uroman* package also includes fonts for Burmese, Tifinagh, Klingon, and Egyptian hieroglyphs, as they are sometimes missing from standard browser font packages.

4 Limitations and Future Work

The current version of *uroman* has a few limitations, some of which we plan to address in future versions. For Japanese, *uroman* currently romanizes hiragana and katakana as expected, but kanji are interpreted as Chinese characters and romanized as such. For Egyptian hieroglyphs, only single-sound phonetic characters and numbers are currently romanized. For Linear B, only phonetic syllabic characters are romanized. For some other extinct scripts such as cuneiform, no romanization is provided.

uroman allows the user to specify an ISO-639-3 source language code, e.g. *uig* for Uyghur. This invokes any language-specific romanization rules for languages that share a script with other languages. Without source language code specification, *uroman* assumes a default language, e.g. Arabic for text in Arabic script. We are considering adding a source language detection component that will automatically determine whether an Arabic-script source text is Arabic, Farsi, or Uyghur etc.

5 Romanization Applications

5.1 Related Work

Gey (2009) reports that romanization based on ALA-LC romanization tables (see Section 2.2) is useful in cross-lingual information retrieval.

There is a body of work mapping text to phonetic representations. Deri and Knight (2016) use Wiktionary and Wikipedia resources to learn text-to-phoneme mappings. Phonetic representations are used in a number of end-to-end transliteration systems (Knight and Graehl, 1998; Yoon et al., 2007). Qian et al. (2010) describe the toolkit *ScriptTranscriber*, which extracts cross-lingual transliteration pairs from comparable corpora. A core component of *ScriptTranscriber* maps text to an ASCII variant of the International Phonetic Alphabet (IPA).

Andy Hu's transliterator[8] is a fairly universal romanizer in JavaScript, limited to romanizing one Unicode character at a time, without context.

5.2 Applications Using *uroman*

Ji et al. (2017) and Mayfield et al. (2017) use *uroman* for named entity recognition. Mayhew et al. (2016) use *uroman* for (end-to-end) transliteration. Cheung et al. (2017) use *uroman* for machine translation of low-resource languages.

uroman has also been used in our aforementioned translation utility (Hermjakob et al., 2018), where humans translate text to another language, with computer support, with high fluency in the target language (English), but no prior knowledge of the source language.

uroman has been partially ported by third parties to Python and Java.[9]

6 Conclusion

Romanization tools have long existed for specific individual languages, but to the best of our knowledge, we present the first publicly available (near) universal romanizer that handles n-to-m character mappings. The tool offers both simple plain text as well as lattice output with alternatives, and includes romanization of numbers in digital form. It has been successfully deployed in a number of multi-lingual natural language systems.

Acknowledgment

This work is supported by DARPA (HR0011-15-C-0115).

---

[8]https://github.com/andyhu/transliteration
[9]https://github.com/BBN-E/bbn-transliterator

References

Leon Cheung, Thamme Gowda, Ulf Hermjakob, Nelson Liu, Jonathan May, Alexandra Mayn, Nima Pourdamghani, Michael Pust, Kevin Knight, Nikolaos Malandrakis, et al. 2017. Elisa system description for LoReHLT 2017.

Aliya Deri and Kevin Knight. 2016. Grapheme-to-phoneme models for (almost) any language. In *Proceedings of the 54th Annual Meeting of the Association for Computational Linguistics (Volume 1: Long Papers)*, volume 1, pages 399–408.

Fredric Gey. 2009. Romanization–an untapped resource for out-of-vocabulary machine translation for CLIR. In *SIGIR Workshop on Information Access in a Multilingual World*, pages 49–51.

Ulf Hermjakob, Jonathan May, Michael Pust, and Kevin Knight. 2018. Translating a language you don't know in the Chinese Room. In *Proceedings of the 56th Annual Meeting of Association for Computational Linguistics, Demo Track*.

Heng Ji, Xiaoman Pan, Boliang Zhang, Joel Nothman, James Mayfield, Paul McNamee, and Cash Costello. 2017. Overview of TAC-KBP2017 13 languages entity discovery and linking. In *Text Analysis Conference – Knowledge Base Population track*.

Kevin Knight and Jonathan Graehl. 1998. Machine transliteration. *Computational Linguistics*, 24(4):599–612.

Vladimir I Levenshtein. 1966. Binary codes capable of correcting deletions, insertions, and reversals. In *Soviet physics doklady*, volume 10, pages 707–710.

James Mayfield, Paul McNamee, and Cash Costello. 2017. Language-independent named entity analysis using parallel projection and rule-based disambiguation. In *Proceedings of the 6th Workshop on Balto-Slavic Natural Language Processing*, pages 92–96.

Stephen Mayhew, Christos Christodoulopoulos, and Dan Roth. 2016. Transliteration in any language with surrogate languages. *arXiv preprint arXiv:1609.04325*.

Lawrence Philips. 2000. The double Metaphone search algorithm. *C/C++ Users J.*, 18(6):38–43.

Ting Qian, Kristy Hollingshead, Su-youn Yoon, Kyoung-young Kim, and Richard Sproat. 2010. A Python toolkit for universal transliteration. In *LREC*.

William E. Winkler. 1990. String comparator metrics and enhanced decision rules in the Fellegi-Sunter model of record linkage. In *Proceedings of the Section on Survey Research Methods*, pages 354–359. ERIC.

Su-Youn Yoon, Kyoung-Young Kim, and Richard Sproat. 2007. Multilingual transliteration using feature based phonetic method. In *Proceedings of the 45th annual meeting of the Association of Computational Linguistics*, pages 112–119.

HarriGT: Linking news articles to scientific literature

James Ravenscroft[1,3,4], Amanda Clare[2] and Maria Liakata[1,3]

[1]Centre for Scientific Computing, University of Warwick, CV4 7AL, United Kingdom
[2]Department of Computer Science, Aberystwyth University, SY23 3DB, United Kingdom
[3]Alan Turing Institute, 96 Euston Rd, London, NW1 2DBB, United Kingdom
[4]Filament AI, CargoWorks, 1-2 Hatfields, London, SE1 9PG, United Kingdom

Abstract

Being able to reliably link scientific works to the newspaper articles that discuss them could provide a breakthrough in the way we rationalise and measure the impact of science on our society. Linking these articles is challenging because the language used in the two domains is very different, and the gathering of online resources to align the two is a substantial information retrieval endeavour. We present HarriGT, a semi-automated tool for building corpora of news articles linked to the scientific papers that they discuss. Our aim is to facilitate future development of information-retrieval tools for newspaper/scientific work citation linking. HarriGT retrieves newspaper articles from an archive containing 17 years of UK web content. It also integrates with 3 large external citation networks, leveraging named entity extraction, and document classification to surface relevant examples of scientific literature to the user. We also provide a tuned candidate ranking algorithm to highlight potential links between scientific papers and newspaper articles to the user, in order of likelihood. HarriGT is provided as an open source tool (`http://harrigt.xyz`).

1 Introduction

For scientists, understanding the ways in which their work is being reported by journalists and the subsequent societal impact of these reports remains an overwhelming task. Research funding councils have also become increasingly interested in the impact that the research that they fund produces. These motivating factors, combined with

suggestions that traditional citation-based metrics such as JIF (Garfield, 2006) and h-index (Hirsch, 2005) are not as transparent as once thought (Cronin, 1984; Bornmann and Daniel, 2008) have catalyzed the development of metrics to measure scientific impact in society, policy and the economy (recently termed "comprehensive scientific impact" (Ravenscroft et al., 2017)). Evaluation programmes such as the UK's Research Excellence Framework (REF) Impact Case Study (REF 2014, 2012) and the United States' STAR Metrics programme (Lane and Bertuzzi, 2010) set the current state of the art in comprehensive scientific impact metrics. However, both processes involve significant manual labour and introduce human subjectivity into their evaluation processes. Ravenscroft et al. (2017) recently showed that there is negligible correlation between citation-based metrics and REF scores and called for the development of an objective, automated metric for measuring comprehensive impact. As part of the US-funded FUSE project, McKeown et al. (2016) developed a method for measuring the use of technical terms over time in scientific works as a proxy for scientific impact. McKeown's work, whilst primarily focusing on scientific literature, represents a significant step towards deeper understanding of scientific impact beyond citations.

Our assumption is that the perception of researchers' work as reflected in the mainstream media is an important means of measuring comprehensive impact, useful both to researchers themselves as well as funding bodies. However, one of the main barriers to building an automated solution to assessing such comprehensive impact is a lack of training data. In this paper, we present and discuss our tool, HarriGT, which facilitates ground truth collection for a corpus of news articles linked to the scientific works that they discuss. In this way we aim to lay the groundwork for future stud-

Proceedings of the 56th Annual Meeting of the Association for Computational Linguistics-System Demonstrations, pages 19–24
Melbourne, Australia, July 15 - 20, 2018. ©2018 Association for Computational Linguistics

ies that help scientists understand societal perception and impact of their work through the media.

2 Background

Citation extraction from news articles reporting on scientific topics remains a challenging and relatively unexplored task. There are no conventions, formal or informal, for citing a scientific work in a news article. Scientific journalists often omit key information about who funded or even carried out a given study from their reports making identification of the work very difficult (Bubela et al., 2009). Journalists also frequently quote academics who were not directly involved in a scientific work in their stories, further confusing attempts to automate citation extraction (Conrad, 1999). Louis and Nenkova (2013) found that the quality of scientific reporting varies greatly even between journalists within the same publishing venue.

On the other hand, parsing and understanding citations between scientific works is a domain that has seen a lot of attention from academia in recent years. Citations in scientific papers are relatively well structured and formulaic. As such, pattern-based extraction mechanisms have been found to yield good citation extraction results (Councill et al., 2008). Disambiguation of the scientific work and authors to which a citation refers can be a much more challenging task. This especially applies in cases where authors have ambiguous names (e.g. J. Smith). One approach is to assign scientific works and authors unique identifiers such that there is no ambiguity in cited works (DOI and ORCID respectively) (Paskin, 2015; Butler, 2012). A more pragmatic approach is needed to disambiguate publications and authors for which no DOI or ORCID ID have been assigned. Huang and Ertekin (2006) present a method for disambiguation of authors using a learned distance metric that takes into account author's known names, affiliations and venues that they typically publish at. Similar approaches have led to the creation of citation networks that store relationships between huge volumes of scientific works. Networks such as CiteSeerX (Wu et al., 2014), Microsoft Academic Knowledge Graph and Scopus provide external access via APIs for research and application development purposes.

Beyond academia, references to scientific work are common across a number of domains. The popular encyclopedia website, Wikipedia, relies upon outbound citation to establish its veracity concerning matters of science (Nielsen, 2007). Whilst DOI links to articles are often used, in many cases, only the title, publication name and author names are provided leading to a structured extraction and disambiguation problem similar to that outlined above. (Nielsen, 2007; Kousha and Thelwall, 2017; Nielsen et al., 2017).

Since academia as a whole has begun to adapt to online publishing, academics have become individually accustomed to sharing work through digital channels and social media. This has led to the development of systems such as Altmetric.com (Adie and Roe, 2013), that monitor social media posts as well as some mainstream media outlets for mentions of scientific works via DOI links. By their own admission, altmetric toolmakers still struggle to identify all mentions of scientific works, focusing only on articles with a DOI or some other unique identifier (Liu and Adie, 2013).

Extraction and disambiguation of references to scientific works in news articles is the task that has motivated the development of HarriGT. We seek to facilitate construction of a human-curated corpus of newspaper articles that have been explicitly linked to scientific works. Such corpora could be used to build machine learning models that are able to connect news articles to scientific works automatically. Using HarriGT we have already started the creation of such a corpus. At time of writing the corpus consists of 304 newspaper articles linked to one or more scientific paper. The corpus is growing incrementally and can be downloaded via the tool.

3 System Overview

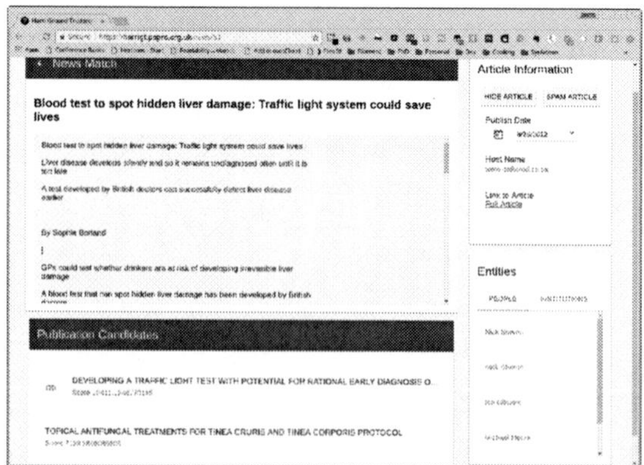

Figure 1: HarriGT Web UI shows a news article and related candidate scientific papers

HarriGT provides a system that brings together historical news articles from web archives stored in the widely used open source WARC format. The system automatically ingests and parses newspaper articles and searches citation graphs for relevant candidate papers that the user is able to **link** or **hide** or mark as **spam**. A diagram explaining this process is available on the HarriGT website. In this paper, we worked with a UK national web archive (JISC and the Internet Archive, 2013) and candidate scientific papers connected to citation graphs from Microsoft, Scopus and Springer. The news article and candidate scientific papers are presented in a web interface, enabling a user to quickly decide whether each candidate is linked to the news article or not. This section discusses the components involved in this process in detail and outlines some of the challenges we faced in the system creation.

3.1 News Corpus Retrieval

In order to build a comprehensive corpus of news articles, we worked with the JISC Web Archive, a comprehensive scrape of the *.uk* top-level domain between 1996 and 2013. Content is stored in Web Archive (WARC) compressed format and an index file containing metadata about every URL that was scraped and a pointer to the related content within the WARC structure was made available. The JISC Web Archive is approximately 62 Terabytes in size, so identifying and filtering relevant content became a primary concern[1].

We initially decided to restrict our investigation to news articles between 2011 and late 2013 which coincided with REF 2014. We compiled a list of web addresses for local and national UK news outlets via a Wikipedia article[2] in order to reduce the number of hostnames that our tool should inspect down to 205. The archive index files also provided metadata about the type of each WARC entry and whether the original scrape was successful or not (e.g. whether the URL was invalid). This brought down the total number of WARC entries to be examined to approximately 11.5 million. Requests to the BLOB store hosting the web archive were optimised through a script that identified batches of URLS archived in the same BLOB.

3.2 News Article Pre-Processing & Filtering

The contents of the archives were typically HTML and thus we needed to extract the title and body of each news story. HTML layouts can vary significantly between sites but news articles follow a typical layout and thus extraction of content fields can be carried out using rules and patterns rather than a machine learning approach. For our purposes we found that the open source library newspaper[3] was highly effective and gave us access to an article's title, authors, publication date and other metadata.

During the process we realised that some news articles had been duplicated in the archive. This can occur when a web crawler retrieves a URL that has been generated erroneously by the scraper script or the website being scraped. This can lead to multiple links to the same content. Examples include incorrectly appending search keywords, pagination information and other parameters into URLs that do not require these parameters.

To get around this problem, we introduced a hashing system, taking the SHA256 hash of the title body text from each article and only accepting new content if its hash is not already known.

We found that using the science section of the newspapers to filter suitable articles led to exclusion of relevant material. A second approach was to only accept articles that pass two high-level keyword filters. The first, simpler check is to see whether or not an article contains one or more keywords: *science, scientist, professor, doctor, academic, journal, research, publish, report*. We deliberately chose these keywords as a simplistic filter to reduce the amount of current affairs/celebrity gossip news that was initially accepted into our system. For the second of our filters, we ran a Named Entity Recognition (NER) algorithm[4] that provided multi-word expression identification and classification for names, locations and geo-political entities. From the results of the NER execution, we only accepted articles with at least one organisation containing *University, College* or *Institute*.

The final step in the pre-processing pipeline is identification of each article's publication date. Publication date is one of the most salient features in our paper candidate scoring algorithm discussed below. Recent digital news articles give their date

---

[1]The JISC Web Archive is accessible for research purposes at `data.webarchive.org.uk/opendata/ukwa.ds.2/`

[2]`https://en.wikipedia.org/wiki/List_of_newspapers_in_the_United_Kingdom`

[3]`http://newspaper.readthedocs.io/en/latest/`

[4]SpaCy 2.0 `https://spacy.io/`

Model Type	Accuracy	F1-Score
SVM	0.94	0.94
Naive Bayes	0.82	0.86

Table 1: Micro-averaged Results from Spam Models. Spam Articles: 2085, Ham Articles: 840

of publication in their HTML metadata. However, for many of the old articles in the web archive, this information was not present. For articles with no known publication date, we first attempted to retrieve the same URL from the live internet where much of the original content is still available but with updated layouts and metadata. If the content can't be found, we used a set of regular expressions (found within the newspaper library mentioned above) to try and find the date in the article HTML. Failing all else, we simply asked the user to try and identify the publication date manually within the user interface.

The retrieval and pre-processing steps are rather time consuming, taking a modern workstation (Intel i7 Quad Core @ 3.5Ghz, 16GB RAM) approximately 24 hours to process 20k news articles. We therefore ingest content into HarriGT in batches using a small Apache Hadoop cluster.

3.3 'Spam' Filtering

Our keyword filter during pre-processing removes a large number of general interest articles that do not discuss scientific work. There are still a number of articles that pass this initial screening that are off topic. We address this issue by including a machine learned "spam" model into HarriGT. Within the user interface, news articles can be marked as **spam** if they contain little relevant scientific content. The model is re-trained using new examples from the **spam** and **link** categories as the user continues to tag articles.

We trained two machine learning models to address the problem, a Naive Bayes classifier and a Support Vector Machine. We used Grid Search to identify the best training hyper-parameters for feature extraction and the models. The optimal feature hyper-parameters were found to be unigram and bigram bag-of-words features with TF-IDF weighting, maximum document frequency of 75% and a maximum vocabulary size of 10,000. We found that an SVM with a linear kernel and $C = 1$ produced the best results and used this model in the live system. Table 3.3 shows our model results after 4 iterations of training and use.

Given the size of the corpus, the hardware en-

vironment that the model was required to support and the positive results from the SVM mode, we decided not to explore deep learning approaches to spam filtering.

3.4 Citation Graph Integration

In order to provide candidate scientific works for each newspaper article, we required integration with rich sources of metadata for as many scientific disciplines as possible. We decided to integrate HarriGT with the Microsoft Academic Knowledge[5], Scopus[6] and Springer[7] APIs. These APIs all provide broad, up to date coverage of known academic works. Each API had a different search endpoint with differing query languages and syntax that had to be catered for.

Each of the APIs returns metadata such as title, names and affiliations of authors, name of publishing venue and date of publication. In most cases each API returned a DOI so that each work could be uniquely identified and hyperlinked via the HarriGT interface. This allowed us to deduplicate items returned by more than one API.

Articles typically talk about the institution that a scientific work was carried out at and independently the name of the author e.g. "Cambridge Researchers have found that... Dr Smith who led the study said..." making automatic extraction of reference information very difficult. Therefore, we use NER to identify all names and institutions in the article and run citation graph queries for each permutation. For example: "A study run by Oxford and Cambridge universities found that... Dr Jones who led the study said..." would yield two queries: (Jones, Oxford), (Jones, Cambridge). Searches are bounded by the article's publication date plus-or-minus 90 days.

3.5 Candidate Scoring Implementation

The retrieval mechanism described above tends to overgenerate links between news articles and scientific publications, resulting in 0.19 precision. Therefore it is important to have a mechanism for ranking these further, to avoid spurious links and only show the user the most prominent ones for further verification. To address this we propose a simple but effective mechanism based on the Levenshtein Ratio. Each news article is associated

---

[5] https://labs.cognitive.microsoft.com/en-us/project-academic-knowledge
[6] https://dev.elsevier.com/index.html
[7] https://dev.springer.com/

with a set of C candidate scientific works c_i where $i \in [0, C]$ are found using the retrieval method discussed above. News articles contain two sets of entity mentions of interest: A set of N peoples' names n_j and a set of O organization names o_j. We also record the number of times each entity is mentioned M_j. For each candidate scientific work c_i, we identify a set of A_i authors' names a_i^k and their respective academic affiliations u_i^k. We also note the publication date of each news article D and the publication date of each candidate scientific work P_i.

For a given news article, we score each candidate scientific work c_i by summing over the square of Levenshtein Ratio ($L_r(x, y)$) of each pair of mentions of names and authors:

$$S_i^{per} = \sum_{j=0}^{N} M_j \sum_{k=0}^{A_i} L_r(n_j, a_k^i)^2$$

A similar calculation is carried out for organisation mentions and affiliations.

$$S_i^{org} = \sum_{j=0}^{O} M_j \sum_{k=0}^{A_i} L_r(o_j, u_k^i)^2$$

The Levenshtein Ratio is a simple, effective measure that has been used for assessing NE similarity (Moreau et al., 2008). We also calculate Δ_D, the number of days between the publication date of the news article, D and the scientific work P_i. In cases where the candidate article has multiple publication dates (for example, online publication versus print publication), Δ_D is calculated for all publication dates and the smallest value is retained.

$$\Delta_D = \min_{n}(\sqrt{(D - P_i^n)^2})$$

Finally, we calculate an overall score S_i for each article by normalizing S_i^{per} and S_i^{org} by their respective numbers of distinct entity mentions and then dividing by Δ_D like so:

$$S_i = (\frac{S_i^{per}}{N} + \frac{S_i^{org}}{O}) \times \frac{1}{\Delta_D}$$

Candidates are ranked according to their S_i score in descending order so that the highest scoring candidates are presented to the user first.

3.6 Candidate Scoring Evaluation

To evaluate our candidate scoring technique, we use it to retrieve the N-best candidates for news articles with known links to one or more scientific papers. For each of the news articles in our ground truth collection, we retrieved all candidate scientific works from the citation graphs as described in section 3.4 above. We then use the scoring algorithm from section 3.5 above to rank the candidates then check to see whether actual linked papers appear in the top 1,3 and 5 results (Top-K accuracy).

	Top-1	**Top-3**	**Top-5**
Accuracy	0.59	0.83	0.90

Table 2: Top-K Accuracy for Scoring Algorithm

We identified a small number of reasons for sub-optimal ranking. Newspaper articles occasionally focus around candidate works published months earlier. In some cases, incorrect publication dates are being reported by the scientific paper APIs. In both cases, our system strongly penalizes candidates in terms of Δ_D. HarriGT's ranking algorithm also weakly penalizes candidates that have multiple authors in cases where only one author (often the lead) is mentioned in the newspaper text. This effect is amplified when work by the same lead author with fewer or no co-authors is also found since these candidates are preferred and filtered to the top of the list.

HarriGT's recall is not bounded by the candidate ranking algorithm but by the queries and results from our integration with Scopus, Microsoft and Springer APIs. HarriGT allows the user to **hide** news articles that are scientific but for which no relevant candidates are recommended. This action is distinct from marking an item as **spam**, which indicates that it has no scientific value and should be excluded from the corpus.

We evaluate the recall of our tool by considering items marked as **link** to be retrieved and deemed relevant and items marked as **hide** to be retrieved but for which no relevant items could be found. Thus defining recall as:

$$recall = \frac{|\{linked\}|}{|\{linked\} \cup \{hidden\}|}$$

At the time of writing, the recall of the system is 0.57. This figure may be lower than the actual figure, since papers are occasionally classified as 'hidden' by annotators if several strong candidates are presented and they are unsure which paper to link to. We expect that this figure will get stronger with more use.

4   Conclusion & Future Work

We have presented HarriGT, the first tool for rapidly establishing links between scientific works and the newspaper articles that discuss them. We have shown that using a combination of NLP techniques and proposing a simple but effective candidate ranking algorithm, it is possible to construct a linked corpus of scientific articles and news articles for future analysis of the impact of scientific articles in news media. The tool could also have other uses such as the discovery of primary sources for scientific news. Future work will explore the role of time and other content in this task. Our open source tool has been constructed with use of the JISC corpus in mind, but could be used with other sources of news also. HarriGT produces useful ranking and good recall and is ready for use with a large corpus. HarriGT is available to try out at `http://www.harrigt.xyz` and we welcome feedback from volunteer users.

Acknowledgments

We thank the EPSRC (grant EP/L016400/1) for funding us through the University of Warwick's CDT in Urban Science, the Alan Turing Institute and British Library for providing resources.

References

E Adie and W Roe. 2013. Altmetric: Enriching scholarly content with article-level discussion and metrics. *Learned Publishing* 26(1):11–17.

L Bornmann and H Daniel. 2008. What do citation counts measure? A review of studies on citing behavior. *Journal of Documentation* 64(1):45–80.

T Bubela et al. 2009. Science communication reconsidered 27(6):514–518.

D Butler. 2012. Scientists: your number is up. *Nature* 485(7400):564–564.

P Conrad. 1999. Uses of expertise: sources, quotes, and voice in the reporting of genetics in the news. *Public Understanding of Science* 8:285–302.

I G Councill et al. 2008. ParsCit: An open-source CRF Reference String Parsing Package. *LREC '08: Proceedings of the 6th International Conference on Language Resources and Evaluation* 2008(3):661–667.

B Cronin. 1984. *The citation process: The role and significance of citations in scientific communication.* T. Graham London.

E Garfield. 2006. History and Meaning of the Journal Impact Factor. *JAMA* 295(1):90–93.

J E Hirsch. 2005. An index to quantify an individual's scientific research output. *Proc Natl Acad Sci USA* 102(46):16569–16572.

J Huang and S Ertekin. 2006. Fast Author Name Disambiguation in CiteSeer .

JISC and the Internet Archive. 2013. JISC UK Web Domain Dataset (1996-2013).

K Kousha and M Thelwall. 2017. Are wikipedia citations important evidence of the impact of scholarly articles and books? *Journal of the Association for Information Science and Technology* 68(3):762–779.

J Lane and S Bertuzzi. 2010. The STAR METRICS project: current and future uses for S&E workforce data. In *Science of Science Measurement Workshop, held Washington DC.*

J Liu and E Adie. 2013. Five challenges in altmetrics: A toolmaker's perspective. *Bulletin of the American Society for Information Science and Technology* 39:31–34.

A Louis and A Nenkova. 2013. A corpus of science journalism for analyzing writing quality. *Dialogue and Discourse* 4(2):87–117.

K McKeown et al. 2016. Predicting the Impact of Scientific Concepts Using Full-Text Features. *Journal of the Association of for Information Science and Technology* 67(11):2684–2696.

E Moreau et al. 2008. Robust Similarity Measures for Named Entities Matching pages 593–600.

F Nielsen et al. 2017. Scholia and scientometrics with Wikidata. In *Joint Proceedings of the 1st International Workshop on Scientometrics and 1st International Workshop on Enabling Decentralised Scholarly Communication.*

F Årup Nielsen. 2007. Scientific citations in Wikipedia. *First Monday* 12(8).

N Paskin. 2015. The digital object identifier: From ad hoc to national to international. In *The Critical Component: Standards in the Information Exchange Environment*, ALCTS (American Library Association Publishing).

J Ravenscroft et al. 2017. Measuring scientific impact beyond academia: An assessment of existing impact metrics and proposed improvements. *PLOS ONE* 12(3):e0173152.

REF 2014. 2012. Assessment framework and guidance on submissions. http://www.ref.ac.uk/2014/pubs/2011-02/.

J Wu et al. 2014. CiteSeerX : AI in a Digital Library Search Engine. *Proceedings of the Twenty-Sixth Annual Conference on Innovative Applications of Artificial Intelligence* 36(3):2930–2937.

Jack the Reader – A Machine Reading Framework

**Dirk Weissenborn[1], Pasquale Minervini[2], Tim Dettmers[3], Isabelle Augenstein[4],
Johannes Welbl[2], Tim Rocktäschel[5], Matko Bošnjak[2], Jeff Mitchell[2],
Thomas Demeester[6], Pontus Stenetorp[2], Sebastian Riedel[2]**

[1]German Research Center for Artificial Intelligence (DFKI), Germany
[2]University College London, United Kingdom
[3]Università della Svizzera italiana, Switzerland
[4]University of Copenhagen, Denmark
[5]University of Oxford, United Kingdom
[6]Ghent University - imec, Ghent, Belgium

Abstract

Many Machine Reading and Natural Language Understanding tasks require reading supporting text in order to answer questions. For example, in Question Answering, the supporting text can be newswire or Wikipedia articles; in Natural Language Inference, premises can be seen as the supporting text and hypotheses as questions. Providing a set of useful primitives operating in a single framework of related tasks would allow for expressive modelling, and easier model comparison and replication. To that end, we present Jack the Reader (JACK), a framework for Machine Reading that allows for quick model prototyping by component reuse, evaluation of new models on existing datasets as well as integrating new datasets and applying them on a growing set of implemented baseline models. JACK is currently supporting (but not limited to) three tasks: Question Answering, Natural Language Inference, and Link Prediction. It is developed with the aim of increasing research efficiency and code reuse.

1 Introduction

Automated reading and understanding of textual and symbolic input, to a degree that enables question answering, is at the core of Machine Reading (*MR*). A core insight facilitating the development of MR models is that most of these tasks can be cast as an instance of the Question Answering (*QA*) task: an input can be cast in terms of *question, support documents* and *answer candidates*, and an output in terms of *answers*. For instance, in case of Natural Language Inference (*NLI*), we can view the hypothesis as a multiple choice question about the underlying premise (support) with predefined set of specific answer candidates (entailment, contradiction, neutral). Link Prediction (*LP*) – a task which requires predicting the truth value about facts represented as *(subject, predicate, object)*-triples – can be conceived of as an instance of QA (see Section 4 for more details). By unifying these tasks into a single framework, we can facilitate the design and construction of multi-component MR pipelines.

There are many successful frameworks such as STANFORD CORENLP (Manning et al., 2014), NLTK (Bird et al., 2009), and SPACY[1] for NLP, LUCENE[2] and SOLR[3] for Information Retrieval, and SCIKIT-LEARN[4], PYTORCH[5] and TENSOR-FLOW (Abadi et al., 2015) for general Machine Learning (*ML*) with a special focus on Deep Learning (*DL*), among others. All of these frameworks touch upon several aspects of Machine Reading, but none of them offers dedicated support for modern MR pipelines. Pre-processing and transforming MR datasets into a format that is usable by a MR model as well as implementing common architecture building blocks all require substantial effort which is not specifically handled by any of the aforementioned solutions. This is due to the fact that they serve a different, typically much broader purpose.

In this paper, we introduce Jack the Reader (JACK), a reusable framework for MR. It allows for the easy integration of novel tasks and datasets by exposing a set of high-level primitives and a common data format. For supported tasks it is straight-forward to develop new models without worrying about the cumbersome implementation

---

[1]`https://spacy.io`
[2]`https://lucene.apache.org`
[3]`http://lucene.apache.org/solr/`
[4]`http://scikit-learn.org`
[5]`http://pytorch.org/`

Proceedings of the 56th Annual Meeting of the Association for Computational Linguistics-System Demonstrations, pages 25–30
Melbourne, Australia, July 15 - 20, 2018. ©2018 Association for Computational Linguistics

of training, evaluation, pre- and post-processing routines. Declarative model definitions make the development of QA and NLI models using common building blocks effortless. JACK covers a large variety of datasets, implementations and pre-trained models on three distinct MR tasks and supports two ML backends, namely PYTORCH and TENSORFLOW. Furthermore, it is easy to train, deploy, and interact with MR models, which we refer to as *readers*.

2 Related Work

Machine Reading requires a tight integration of Natural Language Processing and Machine Learning models. General NLP frameworks include CORENLP (Manning et al., 2014), NLTK (Bird et al., 2009), OPENNLP[6] and SPACY. All these frameworks offer pre-built models for standard NLP preprocessing tasks, such as tokenisation, sentence splitting, named entity recognition and parsing.

GATE (Cunningham et al., 2002) and UIMA (Ferrucci and Lally, 2004) are toolkits that allow quick assembly of baseline NLP pipelines, and visualisation and annotation via a Graphical User Interface. GATE can utilise NLTK and CORENLP models and additionally enable development of rule-based methods using a dedicated pattern language. UIMA offers a text analysis pipeline which, unlike GATE, also includes retrieving information, but does not offer its own rule-based language. It is further worth mentioning the Information Retrieval frameworks APACHE LUCENE and APACHE SOLR which can be used for building simple, keyword-based question answering systems, but offer no ML support.

Multiple general machine learning frameworks, such as SCIKIT-LEARN (Pedregosa et al., 2011), PYTORCH, THEANO (Theano Development Team, 2016) and TENSORFLOW (Abadi et al., 2015), among others, enable quick prototyping and deployment of ML models. However, unlike JACK, they do not offer a simple framework for defining and evaluating MR models.

The framework closest in objectives to JACK is ALLENNLP (Gardner et al., 2017), which is a research-focused open-source NLP library built on PYTORCH. It provides the basic low-level components common to many systems in addition

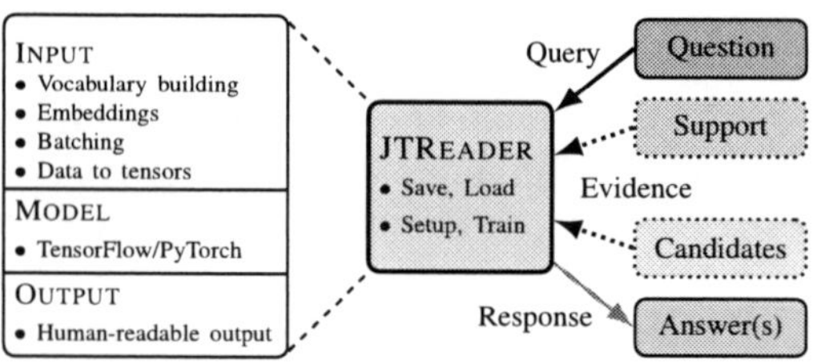

Figure 1: Our core abstraction, the JTREADER. On the left, the responsibilities covered by the INPUT, MODEL and OUTPUT modules that compose a JTREADER instance. On the right, the data format that is used to interact with a JTREADER (dotted lines indicate that the component is optional).

to pre-assembled models for standard NLP tasks, such as coreference resolution, constituency parsing, named entity recognition, question answering and textual entailment. In comparison with ALLENNLP, JACK supports both TENSORFLOW and PYTORCH. Furthermore, JACK can also learn from Knowledge Graphs (discussed in Section 4), while ALLENNLP focuses on textual inputs. Finally, JACK is structured following a modular architecture, composed by input-, model-, and output modules, facilitating code reuse and the inclusion and prototyping of new methods.

3 Overview

In Figure 1 we give a high-level overview of our core abstraction, the JTREADER. It is a task-agnostic wrapper around three typically task-dependent modules, namely the *input*, *model* and *output* modules. Besides serving as a container for modules, a JTREADER provides convenience functionality for interaction, training and serialisation. The underlying modularity is therefore well hidden from the user which facilitates the application of trained models.

3.1 Modules and Their Usage

Our abstract modules have the following high-level responsibilities:

- INPUT MODULES: Pre-processing that transforms a text-based input to tensors.

- MODEL MODULES: Implementation of the actual end-to-end MR model.

- OUTPUT MODULES: Converting predictions into human readable answers.

---

[6]https://opennlp.apache.org

The main design for building models in JACK revolves around functional interfaces between the three main modules: the input-, model-, and output module. Each module can be viewed as a thin wrapper around a (set of) function(s) that additionally provides explicit signatures in the form of *tensor ports* which can be understood as named placeholders for tensors.

The use of explicit signatures helps validate whether modules are correctly implemented and invoked, and to ensure correct behaviour as well as compatibility between modules. Finally, by implementing modules as classes and their interaction via a simple functional interface, JACK allows for the exploitation of benefits stemming from the use of object oriented programming, while retaining the flexibility offered by the functional programming paradigm when combining modules.

Given a list of training instances, corresponding to question-answer pairs, a *input module* is responsible for converting such instances into tensors. Each produced tensor is associated with a pre-defined *tensor port* – a named placeholder for a tensor – which can in turn be used in later modules to retrieve the actual tensor. This step typically involves some shallow forms of linguistic pre-processing such as tokenisation, building vocabularies, etc. The *model module* runs the end-to-end MR model on the now tensorised input and computes a new mapping of output tensor ports to newly computed tensors. Finally, the joint tensor mappings of the input- and model module serve as input to the *output module* which produces a human-readable answer. More in-depth documentation can be found on the project website.

3.2 Distinguishing Features

Module Reusability. Our shallow modularisation of readers into input-, model- and output modules has the advantage that they can be reused easily. Most of nowadays state-of-the-art MR models require the exact same kind of input pre-processing and produce output of the same form. Therefore, existing input- and output modules that are responsible for pre- and post-processing can be reused in most cases, which enables researchers to focus on prototyping and implementing new models. Although we acknowledge that most of the pre-processing can easily be performed by third-party libraries such as CORENLP, NLTK or SPACY, we argue that additional functionality, such as building and controlling vocabularies, padding, batching, etc., and connecting the pre-processed output with the actual model implementation pose time intensive implementation challenges. These can be avoided when working with one of our currently supported tasks – Question Answering, Natural Language Inference, or Link Prediction in Knowledge Graphs. Note that modules are typically task specific and not shared directly between tasks. However, utilities like the pre-processing functions mentioned above and model building blocks can readily be reused even between tasks.

Supported ML Backends. By decoupling modelling from pre- and post-processing we can easily switch between backends for model implementations. At the time of writing, JACK offers support for both TENSORFLOW and PYTORCH. This allows practitioners to use their preferred library for implementing new MR models and allows for the integration of more back-ends in the future.

Declarative Model Definition. Implementing different kinds of MR models can be repetitive, tedious, and error-prone. Most neural architectures are built using a finite set of basic *building blocks* for encoding sequences, and realising interaction between sequences (e.g. via attention mechanisms). For such a reason, JACK allows to describe these models at a high level, as a composition of simpler building blocks [7], leaving concrete implementation details to the framework.

The advantage of using such an approach is that is very easy to change, adapt or even create new models without knowing any implementation specifics of JACK or its underlying frameworks, such as TENSORFLOW and PYTORCH. This solution also offers another important advantage: it allows for easy experimentation of automated architecture search and optimisation (AutoML). JACK already enables the definition of new models purely within configuration files without writing any source code. These are interpreted by JACK and support a (growing) set of pre-defined building blocks. In fact, many models for different tasks in JACK are realised by high-level architecture descriptions. An example of an high-level architecture definition in JACK is available in Appendix A.

---

[7]For instance, see `https://github.com/uclmr/jack/blob/master/conf/nli/esim.yaml`

Dataset Coverage. JACK allows parsing a large number of datasets for QA, NLI, and Link Prediction. The supported QA datasets include SQuAD (Rajpurkar et al., 2016), TriviaQA (Joshi et al., 2017), NewsQA (Trischler et al., 2017), and QAngaroo (Welbl et al., 2017). The supported NLI datasets include SNLI (Bowman et al., 2015), and MultiNLI (Williams et al., 2018). The supported Link Prediction datasets include WN18 (Bordes et al., 2013), WN18RR (Dettmers et al., 2018), and FB15k-237 (Toutanova and Chen, 2015).

Pre-trained Models. JACK offers several pre-trained models. For QA, these include FastQA, BiDAF, and JackQA trained on SQuAD and TriviaQA. For NLI, these include DAM and ESIM trained on SNLI and MultiNLI. For LP, these include DistMult and ComplEx trained on WN18, WN18RR and FB15k-237.

4 Supported MR Tasks

Most end-user MR tasks can be cast as an instance of question answering. The input to a typical question answering setting consists of a *question, supporting texts* and *answers* during training. In the following we show how JACK is used to model our currently supported MR tasks.

Ready to use implementations for these tasks exist which allows for rapid prototyping. Researchers interested in developing new models can define their architecture in TENSORFLOW or PYTORCH, and reuse existing of input- and output modules. New datasets can be tested quickly on a set of implemented baseline models after converting them to one of our supported formats.

Extractive Question Answering. JACK supports the task of *Extractive Question Answering* (EQA), which requires a model to extract an answer for a question in the form of an answer span comprising a document id, token start and -end from a given set of supporting documents. This task is a natural fit for our internal data format, and is thus very easy to represent with JACK.

Natural Language Inference. Another popular MR task is *Natural Language Inference*, also known as Recognising Textual Entailment (RTE). The task is to predict whether a *hypothesis* is entailed by, contradicted by, or neutral with respect to a given *premise*. In JACK, NLI is viewed as an instance of multiple-choice Question Answering problem, by casting the hypothesis as the question, and the premise as the support. The answer candidates to this question are the three possible outcomes or classes – namely *entails, contradicts* or *neutral*.

Link Prediction. A Knowledge Graph is a set of (s, p, o) triples, where s, o denote the *subject* and *object* of the triple, and p denotes its *predicate*: each (s, p, o) triple denotes a fact, represented as a relationship of type p between entities s and o, such as: (LONDON, CAPITALOF, UK). Real-world Knowledge Graphs, such as Freebase (Bollacker et al., 2007), are largely incomplete: the *Link Prediction* task consists in identifying missing (s, p, o) triples that are likely to encode true facts (Nickel et al., 2016).

JACK also supports Link Prediction, because existing LP models can be cast as multiple-choice Question Answering models, where the question is composed of three words – a subject s, a predicate p, and an object o. The answer candidates to these questions are *true* and *false*.

In its original formulation of the Link Prediction task, the support is left empty. However, JACK facilitates enriching the questions with additional support – consisting, for instance, of the neighbourhood of the entities involved in the question, or sentences from a text corpus that include the entities appearing in the triple in question. Such a setup can be interpreted as an instance of NLI, and existing models not originally designed for solving Link Prediction problems can be trained effortlessly.

5 Experiments

Experimental setup and results for different models on the three above-mentioned MR tasks are reported in this section. Note that our re-implementations or training configurations may not be entirely faithful.We performed slight modifications to original setups where we found this to perform better in our experiments, as indicated in the respective task subsections. However, our results still vary from the reported ones, which we believe is due to the extensive hyper-parameter engineering that went into the original settings, which we did not perform. For each experiment, a ready to use training configuration as well as pre-trained models are part of JACK.

Model	Original F1	JACK F1	Speed	#Params
BiDAF	77.3	77.8	1.0x	2.02M
FastQA	76.3	77.4	2.2x	0.95M
JackQA	–	79.6	2.0x	1.18M

Table 1: Metrics on the SQuAD development set comparing F1 metric from the original implementation to that of JACK, number of parameters, and relative speed of the models.

Model	Original	JACK
cBiLSTM (Rocktäschel et al., 2016)	–	82.0
DAM (Parikh et al., 2016)	86.6	84.6
ESIM (Chen et al., 2017)	88.0	87.2

Table 2: Accuracy on the SNLI test set achieved by cBiLSTM, DAM, and ESIM.

Question Answering. For the Question Answering (QA) experiments we report results for our implementations of FastQA (Weissenborn et al., 2017), BiDAF (Seo et al., 2016) and, in addition, our own JackQA implementations. With JackQA we aim to provide a fast and accurate QA model. Both BiDAF and JackQA are realised using high-level architecture descriptions, that is, their architectures are purely defined within their respective configuration files. Results of our models on the SQuAD (Rajpurkar et al., 2016) development set along with additional run-time and parameter metrics are presented in Table 1. Apart from SQuAD, JACK supports the more recent NewsQA (Trischler et al., 2017) and TriviaQA (Joshi et al., 2017) datasets too.

Natural Language Inference. For NLI, we report results for our implementations of conditional BiLSTMs (cBiLSTM) (Rocktäschel et al., 2016), the bidirectional version of conditional LSTMs (Augenstein et al., 2016), the Decomposable Attention Model (DAM, Parikh et al., 2016) and Enhanced LSTM (ESIM, Chen et al., 2017). ESIM was entirely implemented as a *modular* NLI model, i.e. its architecture was purely defined in a configuration file – see Appendix A for more details. Our models or training configurations contain slight modifications from the original which we found to perform better than the original setup. Our results are slightly differ from those reported, since we did not always perform an exhaustive hyper-parameter search.

Dataset	Model	MRR	Hits@3	Hits@10
WN18	DistMult	0.822	0.914	0.936
	ComplEx	0.941	0.936	0.947
WN18RR	DistMult	0.430	0.443	0.490
	ComplEx	0.440	0.461	0.510
FB15k-237	DistMult	0.241	0.263	0.419
	ComplEx	0.247	0.275	0.428

Table 3: Link Prediction results, measured using the Mean Reciprocal Rank (MRR) and Hits@10, for DistMult (Yang et al., 2015), and ComplEx (Trouillon et al., 2016).

Link Prediction. For Link Prediction in Knowledge Graphs, we report results for our implementations of DistMult (Yang et al., 2015) and ComplEx (Trouillon et al., 2016) on various datasets. Results are otlined in Table 3.

6 Demo

We created three tutorial *Jupyter* notebooks at `https://github.com/uclmr/jack/tree/master/notebooks` to demo JACK's use cases. The quick start notebook shows how to quickly set up, load and run the existing systems for QA and NLI. The model training notebook demonstrates training, testing, evaluating and saving QA and NLI models programmatically. However, normally the user will simply use the provided training script from command line. The model implementation notebook delves deeper into implementing new models from scratch by writing all modules for a custom model.

7 Conclusion

We presented Jack the Reader (JACK), a shared framework for Machine Reading tasks that will allow component reuse and easy model transfer across both datasets and domains.

JACK is a new unified Machine Reading framework applicable to a range of tasks, developed with the aim of increasing researcher efficiency and code reuse. We demonstrate the flexibility of our framework in terms of three tasks: Question Answering, Natural Language Inference, and Link Prediction in Knowledge Graphs. With further model additions and wider user adoption, JACK will support faster and reproducible Machine Reading research, enabling a building-block approach to model design and development.

References

Martín Abadi et al. 2015. TensorFlow: Large-scale machine learning on heterogeneous systems. Software available from tensorflow.org. https://www.tensorflow.org/.

Isabelle Augenstein, Tim Rocktäschel, Andreas Vlachos, and Kalina Bontcheva. 2016. Stance detection with bidirectional conditional encoding. In *Proceedings or EMNLP*. pages 876–885.

Steven Bird, Ewan Klein, and Edward Loper. 2009. *Natural language processing with Python: analyzing text with the natural language toolkit.* " O'Reilly Media, Inc.".

Kurt D. Bollacker, Robert P. Cook, and Patrick Tufts. 2007. Freebase: A shared database of structured general human knowledge. In *Proceedings of AAAI*. pages 1962–1963.

Antoine Bordes, Nicolas Usunier, Alberto García-Durán, Jason Weston, and Oksana Yakhnenko. 2013. Translating embeddings for modeling multi-relational data. In *Proceedings of NIPS*. pages 2787–2795.

Samuel R. Bowman, Gabor Angeli, Christopher Potts, and Christopher D. Manning. 2015. A large annotated corpus for learning natural language inference. In *Proceedings of EMNLP*. pages 632–642.

Qian Chen, Xiaodan Zhu, Zhen-Hua Ling, Si Wei, Hui Jiang, and Diana Inkpen. 2017. Enhanced LSTM for natural language inference. In *Proceedings of ACL*. pages 1657–1668.

Hamish Cunningham, Diana Maynard, Kalina Bontcheva, and Valentin Tablan. 2002. GATE: an Architecture for Development of Robust HLT applications. In *Proceedings of ACL*.

Tim Dettmers, Minervini Pasquale, Stenetorp Pontus, and Sebastian Riedel. 2018. Convolutional 2d knowledge graph embeddings. In *Proceedings of AAAI*.

David Ferrucci and Adam Lally. 2004. Uima: an architectural approach to unstructured information processing in the corporate research environment. *Natural Language Engineering* 10(3-4):327–348.

Matt Gardner et al. 2017. AllenNLP: A Deep Semantic Natural Language Processing Platform. White paper.

Mandar Joshi, Eunsol Choi, Daniel S. Weld, and Luke Zettlemoyer. 2017. Triviaqa: A large scale distantly supervised challenge dataset for reading comprehension. In *Proceedings of ACL*. pages 1601–1611.

Christopher Manning et al. 2014. The Stanford CoreNLP Natural Language Processing Toolkit. In *Proceedings of ACL: System Demonstrations*. pages 55–60.

Maximilian Nickel, Kevin Murphy, Volker Tresp, and Evgeniy Gabrilovich. 2016. A review of relational machine learning for knowledge graphs. In *Proceedings of IEEE*. volume 104, pages 11–33.

Ankur P. Parikh, Oscar Täckström, Dipanjan Das, and Jakob Uszkoreit. 2016. A decomposable attention model for natural language inference. In *Proceedings of EMNLP*. pages 2249–2255.

Fabian Pedregosa et al. 2011. Scikit-learn: Machine learning in Python. *JMLR* 12(Oct):2825–2830.

Pranav Rajpurkar, Jian Zhang, Konstantin Lopyrev, and Percy Liang. 2016. SQuAD: 100,000+ Questions for Machine Comprehension of Text. In *Proceedings of EMNLP*. pages 2383–2392.

Tim Rocktäschel, Edward Grefenstette, Karl Moritz Hermann, Tomas Kocisky, and Phil Blunsom. 2016. Reasoning about Entailment with Neural Attention. In *Proceedings of ICLR*.

Min Joon Seo, Aniruddha Kembhavi, Ali Farhadi, and Hannaneh Hajishirzi. 2016. Bidirectional attention flow for machine comprehension. In *Proceedings of ICLR*.

Theano Development Team. 2016. Theano: A Python framework for fast computation of mathematical expressions. *arXiv e-prints* abs/1605.02688.

Kristina Toutanova and Danqi Chen. 2015. Observed versus latent features for knowledge base and text inference. *CVSC workshop, ACL* pages 57–66.

Adam Trischler et al. 2017. NewsQA: A machine comprehension dataset. *Rep4NLP workshop, ACL* .

Théo Trouillon, Johannes Welbl, Sebastian Riedel, Éric Gaussier, and Guillaume Bouchard. 2016. Complex embeddings for simple link prediction. In *Proceedings of ICML*. pages 2071–2080.

Dirk Weissenborn, Georg Wiese, and Laura Seiffe. 2017. Making neural QA as simple as possible but not simpler. In *Proceedings of CoNLL*. pages 271–280.

Johannes Welbl, Pontus Stenetorp, and Sebastian Riedel. 2017. Constructing datasets for multi-hop reading comprehension across documents. *CoRR* abs/1710.06481.

Adina Williams, Nikita Nangia, and Samuel R. Bowman. 2018. A broad-coverage challenge corpus for sentence understanding through inference. In *Proceedings of NAACL*.

Bishan Yang, Wen-tau Yih, Xiaodong He, Jianfeng Gao, and Li Deng. 2015. Embedding Entities and Relations for Learning and Inference in Knowledge Bases. In *Proceedings of ICLR*.

YEDDA: A Lightweight Collaborative Text Span Annotation Tool

Jie Yang, Yue Zhang, Linwei Li, Xingxuan Li
Singapore University of Technology and Design
{jie_yang, linwei_li, xingxuan_li}@mymail.sutd.edu.sg
yue_zhang@sutd.edu.sg

Abstract

In this paper, we introduce YEDDA, a lightweight but efficient and comprehensive open-source tool for text span annotation. YEDDA provides a systematic solution for text span annotation, ranging from collaborative user annotation to administrator evaluation and analysis. It overcomes the low efficiency of traditional text annotation tools by annotating entities through both command line and shortcut keys, which are configurable with custom labels. YEDDA also gives intelligent recommendations by learning the up-to-date annotated text. An administrator client is developed to evaluate annotation quality of multiple annotators and generate detailed comparison report for each annotator pair. Experiments show that the proposed system can reduce the annotation time by half compared with existing annotation tools. And the annotation time can be further compressed by 16.47% through intelligent recommendation.

1 Introduction

Natural Language Processing (NLP) systems rely on large-scale training data (Marcus et al., 1993) for supervised training. However, manual annotation can be time-consuming and expensive. Despite detailed annotation standards and rules, inter-annotator disagreement is inevitable because of human mistakes, language phenomena which are not covered by the annotation rules and the ambiguity of language itself (Plank et al., 2014).

Existing annotation tools (Cunningham et al., 2002; Morton and LaCivita, 2003; Chen and Styler, 2013; Druskat et al., 2014) mainly focus on providing a visual interface for user annotation

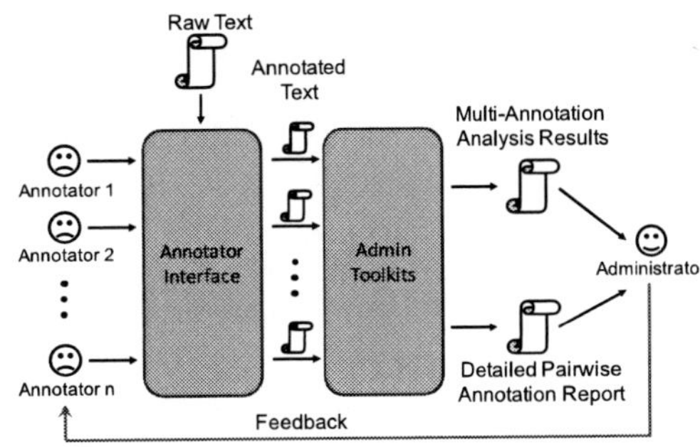

Figure 1: Framework of YEDDA.

process but rarely consider the post-annotation quality analysis, which is necessary due to the inter-annotator disagreement. In addition to the annotation quality, efficiency is also critical in large-scale annotation task, while being relatively less addressed in existing annotation tools (Ogren, 2006; Stenetorp et al., 2012). Besides, many tools (Ogren, 2006; Chen and Styler, 2013) require a complex system configuration on either local device or server, which is not friendly to new users.

To address the challenges above, we propose YEDDA[1], a lightweight and efficient annotation tool for text span annotation. A snapshot is shown in Figure 2. Here text span boundaries are selected and assigned with a label, which can be useful for Named Entity Recognition (NER) (Tjong Kim Sang and De Meulder, 2003), word segmentation (Sproat and Emerson, 2003), chunking (Tjong Kim Sang and Buchholz, 2000) ,etc. To keep annotation efficient and accurate, YEDDA provides systematic solutions across the whole annotation process, which includes the shortcut annotation, batch annotation with a command line, intelligent recommendation, format exporting and

---

[1]Code is available at https://github.com/jiesutd/YEDDA.

Proceedings of the 56th Annual Meeting of the Association for Computational Linguistics-System Demonstrations, pages 31–36
Melbourne, Australia, July 15 - 20, 2018. ©2018 Association for Computational Linguistics

Tool	Operating System			Self Consistency	Command Line Annotation	System Recommendation	Analysis	Size	Language
	MacOS	Linux	Win						
WordFreak	√	√	√	√	×	√	×	1.1M	Java
GATE	√	√	√	√	×	√	×	544M	Java
Knowtator	√	√	√	×	×	×	√	1.5M	Java
Stanford	√	√	√	√	×	×	×	88k	Java
Atomic	√	√	√	√	×	×	×	5.8M	Java
WebAnno	√	√	√	×	×	√	√	13.2M	Java
Anafora	√	√	×	×	×	×	×	1.7M	Python
BRAT	√	√	×	×	×	√	×	31.1M	Python
YEDDA	√	√	√	√	√	√	√	80k	Python

Table 1: Annotation Tool Comparison .

administrator evaluation/analysis.

Figure 1 shows the general framework of YEDDA. It offers annotators with a simple and efficient Graphical User Interface (GUI) to annotate raw text. For the administrator, it provides two useful toolkits to evaluate multi-annotated text and generate detailed comparison report for annotator pair. YEDDA has the advantages of being:
• **Convenient**: it is lightweight with an intuitive interface and does not rely on specific operating systems or pre-installed packages.
• **Efficient**: it supports both shortcut and command line annotation models to accelerate the annotating process.
• **Intelligent**: it offers user with real-time system suggestions to avoid duplicated annotation.
• **Comprehensive**: it integrates useful toolkits to give the statistical index of analyzing multi-user annotation results and generate detailed content comparison for annotation pairs.

This paper is organized as follows: Section 2 gives an overview of previous text annotation tools and the comparison with ours. Section 3 describes the architecture of YEDDA and its detail functions. Section 4 shows the efficiency comparison results of different annotation tools. Finally, Section 5 concludes this paper and give the future plans.

2 Related Work

There exists a range of text span annotation tools which focus on different aspects of the annotation process. Stanford manual annotation tool[2] is a lightweight tool but does not support result analysis and system recommendation. Knowtator (Ogren, 2006) is a general-task annotation tool which links to a biomedical onto ontology to

help identify named entities and relations. It supports quality control during the annotation process by integrating simple inter-annotator evaluation, while it cannot figure out the detailed disagreed labels. WordFreak (Morton and LaCivita, 2003) adds a system recommendation function and integrates active learning to rank the unannotated sentences based on the recommend confidence, while the post-annotation analysis is not supported.

Web-based annotation tools have been developed to build operating system independent annotation environments. GATE[3] (Bontcheva et al., 2013) includes a web-based with collaborative annotation framework which allows users to work collaboratively by annotating online with shared text storage. BRAT (Stenetorp et al., 2012) is another web-based tool, which has been widely used in recent years, it provides powerful annotation functions and rich visualization ability, while it does not integrate the result analysis function. Anafora (Chen and Styler, 2013) and Atomic (Druskat et al., 2014) are also web-based and lightweight annotation tools, while they don't support the automatic annotation and quality analysis either. WebAnno (Yimam et al., 2013; de Castilho et al., 2016) supports both the automatic annotation suggestion and annotation quality monitoring such as inter-annotator agreement measurement, data curation, and progress monitoring. It compares the annotation disagreements only for each sentence and shows the comparison within the interface, while our system can generate a detailed disagreement report in `.pdf` file through the whole annotated content. Besides, those web-based annotation tools need to build a server through complex configurations and some of the servers cannot be deployed on Windows systems.

---

[2] `http://nlp.stanford.edu/software/ stanford-manual-annotation-tool-2004-05-16. tar.gz`

[3] GATE is a general NLP tool which includes annotation function.

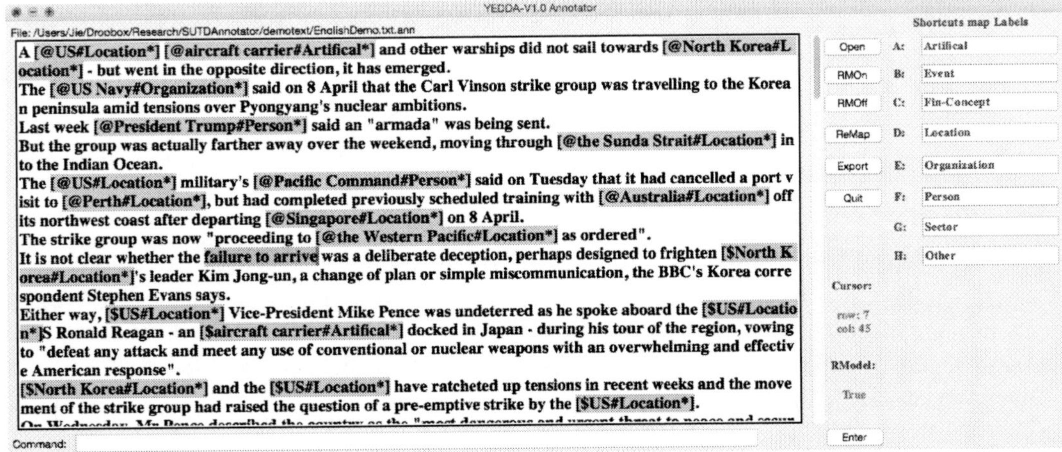

Figure 2: Annotator Interface.

The differences between YEDDA and related work are summarised in Table 1[4]. Here "Self Consistency" represents whether the tool works independently or it relies on pre-installed packages. Compared to these tools, YEDDA provides a lighter but more systematic choice with more flexibility, efficiency and less dependence on system environment for text span annotation. Besides, YEDDA offers administrator useful toolkits for evaluating the annotation quality and analyze the detailed disagreements within annotators.

3 YEDDA

YEDDA is developed based on standard Python GUI library Tkinter[5], and hence needs only Python installation as a prerequisite and is compatible with all Operating System (OS) platforms with Python installation. It offers two user-friendly interfaces for annotators and administrator, respectively, which are introduced in detail in Section 3.1 and Section 3.2, respectively.

3.1 Annotator Client

The client is designed to accelerate the annotation process as much as possible. It supports shortcut annotation to reduce the user operation time. Command line annotation is designed to annotate multi-span in batch. In addition, the client provides system recommendations to lessen the workload of duplicated span annotation.

Figure 2 shows the interface of annotator client on an English entity annotation file. The interface consists of 5 parts. The working area in the up-left which shows the texts with different colors (blue: annotated entities, green: recommended entities and orange: selected text span). The entry at the bottom is the command line which accepts annotation command. There are several control buttons in the middle of the interface, which are used to set annotation model. The status area is below the control buttons, it shows the cursor position and the status of recommending model. The right side shows the shortcut map, where shortcut key "a" or "A" means annotating the text span with "Artificial" type and the same for other shortcut keys. The shortcut map can be configured easily[6]. Details are introduced as follows.

3.1.1 Shortcut Key Annotation

YEDDA provides the function of annotating text span by selecting using mouse and press shortcut key to map the selection into a specific label. It is a common annotation process in many annotation tools (Stenetorp et al., 2012; Bontcheva et al., 2013). It binds each label with one custom shortcut key, this is shown in the "Shortcuts map Labels" part of Figure 2. The annotator needs only two steps to annotate one text span, i.e. "select and press". The annotated file updates simultaneously with each key pressing process.

---

[4]For web-based tools, we list their server-side dependency on operating systems.

[5]https://docs.python.org/2/library/tkinter.html

[6]Type the corresponding labels into the entries following shortcut keys and press "ReMap" button.

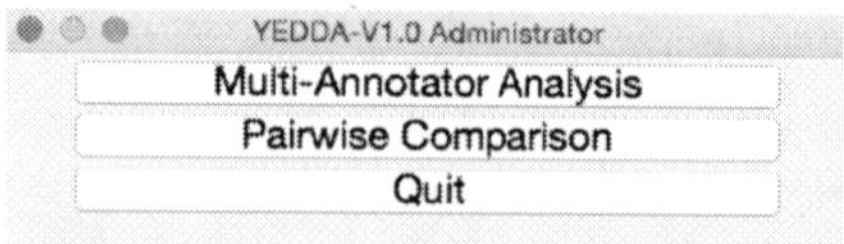

Figure 3: Administrator Interface.

F:Entity/Chunk	UserA	UserB	UserC	UserD	UserE
UserA	100/100	64.1/74.5	70.5/80.9	52.6/62.5	59.0/67.3
UserB	64.1/74.5	100/100	64.8/74.9	58.8/67.1	56.1/66.7
UserC	70.5/80.9	64.8/74.9	100/100	54.7/64.6	57.9/69.2
UserD	52.6/62.5	58.8/67.1	54.7/64.6	100/100	63.7/75.9
UserE	59.0/67.3	56.1/66.7	57.9/69.2	63.7/75.9	100/100

Figure 4: Multiple annotators F1-score matrix.

3.1.2 Command Line Annotation

YEDDA also support the command line annotation function (see the command entry in the bottom of Figure 2) which can execute multi-span annotation at once. The system will parse the command automatically and convert the command into multi-span annotation instructions and execute in batch. It is quite efficient for the tasks of character-based languages (such as Chinese and Japanese) with high entity density. The command follows a simple rule which is "$n1 + key1 + n2 + key2 + n3 + key3 + ...$", where '$n1, n2, n3$' are the length of the entities and '$key1, key2, key3$' is the corresponding shortcut key. For example, command "$2A3D2B$" represents annotating following 2 characters as label 'A' (mapped into a specific label name), the following 3 characters as label 'D' and 2 characters further as label 'B'.

3.1.3 System Recommendation

It has been shown that using pre-annotated text and manual correction increases the annotation efficiency in many annotation tasks (Meurs et al., 2011; Stenetorp et al., 2012). YEDDA offers annotators with system recommendation based on the existing annotation history. The current recommendation system incrementally collects annotated text spans from sentences that have been labeled, thus gaining a dynamically growing lexicon. Using the lexicon, the system automatically annotates sentences that are currently being annotated by leveraging the forward maximum matching algorithm. The automatically suggested text spans and their types are returned with colors in the user interface, as shown in green in Figure 2. Annotators can use the shortcut to confirm, correct or veto the suggestions. The recommending system keeps online updating during the whole annotation process, which learns the up-to-date and in-domain annotation information. The recommending system is designed as "pluggable" which ensures that the recommending algorithm can be easily extended into other sequence labeling models, such as Conditional Random Field (CRF)[7] (Lafferty et al., 2001). The recommendation can be controlled through two buttons "RMOn" and "RMOff", which enables and disables the recommending function, respectively.

3.1.4 Annotation Modification

It is inevitable that the annotator or the recommending system gives incorrect annotations or suggestions. Based on our annotation experience, we found that the time cost of annotation correction cannot be neglected. Therefore, YEDDA provides several efficient modification actions to revise the annotation:

- **Action withdraw**: annotators can cancel their previous action and let system return to the last status by press the shortcut key Ctrl+z.
- **Span label modification**: if the selected span has the correct boundary but receives an incorrect label, annotator only needs to put the cursor inside the span (or select the span) and press the shortcut key of the right label to correct label.
- **Label deletion**: similar to the label modification, the annotator can put the cursor inside the span and press shortcut key q to remove the annotated (recommended) label.

3.1.5 Export Annotated Text

As the annotated file is saved in .ann format, YEDDA provides the "Export" function which exports the annotated text as standard format (ended with .anns). Each line includes one word/character and its label, sentences are separated by an empty line. The exported label can be chosen in either BIO or BIOES format (Ratinov and Roth, 2009).

3.2 Administrator Toolkits

For the administrator, it is important and necessary to evaluate the quality of annotated files and analyze the detailed disagreements of different annotators. Shown in Figure 3, YEDDA provides a

---

[7]Those sequence labeling models work well on big training data. For limited training data, the maximum matching algorithm gives better performance.

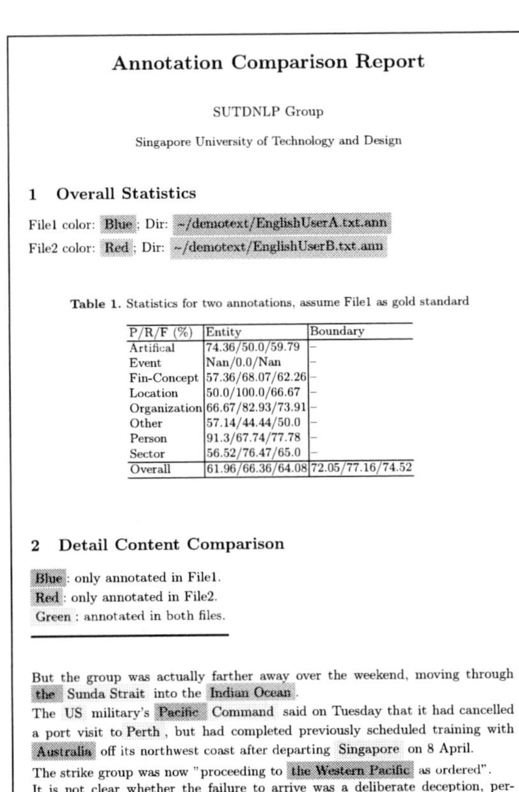

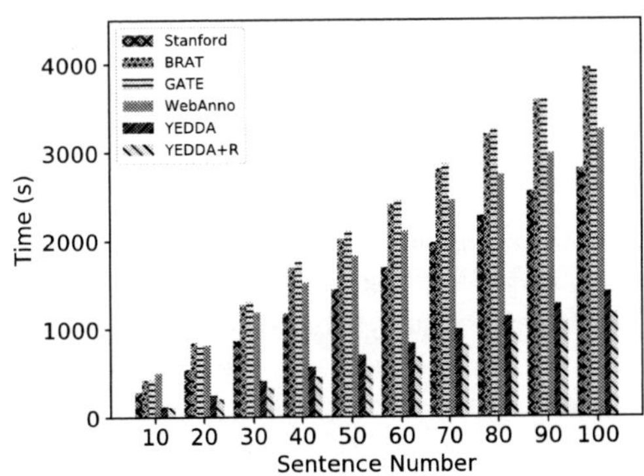

Figure 6: Speed comparison.

Figure 5: Detailed report for annotator pair.

simple interface with several toolkits for administrator monitoring the annotation process.

3.2.1 Multi-Annotator Analysis

To evaluate and monitor the annotation quality of different annotators, our Multi-Annotator Analysis (MAA) toolkit imports all the annotated files and gives the analysis results in a matrix. As shown in Figure 4, the matrix gives the F1-scores in full level (consider both boundary and label accuracy) and boundary level (ignore the label correctness, only care about the boundary accuracy) of all annotator pairs.

3.2.2 Pairwise Annotators Comparison

If an administrator wants to look into the detailed disagreement of annotators, it is quite convenient by using the Pairwise Annotators Comparison (PAC). PAC loads two annotated files and generates a specific comparison report file[8] for the two annotators. As shown in Figure 5, the report

is mainly in two parts:

- **Overall statistics**: it shows the specific precision, recall and F1-score[9] of two files in all labels. It also gives the three accuracy indexes on overall full level and boundary level in the end.
- **Content comparison**: this function gives the detailed comparison of two annotated files in whole content. It highlights the annotated parts of two annotators and assigns different colors for the agreed and disagreed span.

4 Experiments

Here we compare the efficiency of our system with four widely used annotation tools. We extract 100 sentences from CoNLL 2003 English NER (Tjong Kim Sang and De Meulder, 2003) training data, with each sentence containing at least 4 entities. Two undergraduate students without any experience on those tools are invited to annotate those sentences[10]. Their average annotation time is shown in Figure 6, where "YEDDA+R" suggests annotation using YEDDA with the help of system recommendation. The inter-annotator agreements for those tools are closed, which around 96.1% F1-score. As we can see from the figure, our YEDDA system can greatly reduce the annotation time. With the help of system recommendation, the annotation time can be further reduced. We notice that "YEDDA+R" has larger advantage with the increasing numbers of annotated sentences, this is because the system recommendation gives better

---

[8]The report is generated in `.tex` format and can be complied into `.pdf` file.

[9]Notice that we assume "File1" as a gold standard. This only affects the order of precision and recall, while the F1-score keeps same if we choose the other file as gold standard.

[10]We ask the students to annotate those sentences several rounds to get familiar with the entities before they start the final exercise with recording.

suggestions when it learns larger annotated sentences. The "YEDDA+R" gives 16.47% time reduction in annotating 100 sentences[11].

5 Conclusion and Future Work

We have presented a lightweight but systematic annotation tool, YEDDA, for annotating the entities in text and analyzing the annotation results efficiently. In order to reduce the workload of annotators, we are going to integrate active learning strategy in our system recommendation part in the future. A supervised sequence labeling model (such as CRF) is trained based on the annotated text, then unannotated sentences with less confidence (predicted by this model) are reordered in the front to ensure annotators only annotate the most confusing sentences.

6 Acknowledgements

We thank Yanxia Qin, Hongmin Wang, Shaolei Wang, Jiangming Liu, Yuze Gao, Ye Yuan, Lu Cao, Yumin Zhou and other members of SUTDNLP group for their trials and feedbacks. Yue Zhang is the corresponding author. Jie is supported by the YEDDA grant 52YD1314.

References

Kalina Bontcheva, Hamish Cunningham, Ian Roberts, Angus Roberts, Valentin Tablan, Niraj Aswani, and Genevieve Gorrell. 2013. Gate teamware: a web-based, collaborative text annotation framework. *Language Resources and Evaluation* 47(4):1007–1029.

Wei-Te Chen and Will Styler. 2013. Anafora: a web-based general purpose annotation tool. In *NAACL*. volume 2013, page 14.

Hamish Cunningham, Diana Maynard, Kalina Bontcheva, and Valentin Tablan. 2002. Gate: an architecture for development of robust hlt applications. In *ACL*. pages 168–175.

Richard Eckart de Castilho, Eva Mujdricza-Maydt, Seid Muhie Yimam, Silvana Hartmann, Iryna Gurevych, Anette Frank, and Chris Biemann. 2016. A web-based tool for the integrated annotation of semantic and syntactic structures. In *Proceedings of the Workshop on LT4DH*. pages 76–84.

Stephan Druskat, Lennart Bierkandt, Volker Gast, Christoph Rzymski, and Florian Zipser. 2014. Atomic: An open-source software platform for multi-level corpus annotation. In *Proceedings of the 12th Konferenz zur Verarbeitung natürlicher Sprache*.

John Lafferty, Andrew McCallum, and Fernando CN Pereira. 2001. Conditional random fields: Probabilistic models for segmenting and labeling sequence data. In *ICML*. volume 951, pages 282–289.

Mitchell P Marcus, Mary Ann Marcinkiewicz, and Beatrice Santorini. 1993. Building a large annotated corpus of english: The penn treebank. *Computational linguistics* 19(2):313–330.

Marie-Jean Meurs, Caitlin Murphy, Nona Naderi, Ingo Morgenstern, Carolina Cantu, Shary Semarjit, Greg Butler, Justin Powlowski, Adrian Tsang, and René Witte. 2011. Towards evaluating the impact of semantic support for curating the fungus scientific literature. *WS2* page 34.

Thomas Morton and Jeremy LaCivita. 2003. Wordfreak: an open tool for linguistic annotation. In *NAACL: Demo*. pages 17–18.

Philip V Ogren. 2006. Knowtator: a protégé plug-in for annotated corpus construction. In *NAACL: Demo*. Association for Computational Linguistics, pages 273–275.

Barbara Plank, Dirk Hovy, and Anders Søgaard. 2014. Linguistically debatable or just plain wrong? In *ACL*. volume 2, pages 507–511.

Lev Ratinov and Dan Roth. 2009. Design challenges and misconceptions in named entity recognition. In *CoNLL*. pages 147–155.

Richard Sproat and Thomas Emerson. 2003. The first international chinese word segmentation bakeoff. In *Proceedings of the SIGHAN workshop on CLP*. pages 133–143.

Pontus Stenetorp, Sampo Pyysalo, Goran Topić, Tomoko Ohta, Sophia Ananiadou, and Jun'ichi Tsujii. 2012. Brat: a web-based tool for nlp-assisted text annotation. In *EACL: Demo*. pages 102–107.

Erik F Tjong Kim Sang and Sabine Buchholz. 2000. Introduction to the conll-2000 shared task: Chunking. In *Proceedings of the 2nd workshop on Learning language in logic and the 4th conference on Computational natural language learning-Volume 7*. pages 127–132.

Erik F Tjong Kim Sang and Fien De Meulder. 2003. Introduction to the conll-2003 shared task: Language-independent named entity recognition. In *HLT-NAACL*. Association for Computational Linguistics, pages 142–147.

Seid Muhie Yimam, Iryna Gurevych, Richard Eckart de Castilho, and Chris Biemann. 2013. Webanno: A flexible, web-based and visually supported system for distributed annotations. In *ACL: Demo*. pages 1–6.

---

[11]The speed improvement by recommendation depends on the density of text spans. We suggest enabling the recommendation model in the task whose text contains dense and recurring text spans.

NextGen AML: Distributed Deep Learning based Language Technologies to Augment Anti Money Laundering Investigation

Jingguang Han[†], Utsab Barman[†§‡], Jer Hayes[†], Jinhua Du[†§], Edward Burgin[†], Dadong Wan[†]
[†]Accenture Labs Dublin, Ireland
[§]ADAPT Centre, Dublin City University, Ireland
[‡]University College Dublin, Ireland
{jingguang.han, jeremiah.hayes, edward.burgin, dadong.wan}@accenture.com
utsab.barman@ucd.ie, jinhua.du@adaptcentre.ie

Abstract

Most of the current anti money launder-ing (AML) systems, using handcrafted rules, are heavily reliant on existing struc-tured databases, which are not capable of effectively and efficiently identifying hidden and complex ML activities, es-pecially those with dynamic and time-varying characteristics, resulting in a high percentage of false positives. Therefore, analysts[1] are engaged for further inves-tigation which significantly increases hu-man capital cost and processing time. To alleviate these issues, this paper presents a novel framework for the next gener-ation AML by applying and visualiz-ing deep learning-driven natural language processing (NLP) technologies in a dis-tributed and scalable manner to augment AML monitoring and investigation. The proposed distributed framework performs *news and tweet sentiment analysis, en-tity recognition, relation extraction, en-tity linking* and *link analysis* on differ-ent data sources (e.g. news articles and tweets) to provide additional evidence to human investigators for final decision-making. Each NLP module is evaluated on a task-specific data set, and the over-all experiments are performed on synthetic and real-world datasets. Feedback from AML practitioners suggests that our sys-tem can reduce approximately 30% time and cost compared to their previous man-ual approaches of AML investigation.

1 Introduction

Money laundering (ML) is the process of transfer-ring criminal and illegal proceeds into ostensibly legitimate assets, and it has long been considered as the world's third largest "industry". ML is of-ten associated with terrorism financing, drug and human trafficking, so that it is a severe threat to the stability and security of the economy and pol-itics globally. The International Monetary Fund (IMF) estimates that the aggregate size of ML in the world could be somewhere between 2% and 5% of the global Gross Domestic Product (GDP), which is equivalent to $590 billion to $3.2 trillion USD approximately. The annual growth rate of the volume of illicit funds traveling through ML channels is estimated as 2.7% (Jorisch, 2009).

AML is one of the long-standing challenges in the financial sector. A number of systematic frameworks have been proposed for AML sys-tems (Gao and Xu, 2007; Gao and Ye, 2007; Gao and Xu, 2010; Gombiro and Jantjies, 2015) following a multi-stage procedure with data de-scription and transaction evaluation approaches. Moreover, several techniques have been applied in this area: rule-based, link-analysis and risk-classification/scoring-based methods.

In the traditional AML system, financial trans-actions are consistently monitored using complex rules and thresholds to identify suspicious ML pat-terns and generate red alerts, e.g. unexpected high amounts or high frequent transactions. These rules are rigid and restrictive to ensure the blockage of ML transactions, resulting in a high amount of false positives (transactions blocked by mis-take) (Pellegrina et al., 2009; Helmy et al., 2014). Consequently, a significant amount of human re-sources (reviewers/analysts) are engaged to ap-prove or block such red-alerted transactions. This manual validation process is mainly a consultation

---

[1]One of our banking clients has about 10,000 analysts globally to investigate over 400,000 red-alerted transactions weekly. With the data privacy and non-disclosure agreement, we are not entitled to release any clients' or entities' names.

Proceedings of the 56th Annual Meeting of the Association for Computational Linguistics-System Demonstrations, pages 37–42
Melbourne, Australia, July 15 - 20, 2018. ©2018 Association for Computational Linguistics

procedure which involves gathering intelligence information from different sources about the parties involved in a red-alerted transaction. Moreover, the manual process of gathering intelligence involves: (1) news search; (2) name screening; and (3) consultation of existing fraud database or criminal records to determine if any of the parties has a criminal record, fraud offense, or some other suspicious activities. The main drawbacks of most of current AML systems are: (1) a high volume of red ML alerts forces organizations to increase the amount of investigation costs in terms of time and human effort; (2) yet fewer ML alerts result in a limited number of checks, which heavily affects the recall of the system by allowing the suspicious transaction to pass through the compliance procedure (Gao et al., 2006); Several global banking organizations were heavily fined by AML regulators for ineffective AML practices (Martin, 2017).

We propose a novel framework that can drastically decrease the time and effort of *false positive validation* (FPV) for AML solutions. We harness multiple data sources, and apply deep learning-based NLP techniques within a distributed architecture to create a recommendation system to support human analysts for a more efficient and accurate decision-making. The salient contributions of this paper include: (1) Harnessing heterogeneous open data (e.g. social media, news articles and fraud bases) in AML compliance to make it more robust and updated; (2) Using different levels of sentiment analysis (SA) to identify negative evidence of a target entity; (3) Using name entity recognition (NER) and relation extraction (RE) to build the relation network of a target entity, and analyze the hidden and complex connections between the target entity and existing suspicious entities from the fraud bases; and (4) developing a distributed communication architecture for scaling the deployment of various NLP modules.

To the best of our knowledge, harnessing unstructured social and news content to facilitate the investigation and compliance has never been attempted in the recent literature of AML, nor any industrial systems.

2 System Architecture

The proposed novel AML framework follows a distributed architecture to integrate different deep learning-based NLP modules to facilitate the investigations of suspicious ML transactions. The architecture of the system is presented in Figure 1.

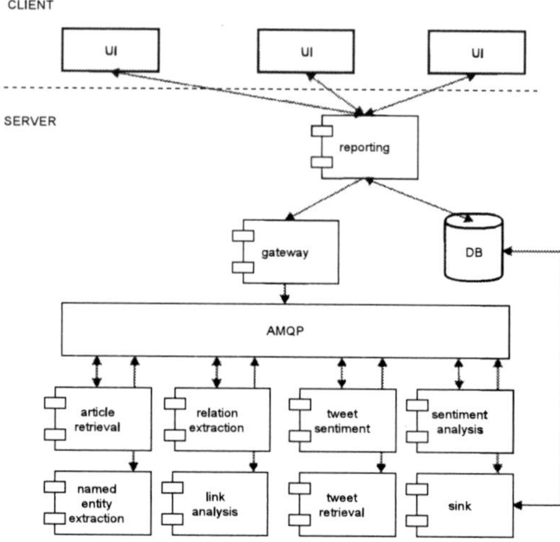

Figure 1: Architecture of the novel AML framework.

The system follows an extensible micro-service oriented distributed architecture where each component acts as a separate micro-service and communicates with others via an Advanced Message Queuing Protocol (AMQP) platform. AMQP is an open standard application layer protocol used for queuing and routing messages between the services in a secure and reliable way[2]. Communications between the components are chained to achieve incremental data processing. This architecture also supports dynamic routing topologies.

In this framework, each AML component is independently configurable, deployable, scalable and replaceable which makes it flexible on where and how to run it. Thus, it can conveniently distribute the AML components over a cluster of machines where allocation of resources could be adjusted on demand depending on the needs regarding the processing time or memory consumption.

In Figure 1, the User Interfaces (UI) connect to the reporting service that provides the results information from the database (DB). The UI can also trigger the processing pipeline, calling the reporting service to make the gateway start processing data regarding new transactions.

The reporting service provides representational state transfer (REST) endpoints for the interaction between the UI and the system. This service allows analysts/experts to retrieve information re-

---

[2]https://www.rabbitmq.com/specification.html

lated to a specific transaction and the set of processed results that will lead to the human analyst to approve or block this transaction.

The information processing pipeline is a combination of different modules (micro-services) via different routings. Different routings encapsulate different customized functionalities for the end user. Using the route configuration file, the route is embedded in the message that is passed around, so the component knows where it should direct the message next.

In this architecture, the data layer is constructed using Cassandra, Neo4j and MySQL along with news and Twitter engines to govern, collect, manage and store various type of data (e.g. banking data and open data). The data layer maintains a bidirectional access with other modules in the system. Two types of data are handled in the data layer: banking and open data. Banking data refers to a wide variety of financial data, for example: data related to Know Your Customer (KYC), client profiles, customer accounts, and real-time transactions. On the other hand open data refers to financial news articles, social media, financial report, existing and open source fraud base etc.

3 Work-flow and Functionalities

The main UI of our system is shown in Figures 2–4. We will explicitly detail the functionality of each NLP module while following the work-flow of the system:

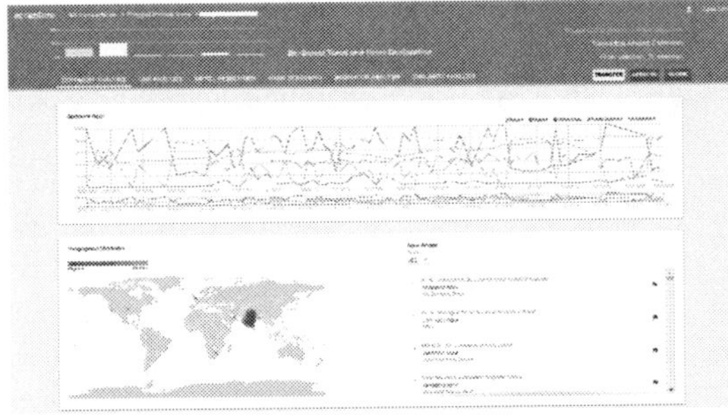

Figure 2: Sentiment Analysis of Target Entity

The system starts with transaction monitoring (TM) that identifies suspicious transaction using complex rules and generates red alerts. Suspicious transactions are flagged and reside in a queue for further investigation. Information such as name, location, account details of the parties (involved in a flagged) are extracted for further usage.

The name screening module filters out ML offenders or criminals have previous records of fraud, illegal activities (e.g. terrorism) and financial crimes by looking at a sanction list or ML cases from bank records and other fraud bases. The name screening employs fuzzy matching techniques as an initial filter like many off-the-self AML solutions. If the target entity is matched with some entities in the list, it will increase the probability of a ML transaction, so the system is triggered for more evidence gathering.

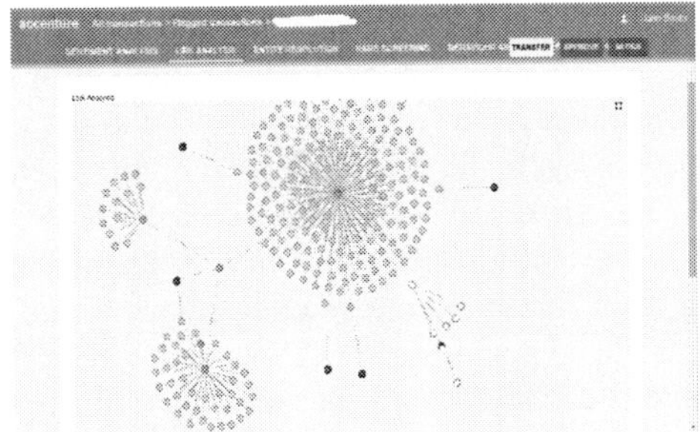

Figure 3: Knowledge Graph of Fraud Base: Each Node is an entity and edges are relations. Sensitive entities are blocked with white boxes according to data privacy agreement.

The target entity with its properties are stored in a knowledge graph (KG) which is constructed from a combination of publicly available fraud/ML bases[3]. Figure 3 shows part of the KG, where each node represents an entity and the edge represents a relation. Persons and organizations that occur in this KG and are red-alerted by the TM system, are strongly considered to be involved in illegal activities. Entity disambiguation is used when the the query of the target entity to the KG is to be made. If the target entity is matched, then we directly submit the evidence to human investigators. The system also considers human judgment in this process, mainly for two reasons: (1) Often fake identities, aliases are captured by analyzing the neighbors of the target entities (e.g. the associate entities remain same) (2) Often indirect connection to a suspicious entity validates the ML claim of a transaction.

Sentiment Analysis is a key module of our system that can be viewed as a sequential and as well

---

[3]https://www.icij.org/investigations/panama-papers/, http://www.fatf-gafi.org/publications/ and https://www.icij.org/investigations/paradise-papers/

as a parallel component for evidence mining. At any given point of time the module starts fetching data from different sources, such as news sources and social media in order to find clues of the target entity, after that it analyses the sentiment of collected news and other data sources and projects the results into a geo-graph and a time-series chart to identify geo and temporal patterns. The goal of this module is to identify potential negative evidence involving crime, fraud and ML etc. As shown in Figure 2, the results are visualized with the time-stamp to reveal the trend. The idea behind viewing the sentiment over time is that *continuously growing* negative enduring sentiment for an entity indicates something suspicious and the necessity of in-depth investigation. In Figure 2, *Red* indicates the negative sentiment, *Green* represents the positive sentiment, and *Yellow* is the average sentiment of target entity's competitors. *Blue* is the averaged sentiment from Twitter data. It can be seen that negative sentiment regarding to financial fraud is dominant for the target entity, and hence an in-depth investigation is necessary. The news are complied and presented along with the graph so that the actual content can also be presented. Geographical distribution in terms of sentiment regarding the target entity is also visualized, which reflects the risks of the target entity involved in the ML activities in terms of location.

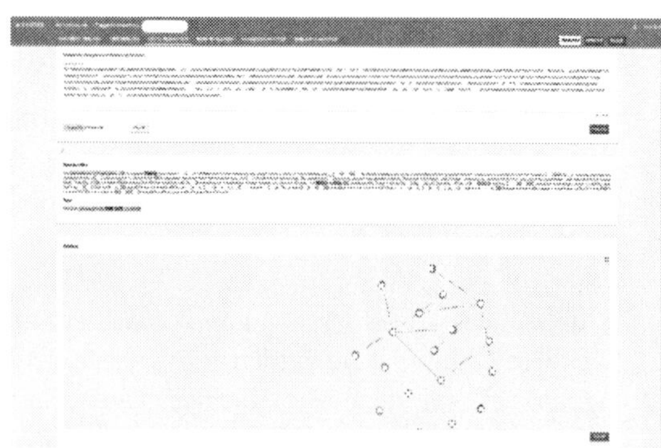

Figure 4: Knowledge Graph from News Article

The next part of our system is designed to perform entity resolution and linking through NER, RE, link analysis (LA). NER and RE are performed over collected unstructured negative news data to extract relational facts in real time and build an entity-specific KG regarding the target entity as shown in Figure 4. Subsequently, these entity-specific KGs are merged with the existing knowledge graph by entity linking. In this process, an entity disambiguation technique is also used to find out the same entity with different mentions. Given the updated KG, we then carry out inspection and reasoning regarding the suspicious entity considering that a direct or indirect connection between a target entity and any number of existing ML/fraud entities. Direct and indirect connections can be a strong evidence implying that the investigated transaction might be illegal. This process not only serves evidence mining for a particular suspicious transaction but also enriches the existing KB continuously by adding a large number of entities that are collected from different sources.

Finally, for a suspicious transaction, confidence scores are generated along with evidences from each module: TM, fraud-base name screening, fraud KB matching, SA trend and entity disambiguation module. The scores are normalized within a range of 0.00 to 1.00 for each module and are presented to a user. Based on these scores, the user approves, blocks or transfers the transaction to higher authorities for action. The goal of our solution is not to replace human compliance personnels, but to augment their capability and to make a more accurate decision efficiently.

4 NLP Models

In this section, we introduce the modeling details for each NLP modules in our system.

4.1 Sentiment Analysis

Sentiment analysis is a task of identifying the polarity of sentiment (e.g. positive, neutral or negative) in a content at different levels, e.g. term, aspect, sentence and document.

For our AML task, we develop two different SA models, namely the document-level and sentence-level models. The former is a multi-channel convolutional neural network (CNN) based sentiment classifier (Kim, 2014) and used to process financial news articles; the latter is also a CNN based model (Tang et al., 2014; Deriu et al., 2016) for social media data.

One challenge for the document-level SA model is that annotated resources in the financial domain are hard to obtain. To solve this problem, we propose a voting scheme to label the training data as follows: Financial news are gathered using a list of keywords[4] and news search APIs, afterwards they

---

[4] https://www3.nd.edu/~mcdonald/Word_

(headlines and the first paragraph of a news) go through some public sentiment APIs to generate the sentiment score. Finally, a voting mechanism is used to obtain the final result in terms of positive or negative sentiment for each document. Our document-level SA classifier, trained on automatic labeled 12,467 of such financial news articles, and it achieves 76.96% in terms of accuracy compared to a public sentiment API[5] on the RT-polarity[6] data set. With respect to the Twitter SA classifier, it is trained and evaluated on SemEval-2016 task 4[7] data set, and achieves 63.10% in terms of accuracy, comparable to the best system (63.30%) in the shared task. Different from previous shared tasks, the SemEval-2016 task 4 is designed to estimate the percentage of tweets that are positive and the percentage of tweets that are negative in a given set of tweets about a topic. Thus, in this circumstance, this dataset is very helpful for us to verify our SA models for AML scenario because in one period there might have many tweets discussing a suspicious entity (e.g. an organisation).

4.2 Relation Extraction

Relation extraction involves the prediction of semantic relations between pairs of nominals or entities in a sentence (Bunescu and Mooney, 2005). We use the pipeline modeling methods for relation extraction tasks, i.e. recognising and disambiguating named entities (Wang et al., 2012) first, and then performing relation extraction on these recognised entities. NER is performed using a combined strategy: (1) Stanford NER Recognizer; (2) a neural NRE which is implemented using a LSTM-CRF framework (Lample et al., 2016); and (3) we combine the recognised named entities from these two models, and select out those that we want based on specific types. Seven different types of named entities are defined in our system, namely *Person*, *Organisation*, *Location*, *Date*, *Time*, *Money* and *Miscellaneous*. Given two entities and a sentence containing these two entities, our LSTM-based model predicts the relation between them. We evaluate it on SemEval 2010 task 8 (Hendrickx et al., 2010) data and it achieves

80.62% in terms of macro-F1 measure.

Moreover, to handle multi-instance problem in the distant supervision RE (i.e. for one entity pair, there exists multiple instances containing this entity pair, where some instances are valid and some are noise), we develop an attentive RNN framework (Lin et al., 2016) with a word-level and a sentence-level attentions for relation prediction, where the word-level attention can learn lexical contexts and the sentence-level attention can select valid instances for relation prediction. We evaluate our model on the publicly available New York Time data set and achives 88.00% accuracy in terms of P@100 measure.

5 Evaluation and Feedbacks from AML Practitioners

As discussed in above section, different validation and evaluation methods are applied to different NLP models, where the tweet SA model, news SA model or attentive RE model achieves or is comparable to the state-of-the-art in terms of accuracy. At present, the entire system is at piloting stage with our banking clients across US, Europe and Asia. It is currently being tested and evaluated by professional AML practitioners for AML and KYC investigations. From the feedbacks that we collected so far, the end users are optimistic on achieving the objective of reducing on average 30% of their time of investigating the red-alerted suspicious transactions and making a decision more efficiently. We have been invited to give keynote talks about different aspects (not the entire one) of this system at highly respected events, such as World Mobile Conference (WMC) 2018, Europe Financial Information Management Conference (FIMA) 2017 etc. Worth mentioning that some of our NLP models were also utilized by our clients in different domains. For instance, one of our diamond clients adopted our news and tweets sentiment analysis models for monitoring their brand reputation. Given the sensitivity of their business, they cannot release the performance metrics to us. However, their overall feedback and experience have been very positive.

6 Conclusions and Future Work

In this paper, we present a novel distributed framework of applying and visualizing different deep learning based NLP technologies to augment the anti money laundering investigation. Our system

---

[5]We use `https://www.ibm.com/watson/alchemy-api.html` and it achieves 75.56% in terms of accuracy.

[6]`https://www.cs.cornell.edu/people/pabo/movie-review-data/rt-polaritydata.README.1.0.txt`

[7]Prediction of five-point scale polarity of a tweet.

is modularized and distributed which enables it to be deployed on scale and on demand. Each component is a micro-service which allows multiple instances of the same module to be created and deployed and used in tandem. By harnessing knowledge graph, sentiment analysis, name screening, named entity recognition, relation extraction, entity linking and link analysis, our system can provide different evidence extracted and analyzed from different data sources to facilitate human investigators. From the human evaluation and clients' feedback, our system can reduce by 30% in terms of human investigation effort.

In the future, we will (1) improve our models with more domain specific data, and fine tune the parameters; (2) scale and deploy the system on cloud-based servers for real-time processing of large volume of data; (3) tailor the solution and evaluate it in other domains such as KYC, and (4) adapt our system to multilingual use cases.

Acknowledgements

Many thanks to the reviewers for their insightful comments and suggestions. This work is supported by Accenture Labs Dublin, Enterprise Ireland under the Research Programme (Grant EI.IP20170626) and Science Foundation Ireland (SFI) Industry Fellowship Programme 2016 (Grant 16/IFB/4490).

References

Razvan Bunescu and Raymond J Mooney. 2005. Subsequence kernels for relation extraction. In *In Proceedings of NIPS*, pages 171–178.

Jan Deriu, Maurice Gonzenbach, Fatih Uzdilli, Aurelien Lucchi, Valeria De Luca, and Martin Jaggi. 2016. Swisscheese at semeval-2016 task 4: Sentiment classification using an ensemble of convolutional neural networks with distant supervision. In *Proceedings of the 10th International Workshop on Semantic Evaluation*, EPFL-CONF-229234, pages 1124–1128.

Shijia Gao and Dongming Xu. 2007. Conceptual modeling and development of an intelligent agent-assisted decision support system for anti-money laundering. *Expert Systems with Applications*.

Shijia Gao and Dongming Xu. 2010. Real-time exception management decision model (rtemdm): applications in intelligent agent-assisted decision support in logistics and anti-money laundering domains. *International Conference on System Sciences*.

Shijia Gao, Dongming Xu, Huaiqing Wang, and Yingfent Wang. 2006. Intelligent anti-money laundering system. *International Conference on Service Operations and Logistics, and Informatics*.

Zengan Gao and Mao Ye. 2007. A framework for data mining-based anti-money laundering research. *Journal of Money Laundering Control*.

Cross Gombiro and Mmaki Jantjies. 2015. A conceptual framework for detecting financial crime in mobile money transactions. *Journal of Governance and Regulation*.

T.H. Helmy, M. Zaki, T. Salah, and B.K. Tarek. 2014. Design of a monitor for detecting money laundering and terrorist financing. *Journal of Theoretical and Applied Information Technology*, 1(1):1–11.

Iris Hendrickx, Su Nam Kim, Zornitsa Kozareva, Preslav Nakov, Diarmuid Ó Séaghdha, Sebastian Padó, Marco Pennacchiotti, Lorenza Romano, and Stan Szpakowicz. 2010. Semeval-2010 task 8: Multi-way classification of semantic relations between pairs of nominals. In *Proceedings of the Workshop on Semantic Evaluations: Recent Achievements and Future Directions*, pages 94–99.

Avi Jorisch. 2009. *Tainted Money: Are we losing the war on money laundering and terrorism financing?* Red Cell Intelligence Group.

Yoon Kim. 2014. Convolutional neural networks for sentence classification. *arXiv preprint arXiv:1408.5882*.

Guillaume Lample, Miguel Ballesteros, Sandeep Subramanian, Kazuya Kawakami, and Chris Dyer. 2016. Neural architectures for named entity recognition. *CoRR*, abs/1603.01360.

Yankai Lin, Shiqi Shen, Zhiyuan Liu, Huanbo Luan, and Maosong Sun. 2016. Neural relation extraction with selective attention over instances. In *Proceedings of the 54th ACL*, pages 2124–2133.

Ben Martin. 2017. Deutsche bank hit with pounds 500m money laundering fines. http://www.telegraph.co.uk/business/2017/01/31/deutsche-bank-hit-500m-money-laundering-fines/.

D. Pellegrina, L. Donato, and M. Donato. 2009. The risk based approach in the new european anti-money laundering legislation: a law and economics view. *Computing Reviews*, 5(2):290–317.

Duyu Tang, Furu Wei, Nan Yang, Ming Zhou, Ting Liu, and Bing Qin. 2014. Learning sentiment-specific word embedding for twitter sentiment classification. In *Proceedings of the 52nd ACL*, pages 1555–1565.

Longyue Wang, Shuo Li, Derek F Wong, and Lidia S Chao. 2012. A joint chinese named entity recognition and disambiguation system. In *Proceedings of the Second CIPS-SIGHAN Joint Conference on Chinese Language Processing*, pages 146–151.

NLP Web Services for Resource-Scarce Languages

M.J. Puttkammer*, E.R. Eiselen[+,] J. Hocking* and F.J. Koen*
*Centre for Text Technology; [+]South African Centre for Digital Language Resources
North-West University, Potchefstroom Campus, South Africa
{Martin.Puttkammer; Justin.Hocking; Frederik.Koen;
Roald.Eiselen}@nwu.ac.za

Abstract

In this paper, we present a project where existing text-based core technologies were ported to Java-based web services from various architectures. These technologies were developed over a period of eight years through various government funded projects for 10 resource-scarce languages spoken in South Africa. We describe the API and a simple web front-end capable of completing various predefined tasks.

1 Introduction

With the establishment of large-scale e-infrastructures, there has been an international move towards making software available as a service. Web services are a way of exposing the functionality of an information system and making it available through standard web technologies (Alonso *et al.*, 2004). A natural language processing (NLP) web service refers to one or more technologies that focus on natural (human) speech or text and that are exposed programmatically to allow anyone with internet access, on multiple platforms, to gain access to the output of the technology. By hosting NLP web services, the development of end-user-facing applications could be facilitated in the sense that software developers and researchers get access to the latest versions of such technologies via simple web queries.

A web service also provides an architecture that will allow human language technologies (HLTs) to be integrated into larger software systems. By adopting a service-orientated architecture, existing resources and tools can also be used to develop complex component-based systems (Boehlke, 2010). Several such systems already exist in Europe and the United States, for example Stanford CoreNLP[1] (Manning *et al.*, 2014), Aylien[2], Web-licht[3] (Hinrichs *et al.*, 2010), and Tanl Pipeline[4] (Attardi *et al.*, 2010). etc. Furthermore, web services can be updated relatively quickly, allowing users to get the latest version of the technologies at all times.

In this paper, we describe a project where 61 existing text-based core technologies were ported to Java-based web services from various architectures. The first part of this paper provides a brief background and details on the relevant languages the technologies were developed for. This is followed by a short description of three previous projects in which the technologies were developed, as well as a description of the technologies themselves. We then describe the API and a simple web front-end capable of completing various predefined tasks in the following sections. We conclude with some information on a current project and future considerations.

2 Background

The South African community, with its rich diversity of 11 official languages, is an emerging market where the development of language resources and HLTs contribute to the promotion of multilingualism and language development. The development of language resources for the official languages contributes significantly to bridging the divide between the privileged and the marginalised in terms of access to information.

There are 11 official languages in South Africa, generally categorised into five language family groups. The conjunctively written Nguni languages include isiZulu (ZU), isiXhosa (XH), isiNdebele (NR), and SiSwati (SS). The disjunctively written languages include the Sotho languages Sesotho (ST), Setswana (TN), Sesotho sa Leboa (NSO), and Tshivenḓa (VE) and the disjunctively written Tswa-Ronga language, Xitsonga (TS). Finally, there are two Germanic languages, English (EN) and Afrikaans (AF)

---

[1] http://nlp.stanford.edu:8080/corenlp/process
[2] http://aylien.com/

[3] http://weblicht.sfs.uni-tuebingen.de/weblichtwiki/
[4] http://tanl.di.unipi.it/en/api

Proceedings of the 56th Annual Meeting of the Association for Computational Linguistics-System Demonstrations, pages 43–49
Melbourne, Australia, July 15 - 20, 2018. ©2018 Association for Computational Linguistics

(Prinsloo & de Schryver, 2002). Apart from English, all South African languages are considered resource-scarce with relatively little data that can be used to develop NLP applications and technologies.

Over the past two decades, the South African government has continuously supported HLT related text and speech projects. These projects have generated NLP resources in the form of data, core technologies, applications and systems that are immensely valuable for the future development of the official South African languages. Although these resources can be obtained in a timely fashion from the Language Resource Management Agency of the South African Centre for Digital Language Resources[5] (SADiLaR), access to these resources can still be considered limited, in the sense that technically proficient persons or organisations are required to utilise these technologies. One way to improve access to these technologies is to make them available as web services. At the Centre for Text Technology, we previously developed freely available web services for machine translation between several South African language pairs[6], and build on this experience to develop the web services.

The web services described in this paper entails the implementation of existing technologies as web services that are accessible via an application programming interface (API) and a user-friendly web application which leverages the API, described in Section 5. These services can process word lists, running text, documents or scanned images as input. The following section provides a brief overview of the individual technologies that have been implemented in the API.

3   Technologies

All the technologies included in the web services were developed over a period of eight years through three projects, NCHLT Text: Phase I, II and III. These projects were initiated and funded by the National Centre for Human Language Technology (NCHLT) of the Department of Arts and Culture (South African government). The technologies and resources described below were only developed for 10 of the South African languages, since there are well known and readily available text-based technologies for English,

such as the Stanford CoreNLP, that can be used on South African English. The three projects and the resulting technologies of each, are briefly described in the following subsections.

3.1   NCHLT Text: Phase I

The first phase of the NCHLT Text project focussed on establishing the foundational resources and technologies for further development of the NLP industry in South Africa. For each language, text corpora from government domain sources were collected to develop a one-million-word corpus for each language. From these corpora, language experts for each of the 10 languages annotated 50,000 tokens per language (and an additional 5,000 tokens for testing) on three levels, namely part of speech (POS), lemma, and morphological composition. In addition to the annotated corpora, five core technologies were developed for each language. These technologies were sentence separators, tokenisers, lemmatisers, morphological decomposers, and POS taggers. Brief descriptions of each technology developed during this phase of the project and ported to web services, are provided below. More detailed descriptions of the technologies are available in Eiselen and Puttkammer (2014).

Sentence separation is a pre-processing step for tokenisation in a typical NLP pipeline. The sentence separators developed during this project are rule-based and split sentences based on language specific characteristics, to ensure that abbreviations and numbering correctly remain part of different sentences.

The tokenisers are also language-specific, rule-based technologies that split sentences into tokens, typically words and punctuation, and are a necessary pre-process for all other NLP tasks.

The POS taggers developed during the project were trained on the 50,000 POS annotated data tokens developed in the project. The implementation uses the open source Hidden Markov Model (HMM) tagger, HunPos (Halácsy *et al.*, 2007). Since HunPos is not a Java-compliant library, it was necessary to port the POS taggers to a Java library, nlp4j[7].

For the initial development and release of the web services, the lemmatisers and morphological decomposers were not included as they are rule-based technologies, with more than 150 rules

---

[5] http://repo.sadilar.org/handle/20.500.12185/7
[6] https://mt.nwu.ac.za/

[7] https://emorynlp.github.io/nlp4j/

each. See Section 7 for more detail on a current project tasked with additional annotation in order to develop machine learning-based technologies.

3.2   NCHLT Text: Phase II

Building on the resources created during the first NCHLT Text project, the second phase focussed on named entity recognition, phrase chunking and language identification. Named entity recognisers and phrase chunkers were developed from an additional 15,000 tokens per language annotated during the project. The language identifier (LID), which was developed to classify text as one of the 11 official languages, was trained on the text corpora collected during the first NCHLT Text project along with an English corpus also collected from government domain sources.

The named entity recognisers were trained using linear-chain conditional random fields (CRF) with L2 regularisation. See Eiselen (2016a) for details on development, evaluation, and accuracy.

The phrase chunkers were also trained with linear-chain CRFs from annotated data, and additionally use the POS tags as a feature by employing the previously developed POS taggers. Eiselen (2016b) provides the full details on development, evaluation, and accuracy of the phrase chunkers.

Both the named entity recognition and phrase chunking core technologies were implemented in the web services using the CRF++[8] Java library.

LID employs character level n-gram language models (n=6) and measures the Euclidean distance between the relative frequencies of a test model and all language models, selecting the one with the lowest distance as the probable language. In the web services, LID is performed on line level, and returns the probable language for each line in the input text. The first version of the LID was implemented in Python, and the web services version was implemented in Java. Evaluation results and implementation details are available in Hocking (2014).

3.3   NCHLT Text: Phase III

The third phase of the NCHLT Text project saw the development of Optical Character Recognition (OCR) models as well as improving access to all the technologies through the development of the web services.

The OCR models for the South African languages were developed using Tesseract[9] and accommodate the diacritic characters required for four of the South African languages. See Hocking and Puttkammer (2016) for the development and evaluation results of these OCR models. For the implementation of OCR in the web services, tess4j[10] was used.

4   Implementation

The web services are implemented as a simple three-tiered Java application, consisting of the API, a Core Technology Manager (Manager for the remainder of the paper) and the individual core technology modules.

The API is responsible for handling all incoming requests, validating parameters and headers, sending parameter data to the Manager for processing and for relaying processing results back to the requestor. The Manager is responsible for initialising and loading the technologies, processing the data from the API, and sending the result back to the API. The core technology modules process the input data and perform the various required analyses. Each of these tiers are described in more detail below.

4.1   NCHLT web services API

The API is a RESTful web service that is both maintainable and scalable. The service is based on the Jersey framework[11], as it is an open source, production quality framework for developing RESTful services in Java. The API is also designed in such a way that new language and technologies can be added at any point without affecting existing API calls. The API uses an authentication process providing restricted access to the available services of the API. The authentication process uses token-based authentication and provides the requestor with a session token that gives the requestor permission to access any future requests made to the API until the requestor's session expires. The access to the list of languages and technologies requests is not protected by the authentication process, and is therefore open to use without obtaining a session token. The API also allows the requestor to request the progress of a

---

[8] https://github.com/taku910/crfpp

[9] https://github.com/tesseract-ocr/

[10] http://tess4j.sourceforge.net

[11] https://jersey.github.io/

technology that is being used to process the requestor's data.

Four functions are supported by the API, which can be accessed by either GET or PUT calls, depending on whether a string of text or a file is sent for processing. The first two calls do not require authentication as described above, and return either the set of languages that are supported for a particular core technology, or a list of core technologies that are supported for a particular language. These two functions ensure that callers can correctly access those technologies that are available for particular languages.

The two functions that require authentication are the call to a specific core technology, and the progress call, which provides progress information on a user's call to a specific technology.

Most of the technologies available via the API require a language parameter in the form of an ISO-639 abbreviation of two or three letters, and some form of textual input in the form of either a list, running text or a file. The OCR module does require a language to be specified, but can only process image files in one of the standard image formats (.png, .jpg, .tiff, or .pdf), while LID only needs text or a file as it returns the language for each line in the input.

The API is called using a GET call[12] and should always consist of the following information:

- the server (and optional port number) on which the service is being hosted;
- the technology, either by number or shortened name;
- the ISO-639 two-letter language code;
- Unicode text that should be processed by the technology; and
- the authentication token included in the request header as the authToken property.

Upon receiving a request, the API validates the parameters and the session token to ensure that all the information needed to use the relevant technology is present. If the request passes the validation, the input and language information is submitted to the Manager that handles the initialisation of the requested core technology module. The Manager then validates the parameter data once again, sends the data for processing by the relevant core technology and returns the result back to the API.

---

[12] http://{server:port}/CTexTWebAPI/services?
core={technology}&lang={code}&text={text}

4.2 Core technology manager

The Manager is tasked with handling the different core technology modules that are loaded for different languages across one or more threads or servers. The Manager controls this by keeping a register of all the modules that have been launched, as well as progress information to determine whether any given module is available for processing when a new request is received from the API. Technologies are loaded in memory as they are requested by the Manager. This allows the technologies to process the data more efficiently and in effect improves the response times to the requestor. Since many of the modules loaded by the Manager require relatively large statistical models to process data, and many of the modules are reused in several of the module pipelines, modules are not immediately discarded. Rather than destroying the loaded module, it is kept in memory to be available for a new call, which significantly reduces the processing time, since it is not necessary to reload the module or its underlying models for each new API call.

In addition to managing the individual modules that are loaded at any given time, the Manager also manages shared tasks, such as file handles and error handling, which can be reused by any of the core technology modules as necessary. This simply ensures that all file upload and download procedures are managed in a consistent, reusable fashion. Finally, it is also important to note that all the modules reuse models and attributes that are shared between multiple instances of the class and are thread-safe. Consequently, running multiple instances simultaneously does not cause any information corruption, race conditions, or related multithreading problems, while limiting the load time and memory required to process data.

4.3 Core technology modules

As mentioned earlier, the development of the web services focussed on transferring existing linguistic core technologies for South African languages to a shared code base that was accessible via a RESTful API. Over the course of the previous projects, various developers used different underlying technologies and programming languages to implement the core technologies. During this project, it was decided to consolidate these disparate technologies into a single code base, with various shared components that will make maintenance and updates of these technologies significantly more efficient.

During the design phase it was decided to port all core technologies to Java, for three reasons. First, Java is supported across most operating systems, allowing the deployment of the technologies and services across many different architectures. Second, Java provides a wide array of freely available and well tested libraries to facilitate the development and distribution of the technologies and web services. A third factor that was taken into consideration is that the core technology modules developed for the web service could also be reused in other user-facing applications, specifically an offline corpus search and processing environment developed in parallel to the web services, CTexTools, version 2[13]. To facilitate distributed computing across multiple servers, each of the core technology modules are also implemented as servlets, which can be initialised by the manager. This allows for multiple versions of the same technology to be run on multiple threads and servers as necessary.

Although the primary focus of transferring the modules was for inclusion in the web services, this transfer also allowed for better integration between the different modules that have been developed at the Centre for Text Technology. All the transferred modules are based on a shared interface class, ICoreTechnology, which in turn implements a shared abstract class CoreTechnology. These are relatively simple shared classes, but have the significant benefit that all the core technologies can be called and handled by the Manager in a systematic, consequent manner. This in turn means that adding technologies to the set of available modules is relatively straightforward, and would immediately iterate through the rest of the API architecture, without requiring updates to the API or Manager itself.

Another consideration in the transfer of the technologies to a shared code base, is the fact that most of the technologies have an interdependence, typically forming pipelines that are required to process a string. As an example, the phrase chunker for a particular language is dependent on the output of the POS tagger as one of its features. The POS tagger in turn is dependent on tokenisation for that language, and tokenisation is dependent on sentence separation to complete its processing. This means that for phrase chunking to be

performed, first sentence separation must be performed, then tokenisation, then POS tagging, and only then can the feature set be created for the string that must be phrase chunked. In the current architecture, this entire chain is inherently implemented, and the phrase chunker only needs to call the POS tagging module for the specific language, which then in turn calls the module(s) that are necessary for tagging to be performed. See Figure 1.

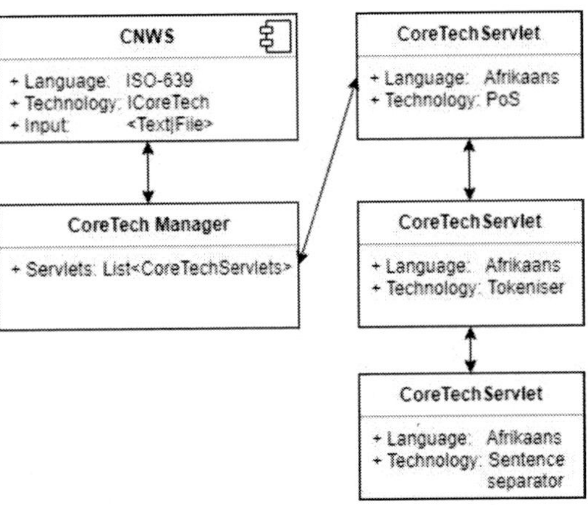

Figure 1: Example of system workflow

The modules required for each technology module are entirely handled by the Manager, which means that core technologies that are typically used in most modules, such as tokenisation, can effectively be reused by various instances of modules that require the shared module.

Due to several factors, the web services are currently only deployed on a single 12 core virtual server with 32Gb memory. In order to test the reliability of the technologies and the responsiveness of the service, a set of load tests were performed on the web services, simulating 70 users simultaneously processing text files of approximately 100,000 tokens, with different technologies in different languages. The entire scenario of processing the approximately 7 million tokens completes within 10 minutes, equating to a processing rate of around 11,700 tokens per second. In a secondary test on the slowest of the technologies, i.e. named entity recognition, for 10 concurrent users, each processing 100,000 words, the service completes in 3.5 minutes, for a rate of 1,400 tokens per second. This is primarily due to the fact that named entity recognition uses the most intricate pipeline, including tokenisation,

---

[13] https://hdl.handle.net/20.500.12185/480

sentence separation, part of speech tagging, and extended feature extraction.

5 Web application

To make the technologies developed during the various phases of the NCHLT project more accessible, a simple web application was also created. This application specifically aims to accommodate users who are unaccustomed to service-orientated architectures, and for whom using these types of architectures can be quite challenging. As such, it was prudent to develop a basic interface to assist users in using the services to complete certain tasks. Thus, we developed a web-based, user-friendly graphical user interface capable of completing various tasks by providing predefined chains of the web services detailed above. For example, if a user needs to perform POS tagging on a document, the user can upload the document and select POS tagging and the relevant language. The system will automatically perform tokenisation and sentence separation before using the POS tagging service to tag the user's document. To facilitate easy and quick processing, a user can provide text, select the required options, process the text, and view or download the results. Detailed documentation on using the API, as well as the web application, is also provided. The tag sets used for all annotation are provided in the help page. The web application is available at http://hlt.nwu.ac.za/.

6 Conclusion and future work

In this paper, we provided an overview of a new web service and application that provides access to 61 different text technologies for South African languages. This implementation allows any developer to access and integrate one of these language technologies in their own environment, while ensuring that the latest versions of these technologies are used at any time. Finally, a simple, user-friendly, web application was described that provides access to predefined chains of NLP technologies for use by end-users who are not as technically proficient, but can use the technologies in their own research work.

Given the flexible nature of the web services and underlying infrastructure, it is foreseen that other language technologies will be included in the service as they become available. The South African government also recently established SADiLaR, a national research infrastructure focussing on the development and distribution of linguistic and natural language processing resources.

There is currently a project underway to extend the set of annotated text corpora from 50,000 to approximately 100,000 tokens. These extended annotated data sets could then be used to create improved core technologies for the South African languages.

7 Acknowledgements

The NCHLT web services project was funded by the Department of Arts and Culture, Government of South Africa. The expansion of the annotated data is funded as a specialisation project by SADiLaR.

References

Alonso, G., Casati, F., Kuno, H. & Machiraju, V. 2004. Web services. Springer-Verlag, Berlin.

Attardi, G., Dei Rossi, S. & Simi, M. 2010. The TANL Pipeline. In *Proceedings of the Seventh International Conference on Language Resources and Evaluation (LREC 2010): Workshop on Web Services and Processing Pipelines in HLT*. European Language Resources Association (ELRA), p. 15-21.

Boehlke, V. 2010. A generic chaining algorithm for NLP webservices. In *Proceedings of the Seventh International Conference on Language Resources and Evaluation (LREC 2010): Workshop on Web Services and Processing Pipelines in HLT*. European Language Resources Association (ELRA), p. 30-36.

Eiselen, R. 2016a. Government Domain Named Entity Recognition for South African Languages. In *Proceedings of the Tenth International Conference on Language Resources and Evaluation (LREC 2016)*. European Language Resources Association (ELRA), p. 3344-3348.

Eiselen, R. 2016b. South African Language Resources: Phrase Chunking. In *Proceedings of the Tenth International Conference on Language Resources and Evaluation (LREC 2016)*. European Language Resources Association (ELRA), p. 689-693.

Eiselen, R. & Puttkammer, M.J. 2014. Developing Text Resources for Ten South African Languages. In *Proceedings of the Ninth International Conference on Language Resources and Evaluation (LREC 2014)*. European Language Resources Association (ELRA), p. 3698-3703.

Halácsy, P., Kornai, A. & Oravecz, C. 2007. HunPos: an open source trigram tagger. In *Proceedings of the 45th Annual Meeting of the Association for Computational Linguistics, Companion Volume: Proceedings of the Demo and Poster Sessions.* Association for Computational Linguistics, p. 209-212.

Hinrichs, E., Hinrichs, M. & Zastrow, T. 2010. WebLicht: Web-based LRT services for German. In *Proceedings of 48th Annual Meeting of the Association for Computational Linguistics: System Demonstrations.* Association for Computational Linguistics, p. 25-29.

Hocking, J. 2014. Language identification for South African languages. In *Proceedings of the Annual Pattern Recognition Association of South Africa and Robotics and Mechatronics International Conference (PRASA-RobMech): Poster session.* Pattern Recognition Association of South Africa, p. 307.

Hocking, J. & Puttkammer, M.J. 2016. Optical character recognition for South African languages. In *Pattern Recognition Association of South Africa and Robotics and Mechatronics International Conference (PRASA-RobMech), 2016.* IEEE, p. 1-5.

Manning, C., Surdeanu, M., Bauer, J., Finkel, J., Bethard, S. & Mcclosky, D. 2014. The Stanford CoreNLP natural language processing toolkit. In *Proceedings of 52nd Annual Meeting of the Association for Computational Linguistics: System Demonstrations.* The Association for Computational Linguistics, p. 55-60.

Prinsloo, D. & De Schryver, G.-M. 2002. Towards an 11 x 11 array for the degree of conjunctivism/disjunctivism of the South African languages. *Nordic Journal of African Studies,* 11(2):249-265.

DCFEE: A Document-level Chinese Financial Event Extraction System based on Automatically Labeled Training Data

Hang Yang[1], Yubo Chen[1], Kang Liu[1,2], Yang Xiao[1] and **Jun Zhao[1,2]**

[1] National Laboratory of Pattern Recognition, Institute of Automation,
Chinese Academy of Sciences, Beijing, 100190, China

[2] University of Chinese Academy of Sciences, Beijing, 100049, China

{hang.yang, yubo.chen, kliu, yang.xiao, jzhao,}@nlpr.ia.ac.cn

Abstract

We present an event extraction framework to detect event mentions and extract events from the document-level financial news. Up to now, methods based on supervised learning paradigm gain the highest performance in public datasets (such as ACE 2005[1], KBP 2015[2]). These methods heavily depend on the manually labeled training data. However, in particular areas, such as financial, medical and judicial domains, there is no enough labeled data due to the high cost of data labeling process. Moreover, most of the current methods focus on extracting events from one sentence, but an event is usually expressed by multiple sentences in one document. To solve these problems, we propose a Document-level Chinese Financial Event Extraction (DCFEE) system which can automatically generate a large scaled labeled data and extract events from the whole document. Experimental results demonstrate the effectiveness of it.

1 Introduction

Event Extraction (EE), a challenging task in Nature Language Processing (NLP), aims at discovering event mentions[3] and extracting events which contain event triggers[4] and event arguments[5] from texts. For example, in the sentence E1[6] as shown in Figure 1, an EE system is expected to discover an *Equity Freeze* event mention (E1 itself) triggered by **frozen** and extract the corresponding five arguments with different roles: *Nagafu Ruihua* (Role=Shareholder Name), *520,000 shares* (Role=Num of Frozen Stock), *People's Court of Dalian city* (Role=Frozen Institution), *May 5,2017* (Role=Freezing Start Date) and *3 years* (Role=Freezing End Date). Extracting event instances from texts plays a critical role in building NLP applications such as Information Extraction (IE), Question Answer (QA) and Summarization (Ahn, 2006). Recently, researchers have built some English EE systems, such as EventRegistry[7] and Stela[8]. However, in financial domain, there is no such effective EE system, especially in Chinese.

Financial events are able to help users obtain competitors' strategies, predict the stock market and make correct investment decisions. For example, the occurrence of an *Equity Freeze* event will have a bad effect on the company and the shareholders should make correct decisions quickly to avoid the losses. In business domain, official announcements released by companies represent the occurrence of major events, such as *Equity Freeze* events, *Equity Trading* events and so on. So it is valuable to discover event mention and extract events from the announcements. However, there are two challenges in Chinese financial EE.

Lack of data: most of the EE methods usually adopted supervised learning paradigm which relies on elaborate human-annotated data, but there is no labeled corpus for EE in the Chinese financial field.

Document-level EE: most of the current methods of EE are concentrated on the sentence-level

---

[1] http://projects.ldc.upenn.edu/ace/

[2] https://tac.nist.gov//2015/KBP/

[3] A sentence that mentions an event, including a distinguished trigger and involving arguments.

[4] The word that most clearly expresses the occurrence of an event.

[5] The entities that fill specific roles in the event.

[6] All the examples in this article are translated from Chinese.

[7] http://eventregistry.org/

[8] https://www.nytsyn.com/

Proceedings of the 56th Annual Meeting of the Association for Computational Linguistics-System Demonstrations, pages 50–55
Melbourne, Australia, July 15 - 20, 2018. ©2018 Association for Computational Linguistics

Figure 1: Example of an *Equity Freeze* event triggered by "frozen" and containing five arguments.

text (Chen et al., 2015) (Nguyen et al., 2016). But an event is usually expressed with multiple sentences in a document. In the financial domain data set constructed in this paper, there are 91% of the cases that the event arguments are distributed in the different sentences. For example, as shown in Figure 1, E1 and E2 describe an *Equity Freeze* event together.

To solve the above two problems, we present a framework named DCFEE which can extract document-level events from announcements based on automatically labeled training data. We make use of Distance Supervision (DS) which has been validated to generate labeled data for EE (Chen et al., 2017) to automatically generate large-scaled annotated data. We use a sequence tagging model to automatically extract sentence-level events. And then, we propose a key-event detection model and an arguments-filling strategy to extract the whole event from the document.

In summary, the contributions of this article are as follows:

- We propose the DCFEE framework which can automatically generate large amounts of labeled data and extract document-level events from the financial announcements.

- We introduce an automatic data labeling method for event extraction and give a series of useful tips for constructing Chinese financial event dataset. We propose a document-level EE system mainly based on a neural sequence tagging model, a key-event detection model, and an arguments-completion strategy. The experimental results show the effectiveness of it.

- The DCFEE system has been successfully built as an online application which can quickly extract events from the financial an-

nouncements [9].

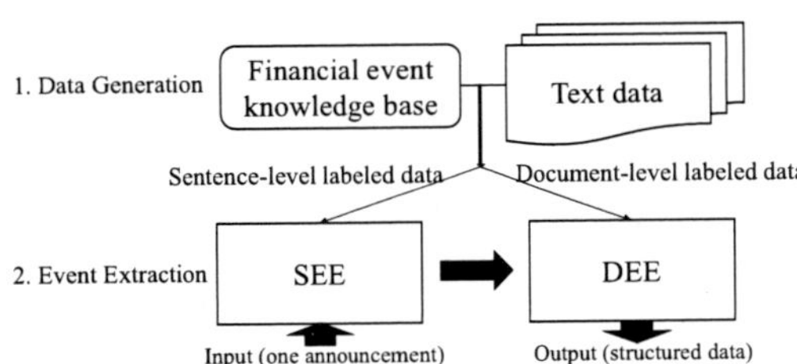

Figure 2: Overview of the DCFEE framework.

2 Methodology

Figure 2 describes the architecture of our proposed DCFEE framework which primarily involves the following two components: (i) Data Generation, which makes use of DS to automatically label event mention from the whole document (document-level data) and annotate triggers and arguments from event mention (sentence-level data); (ii) EE system, which contains Sentence-level Event Extraction (SEE) supported by sentence-level labeled data and Document-level Event Extraction (DEE) supported by document-level labeled data. In the next section, we briefly describe the generation of labeled data and architecture of the EE system.

2.1 Data Generation

Figure 3 describes the process of labeled data generation based on the method of DS. In this section, we first introduce the data sources (structured data and unstructured data) that we use. And then we describe the method of automatically labeling data. Finally, we will introduce some tips that can be used to improve the quality of the labeled data.

---

[9]http://159.226.21.226/financial_graph/online-extract.html

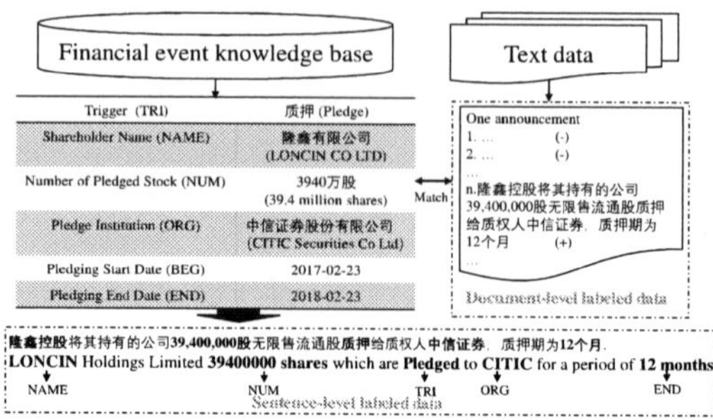

Figure 3: The process of labeled data generation.

Data sources: two types of data resources are required to automatically generate data: a financial event knowledge database containing a lot of structured event data and unstructured text data containing event information. (i) The financial event knowledge database used in this paper is structured data which includes nine common financial event types and is stored in a table format. These structured data which contains key event arguments is summarized from the announcements by financial professionals. An *Equity Pledge* event is taken as an example, as shown on the left of Figure 3, in which key arguments include Shareholder Name (NAME), Pledge Institution (ORG), Number of Pledged Stock (NUM), Pledging Start Date (BEG) and Pledging End Date (END). (ii) The unstructured text data come from official announcements released by the companies which are stored in an unstructured form on the web. We obtain these textual data from Sohu securities net[10].

Method of data generation: annotation data consists of two parts: sentence-level data generated by labeling the event trigger and event arguments in the event mention; document-level data generated by labeling the event mention from the document-level announcement. Now the question is, how to find the event triggers. Event arguments and event mention that correspond to the structured event knowledge database are summarized from a mass of announcements. DS has proved its effectiveness in automatically labeling data for Relation Extraction (Zeng et al., 2015) and Event Extraction (Chen et al., 2017). Inspired by DS, we assume that one sentence contains the most event arguments and driven by a specific trigger is likely to be an event mention in an announcement. And arguments occurring in the event mention are

---

[10]http://q.stock.sohu.com/cn/000001/gsgg.shtml

likely to play the corresponding roles in the event. For each type of financial event, we construct a dictionary of event triggers such as **frozen** in *Equity Freeze* event and **pledged** in *Equity Pledge* event. So the trigger word can be automatically marked by querying the pre-defined dictionary from the announcements. through these pretreatments, structured data can be mapped to the event arguments within the announcements. Therefore, we can automatically identify the event mention and label the event trigger and the event arguments contained in it to generate the sentence-level data, as shown at the bottom of Figure 3. Then, the event mention is automatically marked as a positive example and the rest of the sentences in the announcement are marked as negative examples to constitute the document-level data, as shown on the right of Figure 3. The document-level data and the sentence-level data together form the training data required for the EE system.

Tips: in reality, there are some challenges in data labeling: the correspondence of financial announcements and event knowledge base; the ambiguity and abbreviation of event arguments. There are some tips we used to solve these problems, examples are shown in Figure 3.
(i) Decrease the search space: the search space of candidate announcements can be reduced through retrieving key event arguments such as the publish date and the stock code of the announcements.
(ii) Regular expression: more event arguments can be matched to improve the recall of the labeled data through regular expression. for example, *LONCIN CO LTD* (Role=Shareholder Name) in the financial event database, but *LONCIN* in the announcement. We can solve this problem by regular expression and label the *LONCIN* as an event argument
(iii) Rules: some task-driven rules can be used to automatically annotate data. for example, we can mark *12 months* (Role=Pledging End Date) by calculating the date difference between *2017-02-23* (Role=Pledging Start Date) and *2018-02-23* (Role=Pledging End Date).

2.2 Event Extraction (EE)

Figure 4 depicts the overall architecture of the EE system proposed in this paper which primarily involves the following two components: The sentence-level Event Extraction (SEE) purposes to extract event arguments and event triggers from one sentence; The document-level Event Extraction (DEE) aims to extract event arguments from the whole document based on a key event detection model and an arguments-completion strategy.

2.2.1 Sentence-level Event Extraction (SEE)

We formulate SEE as a sequence tagging task and the training data supported by sentence-level labeled data. Sentences are represented in the BIO format where each character (event triggers, event arguments and others) is labeled as B-label if the token is the beginning of an event argument, I-label if it is inside an event argument or O-label if it is otherwise. In recent years, neural networks have been used in most NLP tasks because it can automatically learn features from the text representation. And the Bi-LSTM-CRF model can produce state of the art (or close to) accuracy on classic NLP tasks such as part of speech (POS), chunking and NER (Huang et al., 2015). It can effectively use both past and future input features thanks to a Bidirectional Long Short-Term Memory (BiLSTM) component and can also use sentence-level tag information thanks to a Conditional Random Field (CRF) layer.

The specific model implementation of the SEE, as shown on the left of Figure 4, is made up of a Bi-LSTM neural network and a CRF layer. Each Chinese character in a sentence is represented by a vector as the input of the Bi-LSTM layer[11] (Mikolov et al., 2013). The output of the Bi-LSTM layer is projected to score for each character. And a CRF layer is used to overcome the label-bias problem. The SEE eventually returns the result of the sentence-level EE for each sentence in the document.

2.2.2 Document-level Event Extraction(DEE)

The DEE is composed of two parts: a key event detection model which aims to discover the event mention in the document and an arguments-completion strategy which aims to pad the missing event arguments.

Key event detection: as shown on the right of figure 4, the input of the event detection is made up of two parts: one is the representation of the event arguments and event trigger come from the output of SEE (blue), and the other is the vector representation of the current sentence(red). The

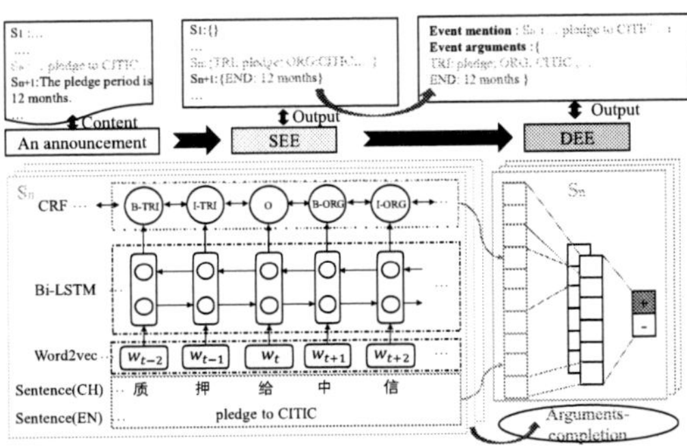

Figure 4: The architecture of event extraction.

two parts are concatenated as the input feature of the Convolutional Neural Networks(CNN) layer. And then the current sentence is classified into two categories: a key event or not.

Arguments-completion strategy: We have obtained the key event which contains most of the event arguments by the DEE, and the event extraction results for each sentence in a document by the SEE. For obtaining complete event information, we use arguments-completion strategy which can automatically pad the missing event arguments from the surrounding sentences. As shown in figure 4, an integrated *Pledge* event contains event arguments in event mention S_n and filled event argument *12 months* obtained from the sentence S_{n+1}.

3 Evaluation

3.1 Dataset

We carry out experiments on four types of financial events: *Equity Freeze (EF)* event, *Equity Pledge (EP)* event, *Equity Repurchase (ER)* event and *Equity Overweight (EO)* event. A total of 2976 announcements have been labeled by automatically generating data. We divided the labeled data into three subsets: the training set (80% of the total number of announcements), development set (10%) and test set (10%). Table 1 shows the statistics of the dataset. NO.ANN represents the number of announcements can be labeled automatically for each event type. NO.POS represents the total number of positive case sentences (event mentions). On the contrary, NO.NEG represents the number of negative case sentences. The positive and negative case sentences constitute the document-level data as the training data for the DEE. The positive sentences which contain event

---

[11]Word vectors are trained with a version of word2vec on Chinese WiKi corpus

trigger and a series of event arguments, are labeled as sentence-level training data for the SEE.

Dataset	NO.ANN	NO.POS	NO.NEG
EF	526	544	2960
EP	752	775	6392
EB	1178	1192	11590
EI	520	533	11994
Total	2976	3044	32936

Table 1: Statistics of automatically labeled data.

We randomly select 200 samples (contain 862 event arguments) to manually evaluate the precision of the automatically labeled data. The average precision is shown in Table 2 which demonstrates that our automatically labeled data is of high quality.

Stage	Mention labeling	Arguments Labeling
Number	200	862
Average Precision	94.50	94.08

Table 2: Manual Evaluation Results.

3.2 Performance of the System

We use the $precision(P)$, $recall(R)$ and (F_1) to evaluate the DCFEE system. Table 3 shows the performance of the pattern-based method[12] and the DCFEE in the extraction of the *Equity Freeze* event. The experimental results show that the performance of the DCFEE is better than that of the pattern-based method in most event arguments extraction.

Method	Pattern-based			DCFEE		
Type	$P(\%)$	$R(\%)$	$F_1(\%)$	$P(\%)$	$R(\%)$	$F_1(\%)$
ORG	79.44	72.22	**75.66**	88.41	61.62	72.62
NUM	57.14	54.55	55.81	59.20	52.02	**56.38**
NAME	63.84	57.07	60.27	89.02	73.74	**80.66**
BEG	65.79	63.13	64.43	81.88	61.62	**70.42**
END	67.62	35.86	46.86	85.00	68.00	**75.56**

Table 3: P, R, F_1 of pattern-based and DCFEE on the *Equity Freeze* event.

Table 4 shows the P, R, F_1 of SEE and DEE on the different event types. It is noteworthy that the golden data used in SEE stage is the automatically generated data and the golden data used in DEE stage comes from the financial event knowledge base. The experimental results show that the effectiveness of SEE and DEE, the acceptable precision

---

[12]Example of a pattern for a freeze event: (*Frozen institution(ORG)+, Trigger word(TRI)+, Shareholder names(NAME)+,time*)

and expansibility of the DCFEE system presented in this paper.

Stage	SEE			DEE		
Type	$P(\%)$	$R(\%)$	$F_1(\%)$	$P(\%)$	$R(\%)$	$F_1(\%)$
EF	90.00	90.41	90.21	80.70	63.40	71.01
EP	93.31	94.36	93.84	80.36	65.91	72.30
ER	92.79	93.80	93.29	88.79	82.02	85.26
EO	88.76	91.88	90.25	80.77	45.93	58.56

Table 4: P, R, F_1 of SEE, DEE on the different event types.

In conclusion, the experiments show that the method based on DS can automatically generate high-quality labeled data to avoid manually labeling. It also validates the DCFEE proposed in this paper, which can effectively extract events from the document-level view.

4 Application of the DCFEE

The application of the DCFEE system: an online EE service for Chinese financial texts. It can help financial professionals quickly get the event information from the financial announcements. Figure 5 shows a screenshot of the online DCFEE system. Different color words represent different event arguments' types, underlined sentences represent the event mention in the document. As shown in figure 5, we can obtain a complete *Equity Freeze* event from unstructured text (an announcement about *Equity Freeze*).

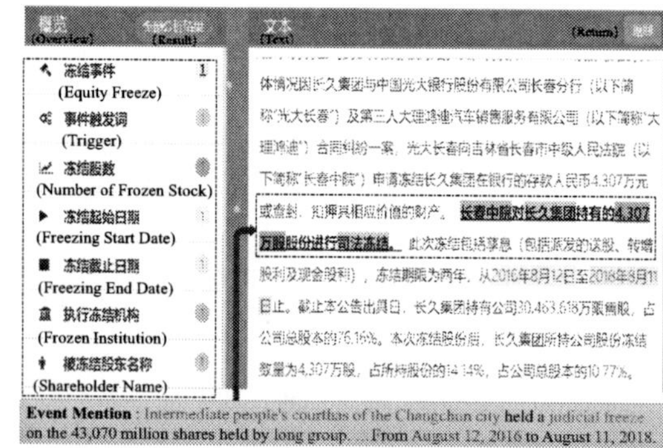

Figure 5: A screen shot of the online DCFEE system[9].

5 Related Work

The current EE approaches can be mainly classified into statistical methods, pattern-based method and hybrid method (Hogenboom et al., 2016).

Statistical method can be divided into two categories: traditional machine learning algorithm based on feature extraction engineering (Ahn, 2006), (Ji and Grishman, 2008), (Liao and Grishman, 2010), (Reichart and Barzilay, 2012) and neural network algorithm based on automatic feature extraction (Chen et al., 2015), (Nguyen et al., 2016), (Liu et al., 2017). The pattern method is usually used in industry because it can achieve higher accuracy, but meanwhile a lower recall. In order to improve recall, there are two main research directions: build relatively complete pattern library and use a semi-automatic method to build trigger dictionary (Chen et al., 2017), (Gu et al., 2016). Hybrid event-extraction methods combine statistical methods and pattern-based methods together (Jungermann and Morik, 2008), (Bjorne et al., 2010). To our best knowledge, there is no system that automatically generates labeled data, and extracts document-level events automatically from announcements in Chinese financial field.

6 Conclusion

We present DCFEE, a framework which is able to extract document-level events from Chinese financial announcements based on automatically labeled data. The experimental results show the effectiveness of the system. We successfully put the system online and users can quickly get event information from the financial announcements through it9.

7 Acknowledgements

This work was supported by the Natural Science Foundation of China (No. 61533018). And this work is also supported by a grant from Ant Financial Services Group.

References

David Ahn. 2006. The stages of event extraction. In *The Workshop on Annotating and Reasoning about Time and Events*, pages 1–8.

Jari Bjorne, Filip Ginter, Sampo Pyysalo, Jun'Ichi Tsujii, and Tapio Salakoski. 2010. Complex event extraction at pubmed scale. *Bioinformatics*, 26(12):i382–i390.

Yubo Chen, Shulin Liu, Xiang Zhang, Kang Liu, and Jun Zhao. 2017. Automatically labeled data generation for large scale event extraction. In *Proceedings of the ACL*, pages 409–419.

Yubo Chen, Liheng Xu, Kang Liu, Daojian Zeng, and Jun Zhao. 2015. Event extraction via dynamic multi-pooling convolutional neural networks. In *Proceedings of the ACL*.

Jiatao Gu, Zhengdong Lu, Hang Li, and O.K. Victor Li. 2016. Incorporating copying mechanism in sequence-to-sequence learning. In *Proceedings of the ACL*, pages 1631–1640.

Frederik Hogenboom, Flavius Frasincar, Uzay Kaymak, Franciska De Jong, and Emiel Caron. 2016. A survey of event extraction methods from text for decision support systems. *Decision Support Systems*, 85(C):12–22.

Zhiheng Huang, Wei Xu, and Kai Yu. 2015. Bidirectional lstm-crf models for sequence tagging. *Computer Science*.

Heng Ji and Ralph Grishman. 2008. Refining event extraction through cross-document inference. In *Proceedings of the ACL*, pages 254–262.

Felix Jungermann and Katharina Morik. 2008. *Enhanced Services for Targeted Information Retrieval by Event Extraction and Data Mining*. Springer Berlin Heidelberg.

Shasha Liao and Ralph Grishman. 2010. Using document level cross-event inference to improve event extraction. In *Proceedings of the ACL*, pages 789–797.

Shulin Liu, Yubo Chen, Kang Liu, and Jun Zhao. 2017. Exploiting argument information to improve event detection via supervised attention mechanisms. In *Proceedings of the ACL*, pages 1789–1798.

Tomas Mikolov, Kai Chen, Greg Corrado, and Jeffrey Dean. 2013. Efficient estimation of word representations in vector space. *Computer Science*.

Thien Huu Nguyen, Kyunghyun Cho, and Ralph Grishman. 2016. Joint event extraction via recurrent neural networks. In *Proceedings of the ACL*, pages 300–309.

Roi Reichart and Regina Barzilay. 2012. Multi event extraction guided by global constraints. In *Proceedings of the NAACL*, pages 70–79.

Daojian Zeng, Kang Liu, Yubo Chen, and Jun Zhao. 2015. Distant supervision for relation extraction via piecewise convolutional neural networks. In *Proceedings of the EMNLP*, pages 1753–1762.

Sentence Suggestion of Japanese Functional Expressions
for Chinese-speaking Learners

Jun Liu[1], Hiroyuki Shindo[1,2] and Yuji Matsumoto[1,2]
[1]Nara Institute of Science and Technology
[2]RIKEN Center for Advanced Intelligence Project (AIP)
{liu.jun.lc3, shindo, matsu}@is.naist.jp

Abstract

We present a computer-assisted learning system, *Jastudy*[1], which is particularly designed for Chinese-speaking learners of Japanese as a second language (JSL) to learn Japanese functional expressions with suggestion of appropriate example sentences. The system automatically recognizes Japanese functional expressions using a free Japanese morphological analyzer MeCab, which is retrained on a Conditional Random Fields (CRF) model. In order to select appropriate example sentences, we apply Support Vector Machines for Ranking (SVMrank) to estimate the complexity of the example sentences using Japanese-Chinese homographs as an important feature. In addition, we cluster the example sentences that contain Japanese functional expressions to discriminate different meanings and usages, based on part-of-speech, conjugation forms and semantic attributes, using the k-means clustering algorithm. Experimental results demonstrate the effectiveness of our approach.

1 Introduction

In the process of Japanese learning, learners must study many vocabulary words as well as various functional expressions. Since a large number of Chinese characters (Kanji characters in Japanese) are commonly used both in Chinese and Japanese, one of the most difficult and challenging problem for Chinese-speaking learners of Japanese as a second language (JSL) is the acquisition of Japanese functional expressions (Dongli Han, and Xin Song. 2011). Japanese has various types of compound functional expressions that consist of more than one word including both content words and functional words, such as "ざるをえ

ない (have to)", "ことができる (be able to)". Due to various meanings and usages of Japanese functional expressions, it is fairly difficult for JSL learners to learn them.

In recent years, certain online Japanese learning systems are developed to support JSL learners, such as Reading Tutor[2], Asunaro[3], Rikai[4], and WWWJDIC[5]. Some of these systems are particularly designed to enable JSL learners to read and write Japanese texts by offering the word information with their corresponding difficulty information or translation information (Ohno et al., 2013; Toyoda 2016). However, learners' native language background has not been taken into account in these systems. Moreover, these systems provide learners with limited information about the various types of Japanese functional expressions, which learners actually intend to learn as a part of the procedure for learning Japanese. Therefore, developing a learning system that can assist JSL learners to learn Japanese functional expressions is crucial in Japanese education.

In this paper, we present *Jastudy*, a computer-assisted learning system, aiming at helping Chinese-speaking JSL learners with their study of Japanese functional expressions. We train a CRF model and use a Japanese morphological analyzer MeCab[6] to detect Japanese functional expressions. To select the appropriate example sentences, we take Japanese-Chinese homographs as an important feature to estimate the complexity of example sentences using SVMrank[7]. In addition, in order to suggest example sentences that contain the target Japanese functional expression with the same meaning and usage, we cluster the

---

[1] http://jastudy.net/jastudy.php

[2] http://language.tiu.ac.jp/

[3] https://hinoki-project.org/asunaro/

[4] http://www.rikai.com/perl/Home.pl

[5] http://nihongo.monash.edu/cgi-bin/wwwjdic?9T

[6] http://taku910.github.io/mecab/

[7] https://www.cs.cornell.edu/people/tj/svm_light/
svm_rank.html

Proceedings of the 56th Annual Meeting of the Association for Computational Linguistics-System Demonstrations, pages 56–61
Melbourne, Australia, July 15 - 20, 2018. ©2018 Association for Computational Linguistics

example sentences, based on part-of-speech, conjugation forms and semantic attributes of the neighboring words, using the k-means clustering algorithm in Scikit-learn[8].

2 General Method

As shown in Figure 1, our proposed system is mainly composed of three processes: automatic detection of Japanese functional expressions, sentence complexity estimation and sentence clustering. In this section, we explain them in detail.

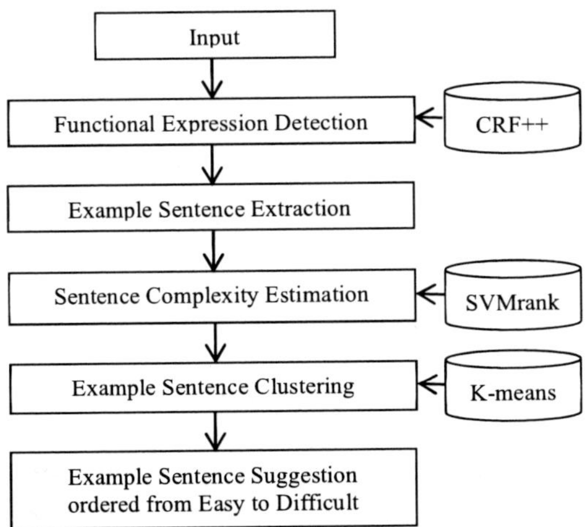

Figure 1: The processing stages of the system

2.1 Detection of Functional Expressions

Several previous researches have been especially paid attention on automatic detection of Japanese functional expressions (Tsuchiya et al., 2006; Shime et al., 2007; Suzuki et al., 2012). However, recognition of Japanese functional expressions is still a difficult problem. For automatic detection of Japanese functional expressions, we apply a Japanese morphological analyzer Mecab, which employs CRF algorithm to build the feature-based statistical model for morphological analysis.

While MeCab provides a pre-trained model using RWCP Text Corpus as well as Kyoto University Corpus (KC), we train a new CRF model using our training corpus, hoping MeCab can detect more Japanese functional expressions. To prepare the training corpus, we firstly referenced certain Japanese grammar dictionaries (Xiaoming Xu and Reika, 2013; Estuko Tomomastu, Jun Miyamoto and Masako Wakuki, 2016) to construct a list of

Japanese functional expressions. As a result, we collected approximately 4,600 types of various surface forms in our list. Then we gathered 21,435 sentences from Tatoeba[9] corpus, HiraganaTime[10] corpus, BCCWJ[11] and some grammar dictionaries (Jamashi and Xu, 2001; Xu and Reika, 2013) and segmented each sentence into word level using MeCab. Finally, we manually annotated part-of-speech information for each Japanese functional expression in our training corpus. Figure 2 shows an example sentence after pre-processing.

お　　　　接頭詞, 名詞接続, *, *, *, *, お, オ, オ
風呂　　　名詞, 一般, *, *, *, *, 風呂, フロ, フロ
に　　　　助詞, 格助詞, 一般, *, *, *, に, ニ, ニ
入っ　　　動詞, 自立, *, *, 五段・ラ行, 連用タ接続, 入る, ハイッ, ハイッ
てから　**助詞, 接続助詞, 機能表現, *, *, *, てから, テカラ, テカラ**
寝　　　　動詞, 自立, *, *, 一段, 連用形, 寝る, ネ, ネ
ます　　　助動詞, *, *, *, 特殊・マス, 基本形, ます, マス, マス
。　　　　記号, 句点, *, *, *, *, 。, 。, 。

Figure 2: An example sentence (I will go to sleep after I take a bath.) after pre-processing. In the sentence, the Japanese functional expression and its part-of-speech information are in bold.

2.2 Sentence Complexity Estimation

There are a large number of Japanese words written with Chinese characters. Most of the words share identical or similar meaning with the Chinese words. We define these words as Japanese-Chinese homographs in our study. For Chinese-speaking learners, it is easy to understand their meanings even though they have never learned Japanese. Therefore, Japanese-Chinese homographs should be considered as an important feature in estimating sentence complexity.

In order to construct a list of Japanese-Chinese homographs, we firstly extracted Japanese words written only with Chinese characters from two Japanese dictionaries: IPA (mecab-ipadic-2.7.0-20070801)[12] and UniDic (unidic-mecab 2.1.2)[13]. These two dictionaries are used as the standard dictionaries for the Japanese morphological analyzer MeCab, with appropriate part-of-speech information for each expression. We then extracted the Chinese translations of these Japanese words from two online dictionary websites: Wiktionary[14]

---

[8] http://scikitlearn.org/stable/modules/clustering.html#clustering

[9] https://tatoeba.org/eng/
[10] http://www.hiraganatiomes.com/
[11] http://pj.ninjal.ac.jp/corpus_center/bccwj/en/
[12] https://sourceforge.net/projects/mecab/files/mecab-ipadic/2.7.0-20070801/mecab-ipadic-2.7.0-20070801.tar.gz/download
[13] http://osdn.net/project/unidic/
[14] http://ja.wictionary.org/wiki/

and Weblio[15]. We compared the character forms of Japanese words with their Chinese translations to identify whether the Japanese word is a Japanese-Chinese homograph or not. Since Japanese words use both the simplified Chinese characters and the traditional Chinese characters, we first replaced all the traditional Chinese characters with the corresponding simplified Chinese characters. If the character form of a Japanese word is the same as the character form of the Chinese translation, the Japanese word is recognized as a Japanese-Chinese homograph, as illustrated in Table 1.

Considering unknown words in the above online dictionaries, we also referenced an online Chinese encyclopedia: Baike Baidu[16] and a Japanese dictionary: Kojien fifth Edition (Shinmura, 1998). If a Japanese word and its corresponding Chinese translation share an identical or a similar meaning, the Japanese word is also identified as a Japanese-Chinese homograph. Ultimately, we created a list of Japanese-Chinese homographs that consists of approximately 14,000 words.

Original Japanese word	Simplified Chinese characters	Chinese translation	Japanese-Chinese homographs
社会 (society)	社会	社会	Yes
緊張 (nervous)	緊张	緊张	Yes
手紙 (letter)	手纸	信件	No

Table 1: Examples of Identification of Japanese–Chinese homographs

To estimate sentence complexity, we follow the standard of the JLPT (Japanese Language Proficiency Test). The JLPT consists of five levels, ranging from N5 (the least difficult level) to N1 (the most difficult level)[17]. We employ the following 12 features as the baseline feature set:

- Numbers of N0–N5 Japanese words in a sentence (Here, N0 implies unknown words in the vocabulary list of JLPT.)
- Numbers of N1–N5 Japanese functional expressions in a sentence
- Length of a sentence

Different from the standard of the JLPT, the words in the list of Japanese–Chinese homographs (JCHs) were categorized separately as a new feature. Ultimately, we combine the following new features with the baseline features (all 17 features), forming our feature set.

- Numbers of JCHs in a sentence
- Numbers of verbs in a sentence
- Numbers of syntactic dependencies in a sentence
- Average length of syntactic dependencies
- Maximum number of child phrases

The last three features are to measure syntactic complexity of a sentence. We used a well-known Japanese dependency structure analyzer CaboCha[18] to divide an example sentence into base phrases (called bunsetsu) and to obtain its syntactic dependency structure. For example, the example sentence "彼は人生に満足して死んだ。(He died content with his life.)" is divided into four phrases: "彼は", "人生に", "満足して", "死んだ". In this sentence, the first, and the third phrases depend on the fourth, and the second phrase depends on the third. The numbers of syntactic dependencies in this sentence is 3. The length of syntactic dependencies is the numbers of phrases between arbitrary phrase and its dependent. In this sentence, the average length of syntactic dependencies is 1.7 (the length of syntactic dependency between the first and the fourth is 3, the length of syntactic dependency between the second and the third is 1, and the length of syntactic dependency between the third and the fourth is 1). The fourth phrase has two child's phrases while the third has only one child phrase, so the maximum number of child phrases in this sentence is 2.

2.3 Sentence Clustering

Some Japanese functional expressions have two or more meanings and usages. For example, the following two example sentences contain the identical Japanese functional expression "そうだ", but have different meanings. However, we can distinguish the meaning of "そうだ" through part-of-speech and conjugation forms of the words that appear just before "そうだ".

雨が降りそうだ。 (**It looks like** it will rain.)
雨が降るそうだ。 (**It's heard that** it will rain.)

To obtain example sentences for each of distinct usages of a functional expression, we apply a

---

[15] http://cjjc.weblio.jp
[16] https://baike.baidu.com
[17] http://jlpt.jp/e/about/levelsummary.html
[18] https://taku910.github.io/cabocha/

clustering algorithm with a small number of known examples (those appear in dictionaries) and a large number of untagged example sentences. For the features of sentence clustering, we utilize the following features: part-of-speech, conjugation form, and semantic attribute of the word that appear just before or after the target Japanese functional expression.

3 Experiments and Results

3.1 Automatically Detecting Japanese Functional Expressions

This experiment evaluates automatic detection of Japanese functional expressions.

We apply CRF++[19], which is an open source implementation of CRF for segmenting sequential data. We utilized nine features including surface forms and their part-of-speech in our training. The training corpus mentioned in Section 2.1 was used in the CRF++. The CRF++ learned the training corpus and outputted a model file as the learning result. We then applied MeCab, trained on our training corpus, to automatically recognize the Japanese functional expressions.

For the test data, we randomly extracted 200 example sentences from Tatoeba, HiraganaTimes and BCCWJ. Table 2 shows some examples of detected Japanese functional expressions by our system. The final evaluation results are shown in Table 3. We obtained 86.5% accuracy, indicating our approach has certain validity.

Correctly detected Japanese functional expressions
Input: 今、雪が降っている。 (It is snowing now.)
Output: 今 、 雪 が 降っ **ている** 。
Input: この箱を開けてください。 (Please open this box.)
Output: この 箱 を 開け **てください** 。
Incorrectly detected Japanese functional expressions
Input: 彼女は火にあたってからだを暖めた。 (She warmed herself by the fire.)
Output: 彼女 は 火 **にあたって** からだ を 暖め た 。

Table 2: Detection of Japanese functional expressions. In the sentences, Japanese functional expressions are in bold and underlined.

Correctly recognized	173 (86.5%)
Incorrectly recognized	27(13.5%)
Total	200 (100%)

Table 3: Experimental results on detection of Japanese functional expressions

[19] https://taku910.github.io/crfpp/

3.2 Estimating Sentence Complexity

This experiment evaluates sentence complexity estimation, using an online machine learning tool SVMrank.

We first collected 5,000 example sentences from Tatoeba, HiraganaTimes, BCCWJ and randomly paired them and constructed 2,500 sentence pairs. Then 15 native Chinese-speaking JSL learners, all of whom have been learning Japanese for about one year, were invited to read the pairs of example sentences and asked to choose the one which is easier to understand. We asked three learners to compare each pair and the final decision was made by majority voting. We finally applied a set of five-fold cross-validations with each combination of 4,000 sentences as the training data and 1,000 sentences as the test data.

The experimental results using baseline features and our method using all of the proposed features are presented in Tables 4 and 5. Compared with the results using the baseline features, our method enhances the average accuracy by 3.3%, partially demonstrating the effectiveness of our features.

Features	Cross-validations	Accuracy
Baseline Features	1	83.2%
	2	84%
	3	80.4%
	4	82%
	5	81.8%
Average		82.3%

Table 4: Experimental results using baseline features.

Features	Cross-validations	Accuracy
Proposed Features	1	87.6%
	2	86.4%
	3	84.6%
	4	83.8%
	5	85.4%
Average		85.6%

Table 5: Experimental results using our proposed features

3.3 Clustering Example Sentences

This experiment evaluates the performance of sentence clustering, using the k-means clustering algorithm in Scikit-learn.

Here in our study, we took five different types of Japanese functional expressions as the examples. For the test data, we collected 10 example sentences, which were used for the reference, from Japanese functional expression dictionaries and 20 example sentences from Tatoeba, HiraganaTimes, and BCCWJ for each type of Japanese functional expressions, respectively. We conducted our experiments with the number of clusters ranging from four to six. The clustering result was evaluated based on whether the test data that was clustered into one cluster share the same usage of a Japanese functional expression. The experimental results are shown in Table 6. The average results of accuracies for the number of clusters ranging from four to six are 89%, 93%, 92%, indicating the usefulness of the sentence clustering method for classifying sentences in the same usage.

Functional Expressions	Numbers of Clusters	Accuracy
そうだ	4	97%
(it looks like /	5	97%
it's heard that)	6	97%
とともに	4	87%
(together with /	5	97%
at the same time)	6	87%
ため（に）	4	83%
(because /	5	83%
in order to)	6	90%
に対して	4	87%
(to / every /	5	93%
in contrast to)	6	93%
次第（だ）	4	93%
(as soon as /	5	93%
depends on)	6	93%
	4	89%
Average	5	93%
	6	92%

Table 6: Experimental results of sentence clustering

4 Featured functions of the Demo

In our proposed demo, we have implemented the following main functions.

1. The function to detect Japanese functional expressions. Given a sentence, *Jastudy* automatically segments the input sentence into individual words using MeCab. Difficult Japanese functional expressions (N2 and above) in the input sentence are simplified with easier Japanese functional expressions (N3 and below) or with phrases and shown in the output sentence, using a "Simple Japanese Replacement List" (Jun Liu and Yuji Matsumoto, 2016). An example is shown in Figure 3. Moreover, *Jastudy* represents detailed information about the surface-form, part-of-speech of each word in the input sentence and the output sentence, respectively.

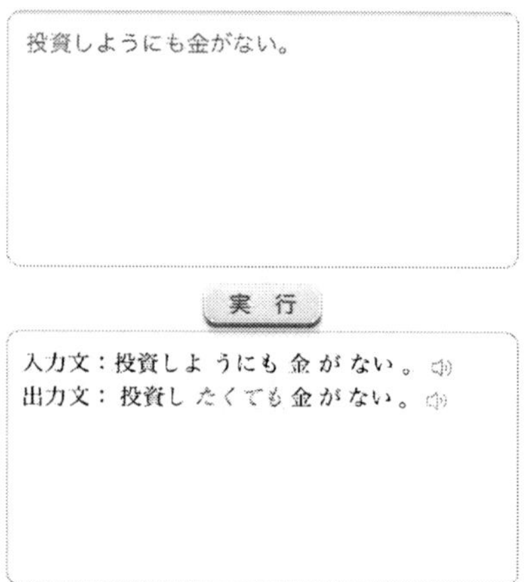

Figure 3: "投資しようにも金がない。(I have no money to invest.)" is typed in the system.

2. The function to provide JSL learners with the detail information about the meaning, usage and example sentences of the Japanese functional expression which appears in the input sentence and the output sentence, respectively. An example is shown in Figure 4. Learners can also choose the Japanese functional expressions they want to learn, based on their Japanese abilities.

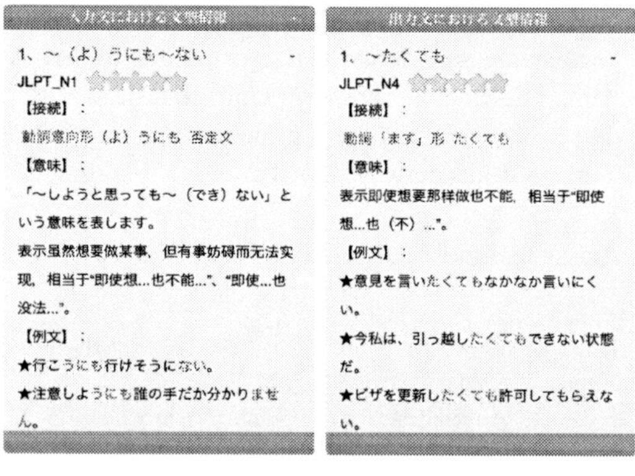

(a) (b)

Figure 4: Detailed information of Japanese functional expressions appeared in the input sentence (a) and the output sentence (b).

3. The function to suggest comprehensive example sentences. The JSL learners can search more example sentences through the following three aspects: 1) only keyword, 2) only usage, 3) both keyword and usage. For example, the learner inputs the Japanese functional expression "そうだ" as a keyword and selects its meaning and usage "it looks like" from drop-down list, a list of

example sentences that contain the functional expression sharing the same meaning are retrieved to form the corpus, as shown in Figure 5. The only sentences whose complexity is equal to or below the learner's level are retrieved.

Figure 5: Example sentences suggested by the system, given "そうだ" with its meaning as "様態(it looks like)"

5   Conclusion and Future Work

In this paper, we presented a computer-assisted leaning system of Japanese language for Chinese-speaking learners with their study of Japanese functional expressions. The system detects Japanese functional expressions using MeCab that employs the CRF model we trained. We apply SVMrank to estimate sentence complexity using the Japanese-Chinese homographs as an important feature to suggest example sentences that are easy to understand for Chinese-speaking JSL learners. Moreover, we cluster example sentences containing the Japanese functional expressions with the same meanings and usages. The experimental results indicate effectiveness of our method.

We plan to examine the run-time effectiveness of the system for JSL learners. This will be our future task for improving the performance of our system.

Acknowledgments

We would like to thank anonymous reviewers for their detailed comments and advice.

References

Dongli Han, and Xin Song. 2011. Japanese Sentence Pattern Learning with the Use of Illustrative Examples Extracted from the Web. *IEEJ Transactions on Electrical and Electronic Engineering*, 6(5): 490–496.

Group Jamashi, Yiping Xu. 2001. Chubunban Nihongo Kukei Jiten-Nihongo Bunkei Jiten (in Chinese and Japanese). *Tokyo: Kurosio Publishers.*

Jun Liu, Yuji matsumoto. 2016. Simplification of Example Sentences for Learners of Japanese Functional Expressions. In *Proceedings of the 3rd Workshop on Natural Language Processing Techniques for Educational Applications*, pages 1–5.

Takahiro Ohno, Zyunitiro Edani, Ayato Inoue, and Dongli Han. 2013. A Japanese Learning Support System Matching Individual Abilities. In *Proceeding of the PACLIC 27 Workshop on Computer-Assisted Language Learning*, pages 556–562.

Takao Shime, Masatoshi Tsuchiya, Suguru Matsuyoshi, Takehito Utsuro, Satoshi Sato. 2007. Automatic Detection of Japanese Compound Functional Expressions and its Application to Statistical Dependency Analysis, *Journal of Natural Language Processing*, Vol (14). No.5: 167-196.

Izuru Shinmura (Ed. In chief). 1998. Kojien 5th Editon (in Japanese). *Tokyo: Iwanani Press.*

Takafumi Suzuki, Yusuke Abe, Itsuki Toyota, Takehito Utsuro, Suguru Matsuyoshi, Masatoshi Tsuchiya. 2012. Detecting Japanese Compound Functional Expressions using Canonical/Derivational Relation, In *Proceedings of the Eighth International Conference on Language Resources and Evaluation (LREC-2012).*

Estuko Tomomastu, Jun Miyamoto and Masako Wakuki. 2016. Japanese Expressions Dictionary. *Aruku Press.*

Etsuko Toyoda. 2016. Evaluation of computerized reading-assistance systems for reading Japanese texts – from a linguistic point of view. *Australasian Journal of Educational Technology*, 32(5): 94-97.

Masatoshi Tsuchiya, Takao Shime, Toshihiro Takagi, Takehito Utsuro, Kiyotaka Uchimoto, Suguru Matsuyoshi, Satoshi Sato, Seiichi Nakagawa. 2006. Chunking Japanese compound functional expressions by machine learning, In *Proceedings of the Workshop on Multi-word-expressions in a Multilingual Context*, pages 25-32.

Xiaoming Xu and Reika. 2013, Detailed introduction of the New JLPT N1-N5 grammar. *East China University of Science and Technology Press.*

Translating a Language You Don't Know in the Chinese Room

Ulf Hermjakob, Jonathan May, Michael Pust, Kevin Knight
Information Sciences Institute & Department of Computer Science
University of Southern California
{ulf, jonmay, pust, knight}@isi.edu

Abstract

In a corruption of John Searle's famous AI thought experiment, the Chinese Room (Searle, 1980), we twist its original intent by enabling humans to translate text, e.g. from Uyghur to English, even if they don't have any prior knowledge of the source language. Our enabling tool, which we call the Chinese Room, is equipped with the same resources made available to a machine translation engine. We find that our superior language model and world knowledge allows us to create perfectly fluent and nearly adequate translations, with human expertise required only for the target language. The Chinese Room tool can be used to rapidly create small corpora of parallel data when bilingual translators are not readily available, in particular for low-resource languages.

1 Introduction

Domain adaptation for machine translation is a well-studied problem.[1] Most works assume a system-builder has an adequate amount of out-of-domain or 'general' domain parallel sentence training data and some smaller corpus of in-domain data that can be used, depending on the size of the in-domain corpus, for additional training, for parameter estimation, or, if the in-domain corpus is very small, simply for system evaluation. Very little, however, is said of the scenario where there is *no* in-domain parallel data available, and yet an in-domain system must be built.

In such scenarios one may try to mine parallel data from comparable corpora (Munteanu and Marcu, 2005), but in cases where even scant (but

not zero) in-domain *monolingual* resources are available this is not a feasible strategy and the only way to obtain any reliably measure of quality is to solicit human translations. However, it may be difficult to recruit translators to prepare such data, if the language is underrepresented or politically sensitive.

Al-Onaizan et al. (2002) describe an experiment where individual humans translated 10 sentences from Tetun to English, without any prior knowledge of Tetun, based solely on an in-domain bitext of 1,102 sentences. Without any prior tools, translation was very tedious, inefficient, and impractical for the 10 sentences, taking about one sentence per hour. But the experiment successfully showed in principle the feasibility of human translation without prior knowledge of the source language.

We introduce a tool, the *Chinese Room*, to facilitate efficient human translation without prior knowledge of a source language. The name is inspired from Searle (1980) who envisioned a monolingual English-speaking human equipped with instructions for answering Chinese questions by manipulating symbols of a Chinese information corpus and the question text to form answers. While Searle used this idea to argue against 'strong' AI, we thought the setup, i.e. giving a human the tools an NLP model is given (in this case, a machine translation model), was a good one for rapidly generating useful translation data.

Apart from generating human translation data, an additional use of the Chinese Room is to support computational linguists in identifying the challenges of machine translation for a specific language pair and language resources. By placing humans in the role of the MT, we may better understand the nature and magnitude of out-of-vocabulary gaps, and whether they might be due to morphological complexity, compounding, assimi-

---

[1] See http://www.statmt.org/survey/Topic/DomainAdaptation for a survey of methodologies.

Proceedings of the 56th Annual Meeting of the Association for Computational Linguistics-System Demonstrations, pages 62–67
Melbourne, Australia, July 15 - 20, 2018. ©2018 Association for Computational Linguistics

lation, spelling variations, insufficient or out-of-domain parallel corpora or dictionaries, etc. We found that the Chinese Room can be a useful tool to help generate new ideas for machine translation research.

1.1 Features

Our Chinese Room tool has the following features:

1. Glosser accommodates a variety of NLP and source language resources
2. User can explore alternative translations
3. Grammar support (such as prefixes, suffixes, function words)
4. Optional romanization of source text
5. Robust to spelling variations
6. Optional confidence levels
7. Propagation of user translations
8. Dictionary search function (allowing regular expressions)
9. User accounts with login, password, worksets, separate workspaces
10. Web-based

2 System Description

2.1 Dictionary and T-table Lookup

The principal glossing resources are dictionaries and translation probability tables (t-tables) that are automatically computed from parallel corpora (Brown et al., 1993). The Chinese Room tool will present the top 10 t-table entries and all dictionary entries, including multi-word entries.

2.2 Out-of-Vocabulary Words

However, particularly for low-resource languages, words will frequently not be found that easily. Due to morphological inflection, affixes, compounding, assimilation, and typos, a source word might not occur in a dictionary or t-table.

Low-resource languages often lack consistent spelling due to dialects, lack of spelling standards, or lack of education. For example, even a small Uyghur corpus included six different spellings for the Uyghur word for *kilometer*: kilometer, kilometir, kilomitir, kilometr, kilomitr, klometir.

It is therefore critical to be able to identify dictionary and t-table entries that approximately match a word or a part hereof. We address this challenge with a combination of multiple indexes and a weighted string similarity metric.

2.3 Multiple Indexes For String Matching

We currently use the following indexing heuristics: (1) stemming, (2) hashing, (3) drop-letter, and (4) long substring. Inspired by phonetic matching (Philips, 2000), our current hash function first removes duplicate letters and then removes vowels, except for any leading vowels that get mapped to a canonical *e*. For example, both *break* and *broke* are hashed to *brk*.

The drop-letter heuristic allows to find entries for words with typos due to letter deletion, addition, substitution and juxtaposition. For example, "crocodile" and "cocodrile" share the drop-letter sequence "cocodile".

The long (7+ letters) substring heuristic finds dictionary entries that contain additional content.

2.4 Weighted String Distance Metric

Traditional edit distance metrics (Levenshtein, 1966) do not consider the particular characters being added, subtracted, or substituted, and will therefore typically assign a higher cost to (*gram, gramme*) than to (*gram, tram*). Such uniform edit distance costs are linguistically implausible.

The Chinese Room Editor therefore uses a modified metric that leverages a resource of edit distance costs. In particular, costs for vowels and duplicate letters are cheap.

```
::s1 o ::s2 u ::cost 0.1
::s1 m ::s2 mm ::cost 0.02
::s1 e ::s2 ::cost 0.1
::s1 e ::s2 ::cost 0.02 ::lc2 fas
::s1 kn ::s2 n ::cost 0.05 ::left1 /^(.* )?$/ ::lc1 eng
```

Table 1: String similarity rule examples.
::s1 = string 1; ::left1 = left context of string 1;
::lc1 = language code of string 1.

The first rule in Table 1 assigns a cost of 0.1 for o/u substitution, well below the default cost of 1. The second and third rule reduce the string distance cost of (*gram, gramme*) to 0.12. Cost entries for pairs of substrings can be restricted to specific left and right contexts or to specific languages. The last rule in Table 1 assigns a low cost to word-initial silent *k* in English. The manually created resource currently has 590 entries, including a core set of 252 language-independent cost entries that are widely applicable.

2.5 Romanization

For a similarity metric to be widely practical, the strings need to be in the same script. We therefore

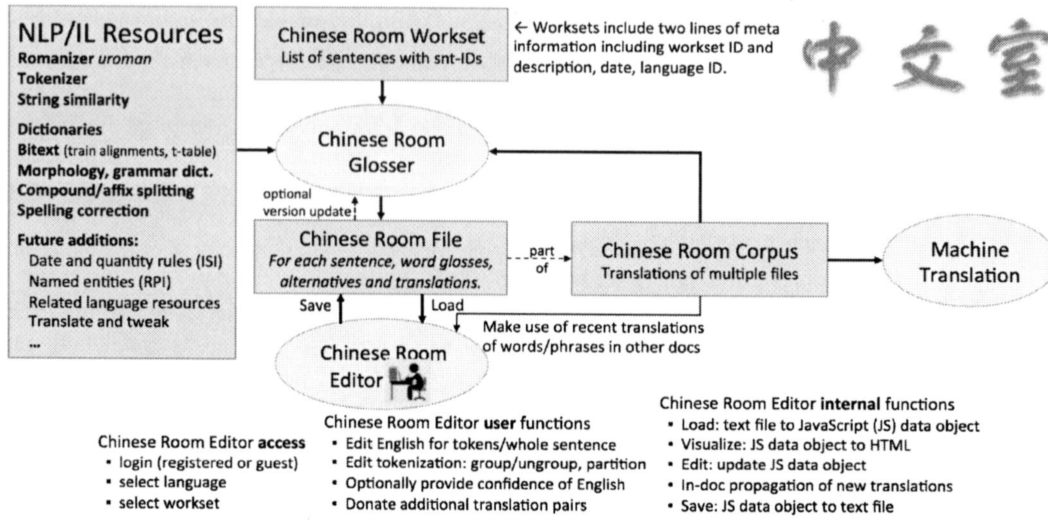

Figure 1: Chinese Room process. Blue rectangles represent data, pink ovals programs and processes.

romanize before computing string similarity.

An additional motivation for romanization in the Chinese Room is based on the observation that foreign scripts present a massive cognitive barrier to humans who are not familiar with them. See Table 2 for examples.

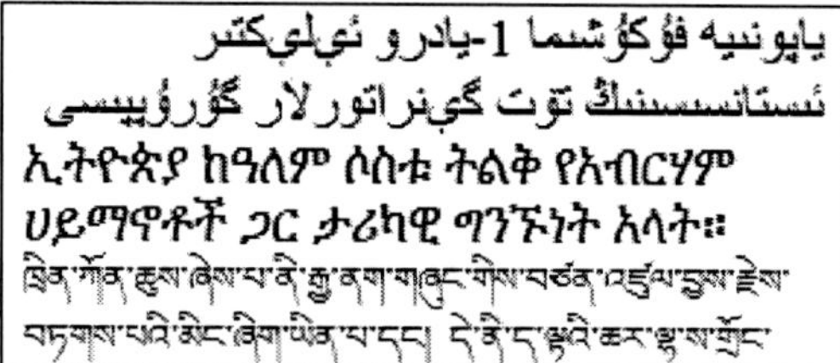

Table 2: Texts in Uyghur, Amharic and Tibetan.

We found that when we asked native English speakers to use the Chinese Room to translate text from languages such as Uyghur or Bengali to English, they strongly preferred working on a romanized version of the source language compared to its original form and indeed found using the native, unfamiliar script to be a nearly impossible task.

By default, we therefore romanize non-Latin-script text, using the universal romanizer *uroman*[2] (Hermjakob et al., 2018). The Chinese Room Editor includes the option to display the original text or both the original and romanized source text. The Uyghur text in Table 2 is romanized as

> yaponie fukushima 1-yadro elektir
>
> istansisining toet genratorlar guruppisi

which facilitates the recognition of cognates.

2.6 Grammar Resource Files

An additional optional resource is a set of grammar entries for affixes and function words that dictionaries and t-tables do not cover very well. Table 3 shows examples for five Hungarian affixes and two Tagalog function words.

::hun ak ::synt plural suffix ::eng -s, -es
::hun at ::synt accusative case suffix
::hun ból ::synt case suffix ::eng from, out of
::hun ből ::synt case suffix ::eng from, out of
::hun el ::synt verb prefix ::eng away; mis-
::tgl ang ::synt definite article ::eng the
::tgl mga ::synt particle ::function plural ::eng -s

Table 3: Grammar entries for Hungarian, Tagalog.

The grammar files have been built manually, typically drawing on external resources such as Wiktionary.[3] The size is language specific, ranging from a few dozen entries to several hundred entries for extremely suffix-rich Hungarian.

2.7 Process

Figure 1 provides an overview of the Chinese Room process. Given a set of NLP resources and a workset of source language sentences, the Chinese Room Glosser builds a Chinese Room File, which can be edited in the Chinese Room Editor. The resulting Chinese Room Corpus can be used for machine translation and other NLP applications.

____

[2]bit.ly/uroman

[3]https://en.wiktionary.org, e.g. https://en.wiktionary.org/wiki/Appendix:Hungarian_suffixes

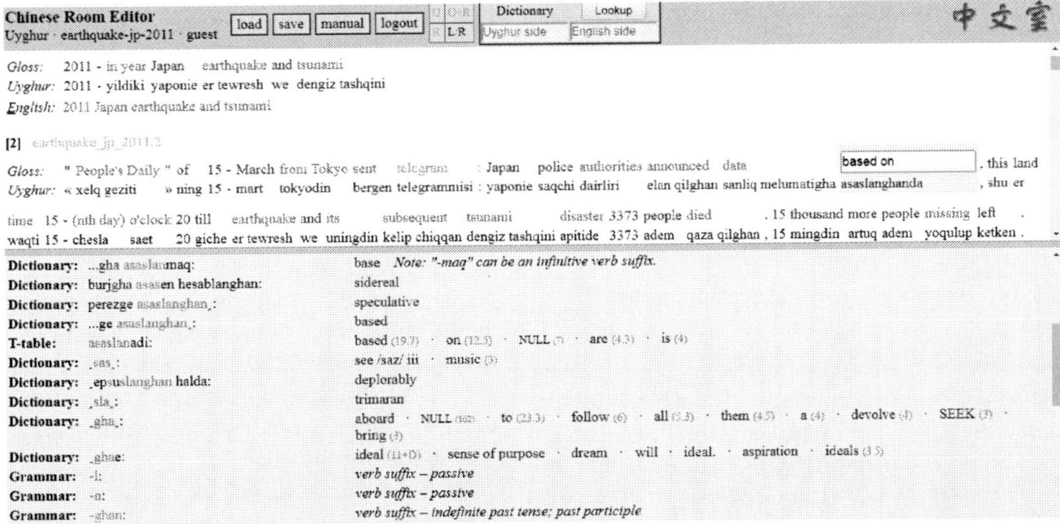

Figure 2: Screenshot of Chinese Room Editor with Uyghur example. Demo site: bit.ly/chinese-room

2.8 Chinese Room Example

Figure 2 shows an example from a Uyghur article about an earthquake. For the (romanized) Uyghur word *asaslanghanda*, the tool shows several relevant entries that guide the translator to the correct gloss *based (on)*. Note the information regarding the suffixes *-maq*, *-ghan*, and *-da*.

2.9 Gloss Propagation

Words and expressions often occur multiple times in a document. When a translator edits a gloss, the edited gloss is propagated to other yet unedited glosses of the same word(s) in a document. The propagated glosses can be overwritten, but that is rarely necessary.

Additionally, the edited glosses are collected as an additional translation resource, which can be compiled and propagated to other documents. This allows the sharing of newly discovered translations between translators.

At times, some sentences will be difficult to fully translate, particularly if there are multiple unknown words. The meaning of some of those words will become apparent in other sentences with a stronger context, which in turn will help comprehension of the original difficult sentence.

The discovery of morphological bridge forms is one such case. In (romanized) Uyghur, for example, a translator might struggle with the meaning of *panahliniwetiptu*, but later in the text find a related word *panahlinish*, which in turn is similar enough to the dictionary entry *panalinish = shelter*

to be found by the tool. With additional grammar guidance for the suffixes *-wet, -ip, -tu,* and *-sh,* the originally hard word can now be glossed and the sentence translated.

3 Chinese Room Editor User Interface[4]

The Chinese Room URL is bit.ly/chinese-room. Temporary visitors are invited to login as *guest*.

3.1 Loading a Workset

To get started, click the *load* button, wait a moment, select a source language (e.g. Uyghur), and a workset (e.g. earthquake-jp-2011-wo-cr-corpus).

3.2 Exploring and Editing Glosses

The initial gloss will often provide a good first idea of what the sentence is about. To explore alternatives to the glosses provided, hover the mouse over a gloss that you want to explore. A blue info box will appear in the lower part of the screen, providing you with a range of entries related to the word. To edit a gloss, or just to fix an info box for subsequent scrolling, click on a gloss, and the gloss becomes editable. To move on to another gloss, click that gloss. To exit gloss editing mode, press *Enter* (while the cursor is in a gloss box). Alternatively, you can click on a translation in the info box to select that translation as a gloss. Double-clicking on a source word will copy it to the gloss; this is

---

[4]For more details, please consult the Chinese Room Editor manual at bit.ly/chinese-room-manual.

useful for words that don't need translations, such as names.

3.3 Editing Sentence Translations

To edit the translation of the full sentence, click on the current translation (in green), initially *empty*. Type text, or adopt a gloss by clicking on it. Press *Enter* to exit sentence editing.

3.4 Grouping, Ungrouping, Confidence

In the *Special ops* section, click on *group* to combine words to a multi-word expression, or *ungroup* to undo. You may optionally assign a confidence level to glosses and sentence translations, which allows you flag uncertainty, for later review by you or somebody else, or to inform a subsequent user (such as a learning algorithm). For more info, hover over a special-op name.

4 Experiments

We have built Chinese Rooms for Bengali, Hungarian, Oromo, Somali, Swahili, Tagalog, Tigrinya, and Uyghur.

For Bengali, two of the authors of this paper translated an article of 10 Bengali sentences to English, without any prior knowledge of Bengali, using the Chinese Room. To evaluate the results, we asked a native speaker from Bangladesh, a graduate student living in the US who is not a professional translator, to first translate the same 10 sentences independently and then to evaluate our translations. According to the native speaker our translations were better; we only missed one Bengali word in translation, and were actually aware of it, but were unable to decode it with the resources at hand.

We used the Chinese Room to create small corpora of parallel data in a time-constrained MT system-building scenario. In this scenario we were required to translate documents from Uyghur to English describing earthquakes and disaster relief efforts. However, we had no parallel data dealing with this topic, and our use of an unrelated test set (see Figure 3) to estimate overall task performance was not reliable. We thus wanted to construct an in-domain Uyghur-English parallel corpus.

In the scenario we were given a small number of one-hour sessions with a *native informant* (NI), a Uyghur native who spoke English and was not a linguistics or computer science expert. We initially asked the NI use the time to translate docu-ments, one sentence at a time. This was accomplished at a rate of 360 words per hour, but required another 30-60 minutes of post-editing to ensure fluency. We next tried typing for the NI (and ensured fluency); this yielded 320 words/hr but did not require post-editing. Finally we used the Chinese Room to translate and asked the NI to point out any errors. This hour yielded 480 words. Machine translation quality on the resulting in-domain set tracked much better with performance on the evaluation set. Later on we built a second in-domain set but did not have any further access to the NI. Using this set of approximate translation to tune parameters yielded a 0.3 BLEU increase in system performance.

We have trained more than 20 people to use the Chinese Room with very good results for the training test case, Somali. We are similarly confident in our translations for Hungarian and Uyghur. Tagalog and Swahili are recent builds, and translations look very promising.

However, we found the dictionary and bitext resources for Tigrinya (to a lesser degree) and Oromo (to a larger degree) to be too small to confidently translate most sentences. We were able to translate some sentences completely, and many others partially, but had to rely on the support of non-professional native speakers to complete the translations. The Chinese Room nevertheless proved to be very useful in this very-low-resource scenario. We could already build glosses for many words and provide a partial translations, so that the native speaker could finish a sentence faster than starting from scratch. The Chinese Room also helped the native speaker to more easily find the English words he/she was looking for, and allowed us to make sure that the translation covered all essential parts of the original text.

5 Related Work

Callison-Burch (2005); Albrecht et al. (2009); Koehn (2010) and Trados[5] have built computer-aided translation systems for high-resource languages, with an emphasis on post-editing.

Hu et al. (2011) describe a *monolingual translation* protocol that combines MT with not only monolingual target language speakers, but, unlike the Chinese Room, also monolingual source language speakers.

---

[5] https://www.sdltrados.com

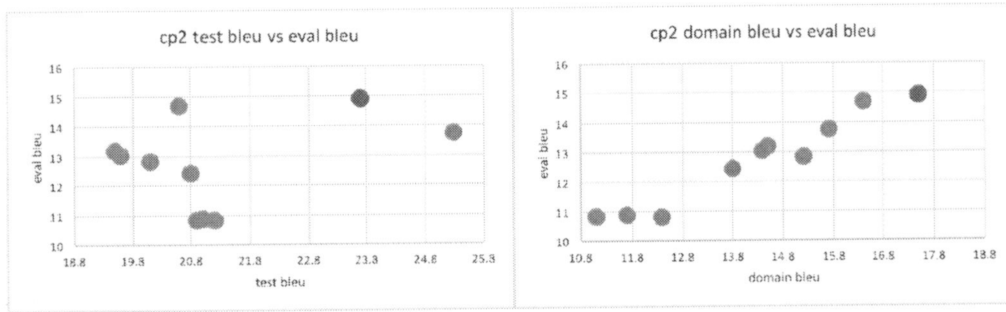

Figure 3: MT performance on an out-of-domain corpus ('test') does not predict performance on the evaluation ('eval') set but performance on our 'domain' data set which comprises NI translations and Chinese Room post-edits, is predictive.

6 Future Work

We have observed that by using the Chinese Room, human translators start to learn some of the vocabulary and grammar of the source language. It might therefore be worthwhile to explore how the Chinese Room tool, with a few modifications, could be used in foreign language learning.

7 Conclusion

We have established the feasibility of a practical system that enables human translation from an unfamiliar language, supporting even low-resource languages. We found that we were able to create perfectly fluent and nearly adequate translations, far exceeding the quality of a state-of-the-art machine translation system (Cheung et al., 2017) using the same resources as the Chinese Room, by exploiting the human translators' target language model and their world knowledge, both of which are still far superior to those of a computer.

Acknowledgments

This work was sponsored by DARPA (HR0011-15-C-0115).

References

Yaser Al-Onaizan, Ulrich Germann, Ulf Hermjakob, Kevin Knight, Philipp Koehn, Daniel Marcu, and Kenji Yamada. 2002. Translation with scarce bilingual resources. *Machine translation*, 17(1):1–17.

Joshua S Albrecht, Rebecca Hwa, and G Elisabeta Marai. 2009. Correcting automatic translations through collaborations between MT and monolingual target-language users. In *EACL*, pages 60–68.

Peter F Brown, Vincent J Della Pietra, Stephen A Della Pietra, and Robert L Mercer. 1993. The mathematics of statistical machine translation: Parameter estimation. *Computational linguistics*, 19(2):263–311.

Chris Callison-Burch. 2005. Linear B system description for the 2005 NIST MT evaluation exercise. In *Proceedings of the NIST 2005 Machine Translation Evaluation Workshop*.

Leon Cheung, Ulf Hermjakob, Jonathan May, Nima Pourdamghani, Michael Pust, Kevin Knight, et al. 2017. Elisa system description for LoReHLT 2017.

Ulf Hermjakob, Jonathan May, and Kevin Knight. 2018. Out-of-the-box universal romanization tool *uroman*. In *Proceedings of the 56th Annual Meeting of Association for Computational Linguistics, Demo Track*.

Chang Hu, Benjamin Bederson, Philip Resnik, and Yakov Kronrod. 2011. Monotrans2: A new human computation system to support monolingual translation. In *SIGCHI Conference on Human Factors in Computing Systems*, pages 1133–1136. ACM.

Philipp Koehn. 2010. Enabling monolingual translators: Post-editing vs. options. In *NAACL Human Language Technologies*, pages 537–545.

Vladimir I Levenshtein. 1966. Binary codes capable of correcting deletions, insertions, and reversals. In *Soviet physics doklady*, volume 10, pages 707–710.

Dragos Stefan Munteanu and Daniel Marcu. 2005. Improving machine translation performance by exploiting non-parallel corpora. *Computational Linguistics*, 31(4):477–504.

Lawrence Philips. 2000. The double Metaphone search algorithm. *C/C++ Users J.*, 18(6):38–43.

John Searle. 1980. Minds, brains, and programs. *Behavioral and Brain Sciences*, 3:417–442.

SANTO: A Web-based Annotation Tool for Ontology-driven Slot Filling

Matthias Hartung[1,*] **Hendrik ter Horst**[1,*] **Frank Grimm**[1],
Tim Diekmann[1], **Roman Klinger**[1,2] and **Philipp Cimiano**[1]
[1]CITEC, Bielefeld University
[2]Institut für Maschinelle Sprachverarbeitung, University of Stuttgart
{mhartung,hterhors,fgrimm,tdiekmann,cimiano}@
techfak.uni-bielefeld.de
roman.klinger@ims.uni-stuttgart.de

Abstract

Supervised machine learning algorithms require training data whose generation for complex relation extraction tasks tends to be difficult. Being optimized for relation extraction at sentence level, many annotation tools lack in facilitating the annotation of relational structures that are widely spread across the text. This leads to non-intuitive and cumbersome visualizations, making the annotation process unnecessarily time-consuming. We propose SANTO, an easy-to-use, domain-adaptive annotation tool specialized for complex slot filling tasks which may involve problems of cardinality and referential grounding. The web-based architecture enables fast and clearly structured annotation for multiple users in parallel. Relational structures are formulated as templates following the conceptualization of an underlying ontology. Further, import and export procedures of standard formats enable interoperability with external sources and tools.

1 Introduction

In most scientific and technical domains, the main medium for knowledge communication is unstructured text. Growing efforts are spent into *literature-based knowledge discovery* (Henry and McInnes, 2017) using information extraction or machine reading approaches for knowledge base population. The goal is to automatically transform the available domain knowledge into structured formats that can be leveraged for downstream analytical tasks.

Recent approaches reduced information extraction problems to binary relation extraction tasks at sentence level (Adel et al., 2016; Zhang et al.,

2017, *i. a.*). In such cases, the annotation procedure is comparably straight-forward to formulate. However, a substantial subset of information extraction tasks can be described as typed n-ary relation extraction or slot filling, in which pre-defined sets of typed slots (templates) need to be assigned from information that may be widely spread across a text (Freitag, 2000). As such templates can contain many slots which may be recursively nested, an appropriate visualization is mandatory during annotation to handle the complexity of the task.

Relevant use cases for template-based information extraction exist in several fields of application: In the biomedical domain, there is a large body of work on database population from text in order to support translational medicine (Zhu et al., 2013; ter Horst et al., 2018, *i. a.*). In digital humanities, there is a vital interest in detecting descriptions of historical events or artifacts from cultural heritage (Ruotsalo et al., 2009; Segers et al., 2011). In the context of manufacturing or retail, structured product descriptions are extracted from web pages or customer reviews (Bing et al., 2016; Petrovski and Bizer, 2017) to enable product comparisons.

In this work, we present SANTO, a lightweight, easy-to-use, domain-adaptive, web-based annotation tool specialized for complex slot filling tasks. SANTO is designed to address particular user needs that are recurrent in such scenarios. It enables data annotation and export into a machine-readable format based on the following features:

- Being based on information models such as ontologies for specifying the template scheme, it can be flexibly adapted to different domains and use cases.
- It enables annotations both at the textual and the template level; it is designed to support fast and seamless instantiation of new templates and their population from textual annotations, particularly in cases where slot fillers

---

*The first two authors contributed equally to this paper.

Proceedings of the 56th Annual Meeting of the Association for Computational Linguistics-System Demonstrations, pages 68–73
Melbourne, Australia, July 15 - 20, 2018. ©2018 Association for Computational Linguistics

pertaining to one template are widely distributed across the text.

- As common in slot filling, the tool builds on top of the fact that extraction models do not need to find every mention of an entity or relation in the text. Instead, the focus is on enabling the user to instantiate the correct cardinality of templates and ensuring referential uniqueness of slot fillers or templates.
- Annotations can be flexibly imported from different external sources. The RDF export of annotated relations within templates is conform to the underlying information model.
- It enables easy curation of annotations (*e. g.*, from multiple imports).
- It is implemented as a web service in order to support remote annotation workflows for multiple users in parallel.

Availability and License. A demo installation is available at `http://psink.techfak.uni-bielefeld.de/santo/`. The source code of the application is publicly available under the Apache 2.0 License at `https://github.com/ag-sc/SANTO`.

2   Related Work

Most annotation frameworks for text focus on the sentence level. Examples include syntactic parsing (Burchardt et al., 2006) or semantic role labeling (Kakkonen, 2006; Yimam et al., 2013). Other tools focus on segmentation annotation tasks, for instance Callisto (Day et al., 2004), WordFreak (Morton and LaCivita, 2003), MMax2 (Müller and Strube, 2006), or GATE Teamware (Bontcheva et al., 2013) (though the latter also supports more complex schemata).

Brat (Stenetorp et al., 2012), WebAnno (Yimam et al., 2013), eHost (South et al., 2012) and CAT (Lenzi et al., 2012) support approaches for relational annotations. These tools are easy to use and highly flexible regarding the specification of annotation schemes. Projects are easy to manage due to administration interfaces and remote annotation is supported. However, these approaches share the limitation that all relational structures need to be anchored at the textual surface. Thus, annotating complex templates as in Figure 1 becomes tedious and visually cumbersome, especially in cases of complex nestings within or across templates, or when fillers are widely dispersed across multiple sentences in a text.

$$
\begin{bmatrix}
\textsc{OrganismModel} & \\
\begin{bmatrix}
\textsc{Age} & \textit{``six-week-old''} \\
\textsc{Species} & \text{SpragueDawleyRat} \\
\textsc{Gender} & \text{Female} \\
\textsc{AgeCategory} & \text{Adult} \\
\textsc{Weight} & \textit{``192–268g``}
\end{bmatrix}
\end{bmatrix}
$$

Figure 1: Example template following a schema derived from the Spinal Cord Injury Ontology.

We propose a tool to frame complex relational annotation problems as slot filling tasks. To our knowledge, the only existing tool for this purpose is the Protégé plugin Knowtator (Ogren, 2006), which is, however, not web-based, comparably difficult to use with multiple annotators, and no longer actively supported since 2009. Thus, our main contribution is an annotation tool which combines the advantages of (i) enabling complex relational slot filling with distant fillers, and (ii) ease of use in web-based environments in order to facilitate remote collaboration.

SANTO is ontology-based, *i. e.*, entity and relation types are derived from an underlying ontology. The same idea is prominent in several annotation tools within the Semantic Web community (*cf.* Oliveira and Rocha, 2013). Contrary to SANTO, these tools support annotations only at the level of individual entities without capturing relational structures as given in template-based slot filling.

3   Use Case: Information Extraction for Database Population

SANTO is designed to create machine-readable annotation data. As a motivating example, our presentation is guided by the use case of generating annotated training data for an ontology-based information extraction system that supports database population in the PSINK project[1] (ter Horst et al., 2018). In this context, our goal is to annotate scientific publications reporting on the outcomes of pre-clinical trials in the spinal cord injury domain. The annotation schema complies to definitions of the Spinal Cord Injury Ontology (SCIO; Brazda et al., 2017). SCIO provides the concept RESULT as a top-level class which subsumes all classes and properties to represent the key parameters of an outcome in a study. Several properties are recursively sub-structured (*e. g.*, EXPERIMENTAL-

---

[1] `http://psink.de`

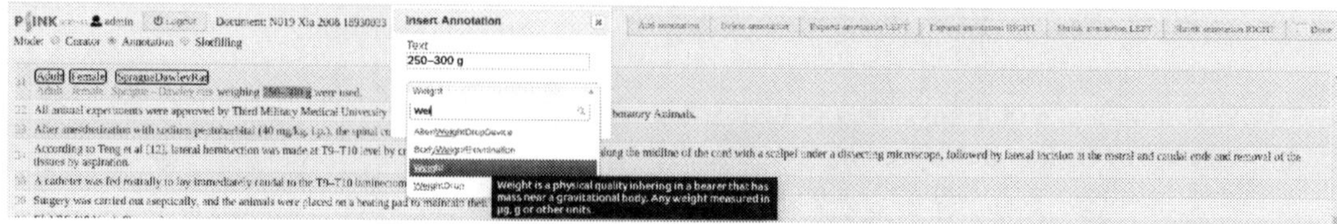

Figure 2: Entity Annotation: Relevant text mentions spanning one or multiple tokens are highlighted in green; entity type annotations are displayed on top of them. A new WEIGHT annotation is being added using the filtered drop-down menu.

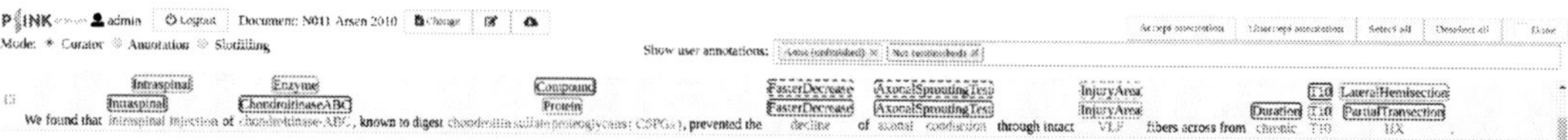

Figure 3: Curation: Annotations of several annotators are displayed colorized. Annotations on the same token are on top of each other. Correct or spurious annotations can be accepted or rejected, respectively. Accepted annotations keep the color code, but are marked with dotted boundaries.

GROUPS, INVESTIGATIONMETHOD, ORGANISM-MODEL). The annotation task is framed as *slot filling*, *i. e.*, pre-defined templates (corresponding to classes in SCIO) need to be populated based on evidence found in the document.

Figure 1 shows an example template which unfolds the ORGANISMMODEL concept from SCIO into slots (corresponding to ontological properties) and their fillers. Fillers for such templates may be distributed across an entire document, which holds in particular for complex, recursively substructured templates such as RESULT.

4 User Interface and Annotation Workflow

Our web application provides three views to the user, which reflect the typical annotation workflow that is encountered in (slot filling) annotation tasks: (i) *entity annotation*, (ii) *curation*, (iii) *template instantiation and slot filling*.

4.1 Entity Annotation

In order to annotate entities at the level of tokens in the text, we support two workflows: Annotations are created by an annotator from scratch, or existing annotations can be imported in order to be altered by the annotator. In SANTO, this is done in the entity annotation view (*cf.* Figure 2). A new annotation can be created by selecting tokens in the text. Being forced to span full tokens, annotations are automatically adjusted to the onset of the first and the offset of the last token. Entity types are

chosen from a drop-down menu[2]. *Discontinuous annotations* are supported as well. Existing annotations can be altered by expanding or shrinking their span, or by changing the entity type (without the need to remove the existing annotation and adding a new one). After a document has been marked as complete by an annotator, it is available for curation.

4.2 Curation

The curation view is designed to help a curator adjudicating possibly divergent mention annotations produced by several annotators. For that purpose, the curator can select annotations of multiple annotators that should be displayed for adjudication. Each annotator corresponds to a unique color. As can be seen from Figure 3, all annotations are arranged on top of each other in order to make divergences clearly visible at a glance. Based on this visualization, the curator can select individual annotations and accept or reject them. Accepted annotations are marked with dotted boundaries while keeping the color. During curation, the original annotations are not altered but cloned into a new curation document which serves as the basis for the subsequent slot filling.[3]

4.3 Template Instantiation and Slot Filling

In this mode, SANTO provides a combined view of curated entity annotations and pre-defined tem-

---

[2]The list can be filtered by name prefixes or taxonomically.

[3]If no curation is needed, all annotations can be easily batch-accepted.

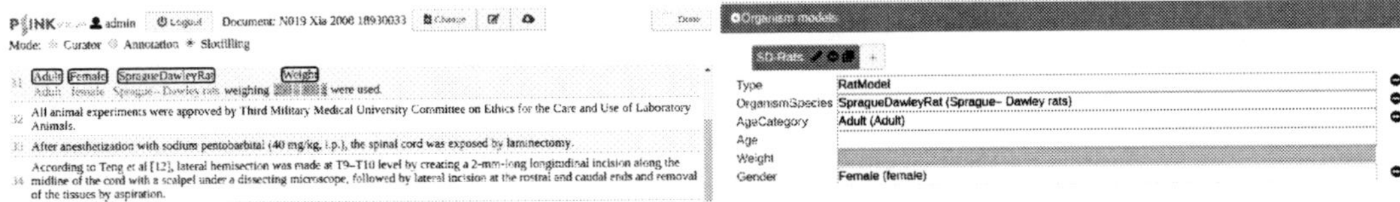

Figure 4: Slot filling view displaying a combined view of curated entity annotations at text level (left) and templates to be filled (right). Type compatibilities between annotated entities and possible target slots are automatically highlighted by the tool.

plates to be filled (*cf.* Figure 4). During template filling, it is no longer possible to change entity annotations. Instead, the goal is to support the user in instantiating the correct *cardinality* of different template types, and *filling their slots* with previously annotated entities, while taking *referential grounding* into account where necessary.

Cardinality of Templates. Often, the number of instantiations of a particular template (*e. g.*, number of EXPERIMENTALGROUPS in a study) is variable and not known a priori. Thus, correctly determining the cardinality of the set of instantiated templates per type is a crucial subproblem in the slot filling task. In SANTO, users can add, remove, or duplicate instances of referential templates and rename them for easy reference (*e. g.*, naming EXPERIMENTALGROUPS as "ChABC-treated group" or "Untreated control group").

Slot Filling. Based on their pre-defined role in the annotation schema, we distinguish three different types of slots in a template: *simple slots*, *recursive slots* and *template slots*.

Simple slots are directly filled with entity annotations (*e. g.*, STATISTICALTEST in Figure 5). In addition to be filled with entity annotations, recursive slots have subordinate slots (*e. g.*, INVESTIGATIONMETHOD in Figure 5, marked with a drop-down symbol on the left). Simple and recursive slots can either be filled by clicking on an existing annotation in the document, or by selecting an annotation from a drop-down menu that appears when clicking on the slot. Here, it is also possible to select an entity type without textual reference, if necessary (*e. g.*, JUDGEMENT in Figure 5). In order to facilitate slot filling, all suitable annotation candidates are highlighted in the document while hovering over a slot and vice versa.[4] Template slots are special cases of recursive slots in order to facilitate referential grounding (see below).

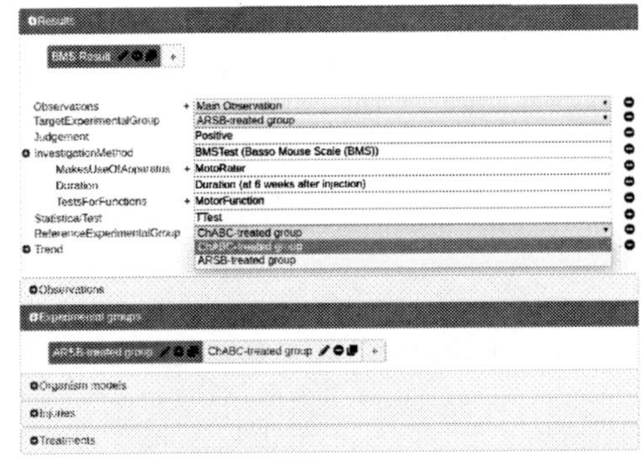

Figure 5: Slot filling view (template pane only) displaying the six main templates according to SCIO. The RESULT template is opened; it includes simple slots (JUDGEMENT), recursive slots (*e. g.*, INVESTIGATIONMETHOD) and template slots (*e. g.*, REFERENCEEXPERIMENTALGROUP, selectable via drop-down).

Slots can be defined to accept multiple annotations from the text. In such cases, a new slot value can be added by clicking on the + symbol (*e. g.*, OBSERVATION or TESTFORFUNCTION in Fig. 5).

Referential Grounding. Slot filling tasks require referential grounding when several instances of complex sub-templates have to be distributed over various governing templates; *e. g.*, an instance of an EXPERIMENTALGROUP might take part in several, but not all of the RESULTs reported in a study. Moreover, the same instance of an EXPERIMENTALGROUP may fill the TARGETEXPERIMENTALGROUP slot in one RESULT and the REFERENCEEXPERIMENTALGROUP in another. SANTO supports these cases by explicitly assigning previously instantiated templates to appropriate template slots via a drop-down menu (*cf.* Figure 5 for slot REFERENCEEXPERIMENTALGROUP), thus ensuring referential uniqueness of fillers. Only templates of the appropriate type are available for selection.

---

[4]Based on type constraints defined in the ontology.

5 Technical Properties

Application Details. The application is hosted on a standard Linux web stack using Apache 2.4, PHP 5.6 with a MySQL (version 5.5) database backend. The frontend uses HTML-5, CSS-3, jQuery[5] with jQuery UI[6] to provide a fast and robust user experience compatible across modern browsers.

Specification of Annotation Scheme. As initial input, the system requires a description of the underlying annotation scheme which can be derived from an ontology. This includes the description of entity types and roles (*Class* vs. *NamedIndividual* etc.), the hierarchical structure of entities (subclass relations) and their relational structure (object-type and data-type properties). Further, the template types that are available for slot filling need to be specified. All specifications are provided in configuration files in CSV format. Thus, instead of a fully-fledged ontology, an ad-hoc information model can be provided as well. Support for automatically translating an RDF ontology to the custom specification format is currently limited to the following syntactic elements: *owl:class*, *rdfs:subClassOf*, *owl:NamedIndividual*, *rdf:type*, *owl:objectTypeProperty*, *owl:dataTypeProperty*, and *rdfs:description*.

Pre-Processing of Input Documents. All documents need to be pre-processed before being uploaded to the application. This includes sentence splitting and tokenization. Note that entity annotations are limited to sentence boundaries and only full tokens can be annotated.

Import and Export of Annotations. For each document, it is possible to import entity annotations for individual annotators from different sources (*e. g.*, external annotation platforms or automated systems). The syntactic format for importing annotations is based on a shallow tab-separated formalism in order to facilitate a wide range of annotation sources such as existing information extraction tools, lexicon matching routines, or manual workflows. Entity and template annotations can be easily exported. While entity annotations are simply described in a CSV-structured file, template annotations are exported as RDF following the underlying ontology and annotation schema.

User Management. User roles in SANTO comprise *annotators* and *curators*. Individual views per annotator and curator enable multiple annotations, curations and slot fillings for each document. The web-based architecture supports multiple annotations in parallel.

6 Conclusion

We have presented SANTO, the first web-based annotation tool which enables easy annotation of complex relational structures in a template-based slot filling setting. The tool is web-based and flexibly configurable. Being designed in order to address typical user needs in slot filling workflows, we expect SANTO to have a positive impact on research aiming at automated acquisition of comprehensive, highly structured domain knowledge from textual sources, as in biomedical information extraction, digital humanities, or similar fields.

Acknowledgments

This work has been funded by the Federal Ministry of Education and Research (BMBF, Germany) in the PSINK project (grant 031L0028A). We thank our PSINK colleagues Nicole Brazda, Veronica Estrada, Jessica Schira and Hans Werner Müller for helping shape the user requirements for SANTO.

References

Heike Adel, Benjamin Roth, and Hinrich Schütze. 2016. Comparing convolutional neural networks to traditional models for slot filling. In *Proc. of the 2016 Conference of the North American Chapter of the Association for Computational Linguistics: Human Language Technologies*, pages 828–838, San Diego, California.

Lidong Bing, Tak-Lam Wong, and Wai Lam. 2016. Unsupervised extraction of popular product attributes from e-commerce web sites by considering customer reviews. *ACM Trans. Internet Technol.*, 16(2):12:1–12:17.

Kalina Bontcheva, Hamish Cunningham, Ian Roberts, Angus Roberts, Valentin Tablan, Niraj Aswani, and Genevieve Gorrell. 2013. GATE Teamware: a web-based, collaborative text annotation framework. *Language Resources and Evaluation*, 47(4):1007–1029.

Nicole Brazda, Hendrik ter Horst, Matthias Hartung, Cord Wiljes, Veronica Estrada, Roman Klinger, Wolfgang Kuchinke, Hans Werner Müller, and Philipp Cimiano. 2017. SCIO: An Ontology to Support the Formalization of Pre-Clinical Spinal Cord

---

[5] https://jquery.com
[6] https://jqueryui.com

Injury Experiments. In *Proc. of the 3rd JOWO Workshops: Ontologies and Data in the Life Sciences*.

Aljoscha Burchardt, Katrin Erk, Anette Frank, Andrea Kowalski, and Sebastian Pado. 2006. SALTO: A versatile multi-level annotation tool. In *Proc. of LREC-2006*, Genoa, Italy.

David Day, Chad McHenry, Robyn Kozierok, and Laurel Riek. 2004. Callisto: A configurable annotation workbench. In *Proc. of the Internation Conference on Language Resources and Evaluation*.

Dayne Freitag. 2000. Machine learning for information extraction in informal domains. *Machine Learning*, 39(2-3):169–202.

Sam Henry and Bridget T. McInnes. 2017. Literature based discovery: Models, methods, and trends. *J Biomed Inform*, 74:20–32.

Hendrik ter Horst, Matthias Hartung, Roman Klinger, Nicole Brazda, Hans Werner Müller, and Philipp Cimiano. 2018. Assessing the impact of single and pairwise slot constraints in a factor graph model for template-based information extraction. In Max Silberztein and Elisabeth Métais, editors, *Proc. of NLDB 2018*, volume 10859 of *Lecture Notes in Computer Science*, pages 179–190. Springer.

Tuomo Kakkonen. 2006. DepAnn – An Annotation Tool for Dependency Treebanks. In *Proc. of the 11th ESSLLI Student Session*, Malaga, Spain. 18th European Summer School in Logic, Language and Information (ESSLLI 2006).

Valentina Bartalesi Lenzi, Giovanni Moretti, and Rachele Sprugnoli. 2012. CAT: the CELCT Annotation Tool. In *Proc. of the Eighth International Conference on Language Resources and Evaluation (LREC-2012)*, pages 333–338, Istanbul, Turkey. European Language Resources Association (ELRA). ACL Anthology Identifier: L12-1072.

Thomas Morton and Jeremy LaCivita. 2003. Wordfreak: An open tool for linguistic annotation. In *Proc. of the 2003 Conference of the North American Chapter of the Association for Computational Linguistics on Human Language Technology: Demonstrations - Volume 4*, NAACL-Demonstrations '03, pages 17–18, Stroudsburg, PA, USA.

Christoph Müller and Michael Strube. 2006. Multi-level annotation of linguistic data with MMAX2. In Sabine Braun, Kurt Kohn, and Joybrato Mukherjee, editors, *Corpus Technology and Language Pedagogy: New Resources, New Tools, New Methods*, pages 197–214. Peter Lang, Frankfurt, Germany.

Philip V. Ogren. 2006. Knowtator: a Protégé plug-in for annotated corpus construction. In *Proc. of the 2006 Conference of the North American Chapter of the Association for Computational Linguistics on Human Language Technology*, pages 273–275, Morristown, NJ, USA.

Pedro Oliveira and João Rocha. 2013. Semantic annotation tools survey. *2013 IEEE Symposium on Computational Intelligence and Data Mining (CIDM)*, pages 301–307.

Petar Petrovski and Christian Bizer. 2017. Extracting attribute-value pairs from product specifications on the web. In *Proc. of the International Conference on Web Intelligence*, pages 558–565, Leipzig, Germany.

Tuukka Ruotsalo, Lora Aroyo, and Guus Schreiber. 2009. Knowledge-based linguistic annotation of digital cultural heritage collections. *IEEE Intelligent Systems*, 24(2):64–75.

Roxane Segers, Marieke van Erp, Lourens van der Meij, Lora Aroyo, Guus Schreiber, Bob Wielinga, Jacco van Ossenbruggen, Johan Oomen, and Geertje Jacobs. 2011. Hacking history: Automatic historical event extraction for enriching cultural heritage multimedia collections. In *Proc. of the Workhop on Detection, Representation, and Exploitation of Events in the Semantic Web (DeRiVE 2011)*, Bonn, Germany.

Brett South, Shuying Shen, Jianwei Leng, Tyler Forbush, Scott DuVall, and Wendy Chapman. 2012. A prototype tool set to support machine-assisted annotation. In *BioNLP: Proc. of the 2012 Workshop on Biomedical Natural Language Processing*, pages 130–139, Montréal, Canada. Association for Computational Linguistics.

Pontus Stenetorp, Sampo Pyysalo, Goran Topić, Tomoko Ohta, Sophia Ananiadou, and Jun'ichi Tsujii. 2012. Brat: a Web-based Tool for NLP-Assisted Text Annotation. In *Proc. of the Demonstrations at the 13th Conference of the European Chapter of the Association for Computational Linguistics*, pages 102–107, Avignon, France.

Seid Muhie Yimam, Iryna Gurevych, Richard Eckart de Castilho, and Chris Biemann. 2013. Webanno: A flexible, web-based and visually supported system for distributed annotations. In *Proc. of the 51st Annual Meeting of the Association for Computational Linguistics: System Demonstrations*, pages 1–6, Sofia, Bulgaria.

Yuhao Zhang, Victor Zhong, Danqi Chen, Gabor Angeli, and Christopher D. Manning. 2017. Position-aware attention and supervised data improve slot filling. In *Proc. of the 2017 Conference on Empirical Methods in Natural Language Processing*, pages 35–45, Copenhagen, Denmark.

Fei Zhu, Preecha Patumcharoenpol, Cheng Zhang, Yang Yang, Jonathan Chan, Asawin Meechai, Wanwipa Vongsangnak, and Bairong Shen. 2013. Biomedical text mining and its applications in cancer research. *Journal of Biomedical Informatics*, 46(2):200 – 211.

NCRF++: An Open-source Neural Sequence Labeling Toolkit

Jie Yang and **Yue Zhang**
Singapore University of Technology and Design
`jie_yang@mymail.sutd.edu.sg`
`yue_zhang@sutd.edu.sg`

Abstract

This paper describes NCRF++, a toolkit for neural sequence labeling. NCRF++ is designed for quick implementation of different neural sequence labeling models with a CRF inference layer. It provides users with an inference for building the custom model structure through configuration file with flexible neural feature design and utilization. Built on PyTorch[1], the core operations are calculated in batch, making the toolkit efficient with the acceleration of GPU. It also includes the implementations of most state-of-the-art neural sequence labeling models such as LSTM-CRF, facilitating reproducing and refinement on those methods.

1 Introduction

Sequence labeling is one of the most fundamental NLP models, which is used for many tasks such as named entity recognition (NER), chunking, word segmentation and part-of-speech (POS) tagging. It has been traditionally investigated using statistical approaches (Lafferty et al., 2001; Ratinov and Roth, 2009), where conditional random fields (CRF) (Lafferty et al., 2001) has been proven as an effective framework, by taking discrete features as the representation of input sequence (Sha and Pereira, 2003; Keerthi and Sundararajan, 2007).

With the advances of deep learning, neural sequence labeling models have achieved state-of-the-art for many tasks (Ling et al., 2015; Ma and Hovy, 2016; Peters et al., 2017). Features are extracted automatically through network structures including long short-term memory (LSTM) (Hochreiter and Schmidhuber, 1997) and convolution neural network (CNN) (LeCun et al., 1989),

```
##NetworkConfiguration##
use_crf=True
word_seq_feature=LSTM
word_seq_layer=1
char_seq_feature=CNN
feature=[POS] emb_dir=None emb_size=10
feature=[Cap] emb_dir=%(cap_emb_dir)
##Hyperparameters##
...
```

Figure 1: Configuration file segment

with distributed word representations. Similar to discrete models, a CRF layer is used in many state-of-the-art neural sequence labeling models for capturing label dependencies (Collobert et al., 2011; Lample et al., 2016; Peters et al., 2017).

There exist several open-source statistical CRF sequence labeling toolkits, such as CRF++[2], CRF-Suite (Okazaki, 2007) and FlexCRFs (Phan et al., 2004), which provide users with flexible means of feature extraction, various training settings and decoding formats, facilitating quick implementation and extension on state-of-the-art models. On the other hand, there is limited choice for neural sequence labeling toolkits. Although many authors released their code along with their sequence labeling papers (Lample et al., 2016; Ma and Hovy, 2016; Liu et al., 2018), the implementations are mostly focused on specific model structures and specific tasks. Modifying or extending can need enormous coding.

In this paper, we present Neural CRF++ (NCRF++)[3], a neural sequence labeling toolkit based on PyTorch, which is designed for solving general sequence labeling tasks with effective and efficient neural models. It can be regarded as the neural version of CRF++, with both take the CoNLL data format as input and can add hand-

---

[1] `http://pytorch.org/`

[2] `https://taku910.github.io/crfpp/`
[3] Code is available at `https://github.com/jiesutd/NCRFpp`.

Proceedings of the 56th Annual Meeting of the Association for Computational Linguistics-System Demonstrations, pages 74–79
Melbourne, Australia, July 15 - 20, 2018. ©2018 Association for Computational Linguistics

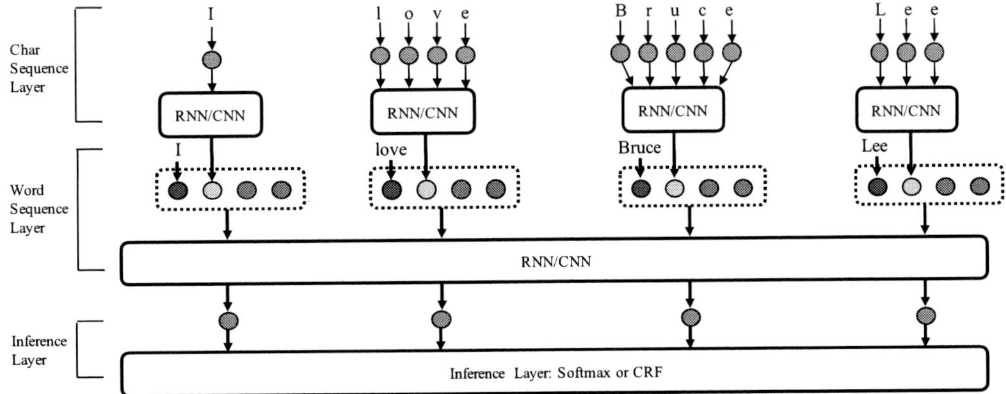

Figure 2: NCRF++ for sentence "I love Bruce Lee". Green, red, yellow and blue circles represent character embeddings, word embeddings, character sequence representations and word sequence representations, respectively. The grey circles represent the embeddings of sparse features.

crafted features to CRF framework conveniently. We take the layerwise implementation, which includes character sequence layer, word sequence layer and inference layer. NCRF++ is:

- **Fully configurable**: users can design their neural models only through a configuration file without any code work. Figure 1 shows a segment of the configuration file. It builds a LSTM-CRF framework with CNN to encode character sequence (the same structure as Ma and Hovy (2016)), plus POS and Cap features, within 10 lines. This demonstrates the convenience of designing neural models using NCRF++.

- **Flexible with features**: human-defined features have been proved useful in neural sequence labeling (Collobert et al., 2011; Chiu and Nichols, 2016). Similar to the statistical toolkits, NCRF++ supports user-defined features but using distributed representations through lookup tables, which can be initialized randomly or from external pretrained embeddings (embedding directory: emb_dir in Figure 1). In addition, NCRF++ integrates several state-of-the-art automatic feature extractors, such as CNN and LSTM for character sequences, leading easy reproduction of many recent work (Lample et al., 2016; Chiu and Nichols, 2016; Ma and Hovy, 2016).

- **Effective and efficient**: we reimplement several state-of-the-art neural models (Lample et al., 2016; Ma and Hovy, 2016) using NCRF++. Experiments show models built in NCRF++ give comparable performance with reported results in the literature. Besides, NCRF++ is implemented

using batch calculation, which can be accelerated using GPU. Our experiments demonstrate that NCRF++ as an effective and efficient toolkit.

- **Function enriched**: NCRF++ extends the Viterbi algorithm (Viterbi, 1967) to enable decoding n best sequence labels with their probabilities.

Taking NER, Chunking and POS tagging as typical examples, we investigate the performance of models built in NCRF++, the influence of human-defined and automatic features, the performance of *nbest* decoding and the running speed with the batch size. Detail results are shown in Section 3.

2 NCRF++ Architecture

The framework of NCRF++ is shown in Figure 2. NCRF++ is designed with three layers: a character sequence layer; a word sequence layer and inference layer. For each input word sequence, words are represented with word embeddings. The character sequence layer can be used to automatically extract word level features by encoding the character sequence within the word. Arbitrary handcrafted features such as capitalization [Cap], POS tag [POS], prefixes [Pre] and suffixes [Suf] are also supported by NCRF++. Word representations are the concatenation of word embeddings (red circles), character sequence encoding hidden vector (yellow circles) and handcrafted neural features (grey circles). Then the word sequence layer takes the word representations as input and extracts the sentence level features, which are fed into the inference layer to assign a label to each word. When building the network, users only need to edit the configuration file to configure the model structure, training settings and hyperparameters. We use layer-wised encapsulation in our implementation. Users can extend NCRF++ by defining their own structure in any layer and integrate it into NCRF++ easily.

2.1 Layer Units

2.1.1 Character Sequence Layer

The character sequence layer integrates several typical neural encoders for character sequence information, such as RNN and CNN. It is easy to select our existing encoder through the configuration file (by setting `char_seq_feature` in Figure 1). Characters are represented by character embeddings (green circles in Figure 2), which serve as the input of character sequence layer.

• **Character RNN** and its variants Gated Recurrent Unit (GRU) and LSTM are supported by NCRF++. The character sequence layer uses bidirectional RNN to capture the left-to-right and right-to-left sequence information, and concatenates the final hidden states of two RNNs as the encoder of the input character sequence.

• **Character CNN** takes a sliding window to capture local features, and then uses a *max-pooling* for aggregated encoding of the character sequence.

2.1.2 Word Sequence Layer

Similar to the character sequence layer, NCRF++ supports both RNN and CNN as the word sequence feature extractor. The selection can be configurated through `word_seq_feature` in Figure 1. The input of the word sequence layer is a word representation, which may include word embeddings, character sequence representations and handcrafted neural features (the combination depends on the configuration file). The word sequence layer can be stacked, building a deeper feature extractor.

• **Word RNN** together with GRU and LSTM are available in NCRF++, which are popular structures in the recent literature (Huang et al., 2015; Lample et al., 2016; Ma and Hovy, 2016; Yang et al., 2017). Bidirectional RNNs are supported to capture the left and right contexted information of each word. The hidden vectors for both directions on each word are concatenated to represent the corresponding word.

• **Word CNN** utilizes the same sliding window as character CNN, while a nonlinear function (Glorot et al., 2011) is attached with the extracted features. Batch normalization (Ioffe and Szegedy, 2015) and dropout (Srivastava et al., 2014) are also supported to follow the features.

2.1.3 Inference Layer

The inference layer takes the extracted word sequence representations as features and assigns labels to the word sequence. NCRF++ supports both softmax and CRF as the output layer. A linear layer firstly maps the input sequence representations to label vocabulary size scores, which are used to either model the label probabilities of each word through simple softmax or calculate the label score of the whole sequence.

• **Softmax** maps the label scores into a probability space. Due to the support of parallel decoding, softmax is much more efficient than CRF and works well on some sequence labeling tasks (Ling et al., 2015). In the training process, various loss functions such as negative likelihood loss, cross entropy loss are supported.

• **CRF** captures label dependencies by adding transition scores between neighboring labels. NCRF++ supports CRF trained with the sentence-level maximum log-likelihood loss. During the decoding process, the Viterbi algorithm is used to search the label sequence with the highest probability. In addition, NCRF++ extends the decoding algorithm with the support of *nbest* output.

2.2 User Interface

NCRF++ provides users with abundant network configuration interfaces, including the network structure, input and output directory setting, training settings and hyperparameters. By editing a configuration file, users can build most state-of-the-art neural sequence labeling models. On the other hand, all the layers above are designed as "plug-in" modules, where user-defined layer can be integrated seamlessly.

2.2.1 Configuration

• **Networks** can be configured in the three layers as described in Section 2.1. It controls the choice of neural structures in character and word levels with `char_seq_feature` and `word_seq_feature`, respectively. The inference layer is set by `use_crf`. It also defines the usage of handcrafted features and their properties in `feature`.

• **I/O** is the input and output file directory configuration. It includes `training_dir`,

Models	NER	chunking	POS
	F1-value	F1-value	Acc
Nochar+WCNN+CRF	88.90	94.23	96.99
CLSTM+WCNN+CRF	90.70	94.76	97.38
CCNN+WCNN+CRF	90.43	94.77	97.33
Nochar+WLSTM+CRF	89.45	94.49	97.20
CLSTM+WLSTM+CRF	91.20	95.00	97.49
CCNN+WLSTM+CRF	**91.35**	**95.06**	97.46
Lample et al. (2016)	90.94	–	97.51
Ma and Hovy (2016)	91.21	–	**97.55**
Yang et al. (2017)	91.20	94.66	**97.55**
Peters et al. (2017)	90.87	95.00	–

Table 1: Results on three benchmarks.

dev_dir, test_dir, raw_dir, pretrained character or word embedding (char_emb_dim or word_emb_dim), and decode file directory (decode_dir).

- **Training** includes the loss function (loss_function), optimizer (optimizer)[4] shuffle training instances train_shuffle and average batch loss ave_batch_loss.

- **Hyperparameter** includes most of the parameters in the networks and training such as learning rate (lr) and its decay (lr_decay), hidden layer size of word and character (hidden_dim and char_hidden_dim), *nbest* size (nbest), batch size (batch_size), dropout (dropout), etc. Note that the embedding size of each hand-crafted feature is configured in the networks configuration (feature=[POS] emb_dir=None emb_size=10 in Figure 1).

2.2.2 Extension

Users can write their own custom modules on all three layers, and user-defined layers can be integrated into the system easily. For example, if a user wants to define a custom character sequence layer with a specific neural structure, he/she only needs to implement the part between input character sequence indexes to sequence representations. All the other networks structures can be used and controlled through the configuration file. A README file is given on this.

3 Evaluation

3.1 Settings

To evaluate the performance of our toolkit, we conduct the experiments on several datasets. For NER task, CoNLL 2003 data (Tjong Kim Sang

Features		P	R	F
Baseline	WLSTM+CRF	80.44	87.88	89.15
Human Feature	+POS	90.61	89.28	89.94
	+Cap	90.74	90.43	90.58
	+POS+Cap	90.92	90.27	90.59
Auto Feature	+CLSTM	91.22	91.17	91.20
	+CCNN	91.66	91.04	91.35

Table 2: Results using different features.

and De Meulder, 2003) with the standard split is used. For the chunking task, we perform experiments on CoNLL 2000 shared task (Tjong Kim Sang and Buchholz, 2000), data split is following Reimers and Gurevych (2017). For POS tagging, we use the same data and split with Ma and Hovy (2016). We test different combinations of character representations and word sequence representations on these three benchmarks. Hyperparameters are mostly following Ma and Hovy (2016) and almost keep the same in all these experiments[5]. Standard SGD with a decaying learning rate is used as the optimizer.

3.2 Results

Table 1 shows the results of six CRF-based models with different character sequence and word sequence representations on three benchmarks. State-of-the-art results are also listed. In this table, "Nochar" suggests a model without character sequence information. "CLSTM" and "CCNN" represent models using LSTM and CNN to encode character sequence, respectively. Similarly, "WLSTM" and "WCNN" indicate that the model uses LSTM and CNN to represent word sequence, respectively.

As shown in Table 1, "WCNN" based models consistently underperform the "WLSTM" based models, showing the advantages of LSTM on capturing global features. Character information can improve model performance significantly, while using LSTM or CNN give similar improvement. Most of state-of-the-art models utilize the framework of word LSTM-CRF with character LSTM or CNN features (correspond to "CLSTM+WLSTM+CRF" and "CCNN+WLSTM+CRF" of our models) (Lample et al., 2016; Ma and Hovy, 2016; Yang et al., 2017; Peters et al., 2017). Our implementations can achieve comparable results, with better NER and

---

[4]Currently NCRF++ supports five optimizers: SGD/AdaGrad/AdaDelta/RMSProp/Adam.

[5]We use a smaller learning rate (0.005) on CNN based word sequence representation.

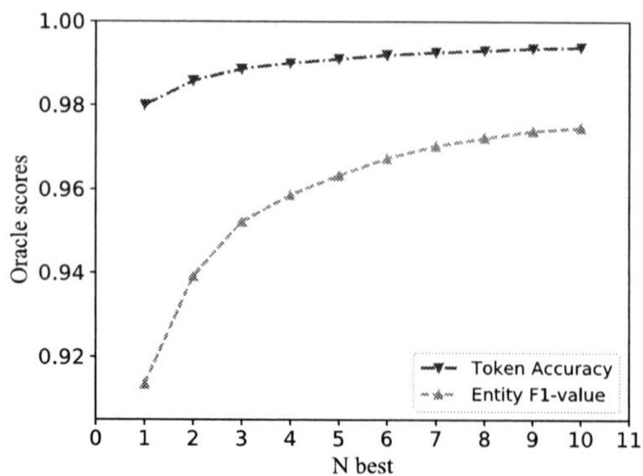

Figure 3: Oracle performance with nbest.

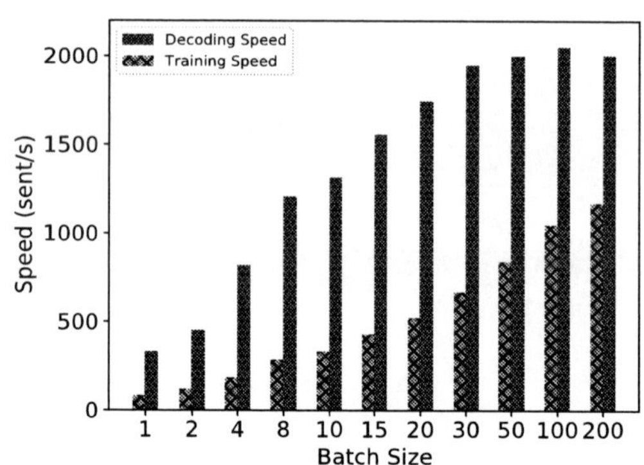

Figure 4: Speed with batch size.

chunking performances and slightly lower POS tagging accuracy. Note that we use almost the same hyperparameters across all the experiments to achieve the results, which demonstrates the robustness of our implementation. The full experimental results and analysis are published in Yang et al. (2018).

3.3 Influence of Features

We also investigate the influence of different features on system performance. Table 2 shows the results on the NER task. POS tag and capital indicator are two common features on NER tasks (Collobert et al., 2011; Huang et al., 2015; Strubell et al., 2017). In our implementation, each POS tag or capital indicator feature is mapped as 10-dimension feature embeddings through randomly initialized feature lookup table [6]. The feature embeddings are concatenated with the word embeddings as the representation of the corresponding word. Results show that both human features [POS] and [Cap] can contribute the NER system, this is consistent with previous observations (Collobert et al., 2011; Chiu and Nichols, 2016). By utilizing LSTM or CNN to encode character sequence automatically, the system can achieve better performance on NER task.

3.4 N best Decoding

We investigate *nbest* Viterbi decoding on NER dataset through the best model "CCNN+WLSTM+CRF". Figure 3 shows the oracle entity F1-values and token accuracies with different *nbest* sizes. The oracle F1-value

rises significantly with the increasement of *nbest* size, reaching 97.47% at $n = 10$ from the baseline of 91.35%. The token level accuracy increases from 98.00% to 99.39% in *10-best*. Results show that the *nbest* outputs include the gold entities and labels in a large coverage, which greatly enlarges the performance of successor tasks.

3.5 Speed with Batch Size

As NCRF++ is implemented on batched calculation, it can be greatly accelerated through parallel computing through GPU. We test the system speeds on both training and decoding process on NER dataset using a Nvidia GTX 1080 GPU. As shown in Figure 4, both the training and the decoding speed can be significantly accelerated through a large batch size. The decoding speed reaches saturation at batch size 100, while the training speed keeps growing. The decoding speed and training speed of NCRF++ are over 2000 sentences/second and 1000 sentences/second, respectively, demonstrating the efficiency of our implementation.

4 Conclusion

We presented NCRF++, an open-source neural sequence labeling toolkit, which has a CRF architecture with configurable neural representation layers. Users can design custom neural models through the configuration file. NCRF++ supports flexible feature utilization, including handcrafted features and automatically extracted features. It can also generate *nbest* label sequences rather than the best one. We conduct a series of experiments and the results show models built on NCRF++ can achieve state-of-the-art results with an efficient running speed.

---

⁶`feature=[POS] emb_dir=None emb_size=10`
`feature=[Cap] emb_dir=None emb_size=10`

References

Jason Chiu and Eric Nichols. 2016. Named entity recognition with bidirectional LSTM-CNNs. *Transactions of the Association for Computational Linguistics* 4:357–370. https://transacl.org/ojs/index.php/tacl/article/view/792.

Ronan Collobert, Jason Weston, Léon Bottou, Michael Karlen, Koray Kavukcuoglu, and Pavel Kuksa. 2011. Natural language processing (almost) from scratch. *Journal of Machine Learning Research* 12(Aug):2493–2537.

Xavier Glorot, Antoine Bordes, and Yoshua Bengio. 2011. Deep sparse rectifier neural networks. In *International Conference on Artificial Intelligence and Statistics*. pages 315–323.

Sepp Hochreiter and Jürgen Schmidhuber. 1997. Long short-term memory. *Neural computation* 9(8):1735–1780.

Zhiheng Huang, Wei Xu, and Kai Yu. 2015. Bidirectional LSTM-CRF models for sequence tagging. *arXiv preprint arXiv:1508.01991* .

Sergey Ioffe and Christian Szegedy. 2015. Batch normalization: Accelerating deep network training by reducing internal covariate shift. In *International Conference on Machine Learning*. pages 448–456.

S Sathiya Keerthi and Sellamanickam Sundararajan. 2007. Crf versus svm-struct for sequence labeling. *Yahoo Research Technical Report* .

John Lafferty, Andrew McCallum, and Fernando CN Pereira. 2001. Conditional random fields: Probabilistic models for segmenting and labeling sequence data. In *International Conference on Machine Learning*. volume 1, pages 282–289.

Guillaume Lample, Miguel Ballesteros, Sandeep Subramanian, Kazuya Kawakami, and Chris Dyer. 2016. Neural architectures for named entity recognition. In *NAACL-HLT*. pages 260–270.

Yann LeCun, Bernhard Boser, John S Denker, Donnie Henderson, Richard E Howard, Wayne Hubbard, and Lawrence D Jackel. 1989. Backpropagation applied to handwritten zip code recognition. *Neural computation* 1(4):541–551.

Wang Ling, Chris Dyer, Alan W Black, Isabel Trancoso, Ramon Fermandez, Silvio Amir, Luis Marujo, and Tiago Luis. 2015. Finding function in form: Compositional character models for open vocabulary word representation. In *EMNLP*. pages 1520–1530.

Liyuan Liu, Jingbo Shang, Frank Xu, Xiang Ren, Huan Gui, Jian Peng, and Jiawei Han. 2018. Empower sequence labeling with task-aware neural language model. In *AAAI*.

Xuezhe Ma and Eduard Hovy. 2016. End-to-end sequence labeling via Bi-directional LSTM-CNNs-CRF. In *ACL*. volume 1, pages 1064–1074.

Naoaki Okazaki. 2007. Crfsuite: a fast implementation of conditional random fields (crfs) .

Matthew Peters, Waleed Ammar, Chandra Bhagavatula, and Russell Power. 2017. Semi-supervised sequence tagging with bidirectional language models. In *ACL*. volume 1, pages 1756–1765.

Xuan-Hieu Phan, Le-Minh Nguyen, and Cam-Tu Nguyen. 2004. Flexcrfs: Flexible conditional random fields.

Lev Ratinov and Dan Roth. 2009. Design challenges and misconceptions in named entity recognition. In *CoNLL*. pages 147–155.

Nils Reimers and Iryna Gurevych. 2017. Reporting score distributions makes a difference: Performance study of lstm-networks for sequence tagging. In *EMNLP*. pages 338–348.

Fei Sha and Fernando Pereira. 2003. Shallow parsing with conditional random fields. In *NAACL-HLT*. pages 134–141.

Nitish Srivastava, Geoffrey E Hinton, Alex Krizhevsky, Ilya Sutskever, and Ruslan Salakhutdinov. 2014. Dropout: a simple way to prevent neural networks from overfitting. *Journal of Machine Learning Research* 15(1):1929–1958.

Emma Strubell, Patrick Verga, David Belanger, and Andrew McCallum. 2017. Fast and accurate entity recognition with iterated dilated convolutions. In *EMNLP*. pages 2670–2680.

Erik F Tjong Kim Sang and Sabine Buchholz. 2000. Introduction to the conll-2000 shared task: Chunking. In *Proceedings of the 2nd workshop on Learning language in logic and the 4th conference on Computational natural language learning-Volume 7*. pages 127–132.

Erik F Tjong Kim Sang and Fien De Meulder. 2003. Introduction to the conll-2003 shared task: Language-independent named entity recognition. In *HLT-NAACL*. pages 142–147.

Andrew Viterbi. 1967. Error bounds for convolutional codes and an asymptotically optimum decoding algorithm. *IEEE transactions on Information Theory* 13(2):260–269.

Jie Yang, Shuailong Liang, and Yue Zhang. 2018. Design challenges and misconceptions in neural sequence labeling. In *COLING*.

Zhilin Yang, Ruslan Salakhutdinov, and William W Cohen. 2017. Transfer learning for sequence tagging with hierarchical recurrent networks. In *International Conference on Learning Representations*.

TALEN: Tool for Annotation of Low-resource ENtities

Stephen Mayhew
University of Pennsylvania
Philadelphia, PA
mayhew@seas.upenn.edu

Dan Roth
University of Pennsylvania
Philadelphia, PA
danroth@seas.upenn.edu

Abstract

We present a new web-based interface, TALEN, designed for named entity annotation in low-resource settings where the annotators do not speak the language. To address this non-traditional scenario, TALEN includes such features as in-place lexicon integration, TF-IDF token statistics, Internet search, and entity propagation, all implemented so as to make this difficult task efficient and frictionless. We conduct a small user study to compare against a popular annotation tool, showing that TALEN achieves higher precision and recall against ground-truth annotations, and that users strongly prefer it over the alternative.

TALEN is available at:
`github.com/CogComp/talen`.

1 Introduction

Named entity recognition (NER), the task of finding and classifying named entities in text, has been well-studied in English, and a select few other languages, resulting in a wealth of resources, particularly annotated training data. But for most languages, no training data exists, and annotators who speak the language can be hard or impossible to find. This low-resource scenario calls for new methods for gathering training data. Several works address this with automatic techniques (Tsai et al., 2016; Zhang et al., 2016; Mayhew et al., 2017), but often a good starting point is to elicit manual annotations from annotators who do not speak the target language.

Language annotation strategies and software have historically assumed that annotators speak the language in question. Although there has been work on *non-expert* annotators for natural language tasks (Snow et al., 2008), where the annotators lack specific skills related to the task, there has been little to no work on situations where annotators, expert or not, do not speak the language. To this end, we present a web-based interface designed for users to annotate text quickly and easily in a language they do not speak.

TALEN aids non-speaker annotators[1] with several different helps and nudges that would be unnecessary in cases of a native speaker. The main features, described in detail in Section 2, are a Named Entity (NE) specific interface, entity propagation, lexicon integration, token statistics information, and Internet search.

The tool operates in two separate modes, each with all the helps described above. The first mode displays atomic documents in a manner analogous to nearly all prior annotation software. The second mode operates on the sentence level, patterned on bootstrapping with a human in the loop, and designed for efficient discovery and annotation.

In addition to being useful for non-speaker annotations, TALEN can be used as a lightweight inspection and annotation tool for within-language named entity annotation. TALEN is agnostic to labelset, which means that it can also be used for a wide variety of sequence tagging tasks.

2 Main Features

In this section, we describe the main features individually in detail.

Named Entity-Specific Interface

The interface is designed specifically for Named Entity (NE) annotation, where entities are rela-

---

[1] We use 'non-speaker' to denote a person who does not speak or understand the language, in contrast with 'non-native speaker', which implies at least a shallow understanding of the language.

80

Proceedings of the 56th Annual Meeting of the Association for Computational Linguistics-System Demonstrations, pages 80–86
Melbourne, Australia, July 15 - 20, 2018. ©2018 Association for Computational ENtuistics

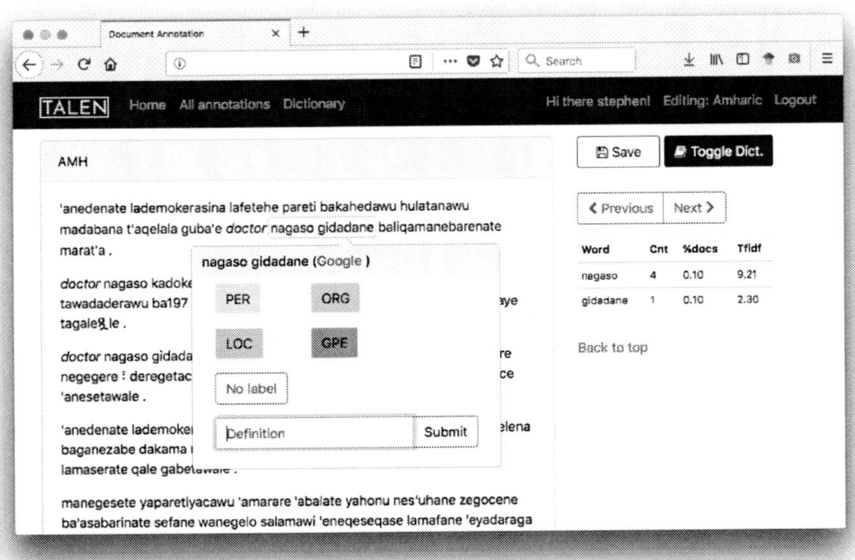

Figure 1: Document-based annotation screen. A romanized document from an Amharic corpus is shown. The user has selected "nagaso gidadane" (Negasso Gidada) for tagging, indicated by the thin gray border, and by the popover component. The lexicon (dictionary) is active, and is displaying the definition (in italics) for "doctor" immediately prior to "nagaso". (URL and document title are obscured).

tively rare in the document. The text is intentionally displayed organically, in a way that is familiar and compact, so that the annotator can see as much as possible on any given screen. This makes it easy for an annotator to make document-level decisions, for example, if an unusual-looking phrase appears several times. To add an annotation, as shown in Figure 1, the annotator clicks (and drags) on a word (or phrase), and a popover appears with buttons corresponding to label choices as defined in the configuration file. Most words are not names, so a default label of non-name (O) is assigned to all untouched tokens, keeping the number of clicks to a minimum. In contrast, a part-of-speech (POS) annotation system, SAWT (Samih et al., 2016), for example, is designed so that every token requires a decision and a click.

Entity Propagation

In a low-resource scenario, it can be difficult to discover and notice names because all words look unfamiliar. To ease this burden, and to save on clicks, the interface propagates all annotation decisions to every matching surface in the document. For example, if *'iteyop'eya* (Ethiopia) shows up many times in a document, then a single click will annotate all of them.

In the future, we plan to make this entity propagation smarter by allowing propagation to near surface forms (in cases where a suffix or prefix differs from the target phrase) or to cancel propagation on incorrect phrases, such as stopwords.

Lexicon Integration

The main difficulty for non-speakers is that they do not understand the text they are annotating. An important feature of TALEN is in-place lexicon integration, which replaces words in the annotation screen with their translation from the lexicon. For example, in Figure 1, the English word *doctor* is displayed in line (translations are marked by italics). As before, this is built on the notion that annotation is easiest when text looks organic, with translations seamlessly integrated. Users can click on a token and add a definition, which is immediately saved to disk. The next time the annotator encounters this word, the definition will be displayed. If available, a bilingual lexicon (perhaps from PanLex (Kamholz et al., 2014)), can kickstart the process. A side effect of the definition addition feature is a new or updated lexicon, which can be shared with other users, or used for other tasks.

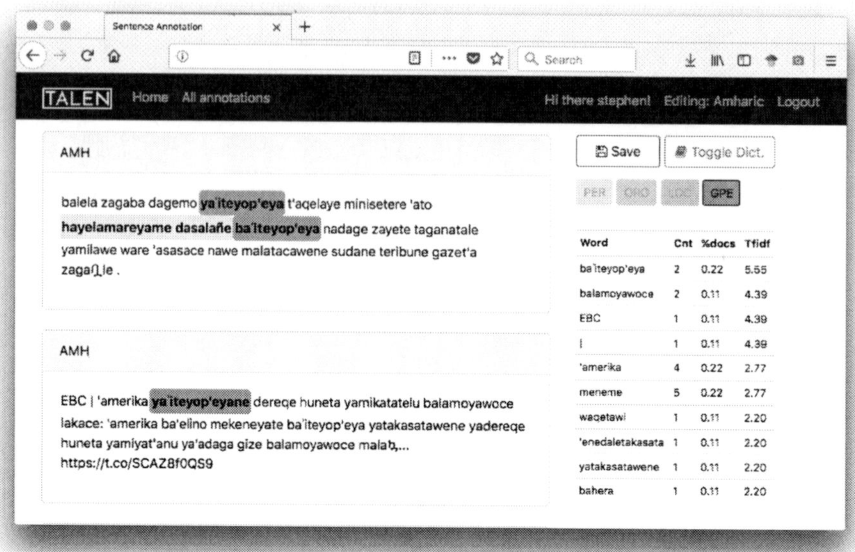

Figure 2: Sentence-based annotation screen, with sentences corresponding to seed term *ba'iteyop'eya* (annotated in the first sentence, not in the second). Two sentences are shown, and the remaining three sentences associated with this seed term are lower on the page. Notice that *hayelamareyame dasalañe* (Hailemariam Desalegn) has also been annotated in the first sentence. This will become a new seed term for future iterations. (URL and sentence IDs are obscured).

Token Statistics

When one has no knowledge of a language, it may be useful to know various statistics about tokens, such as document count, corpus count, or TF-IDF. For example, if a token appears many times in every document, it is likely not a name. Our annotation screen shows a table with statistics over tokens, including document count, percentage of documents containing it, and TF-IDF. At first, it shows the top 10 tokens by TF-IDF, but the user can click on any token to get individual statistics. For example, in Figure 1, *nagaso* appears 4 times in this document, appears in 10% of the total documents, and has a TF-IDF score of 9.21. In practice, we have found that this helps to give an idea of the topic of the document, and often names will have high TF-IDF in a document.

Internet Search

Upon selection of any token or phrase, the popover includes an external link to search the Internet for that phrase. This can be helpful in deciding if a phrase is a name or not, as search results may return images, or even autocorrect the phrase to an English standard spelling.

3 Annotation Modes

There are two annotation modes: a document-based mode, and a sentence-based mode. Each has all the helps described above, but they display documents and sentences to users in different ways.

3.1 Document-based Annotation

The document-based annotation is identical to the common paradigm of document annotation: the administrator provides a group of documents, and creates a configuration file for that set. The annotator views one document at a time, and moves on to the next when they are satisfied with the annotations. Annotation proceeds in a linear fashion, although annotators may revisit old documents to fix earlier mistakes. Figure 1 shows an example of usage in the document-based annotation mode.

3.2 Sentence-based Annotation

The sentence-based annotation mode is modeled after bootstrapping methods. In this mode, the configuration file is given a path to a corpus of documents (usually a very large corpus) and a small number (less than 10) seed entities, which

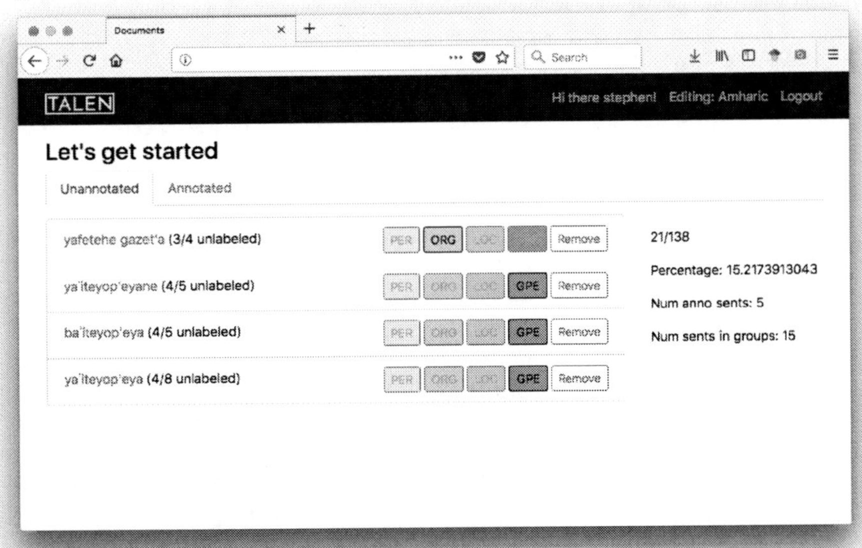

Figure 3: Sentence-based annotation screen showing 4 seed terms available for annotation. Notice the *Unannotated* and *Annotated* tabs. These terms are in the active *Unannotated* tab because each term has some sentences that have not yet been labeled with that seed term. For example, of the 5 sentences found for *ba'iteyop'eya*, only 1 has this seed term labeled (see Figure 2).

can be easily acquired from Wikipedia. This corpus is indexed at the sentence level, and for each seed entity, k sentences are retrieved. These are presented to the annotator, as in Figure 2, who will mark all names in the sentences, starting with the entity used to gather the sentence, and hopefully discover other names in the process. As names are discovered, they are added to the list of seed entities, as shown in Figure 3. New sentences are then retrieved, and the process continues until a predefined number of sentences has been retrieved. At this point, the data set is frozen, no new sentences are added, and the annotator is expected to thoroughly examine each sentence to discover all named entities.

In practice, we found that the size of k, which is the number of sentences retrieved per seed term, affects the overall corpus diversity. If k is large relative to the desired number of sentences, then the annotation is fast (because entity propagation can annotate all sentences with one click), but the method produces a smaller number of unique entities. However, if k is small, annotation may be slower, but return more diverse entities. In practice, we use a default value of $k = 5$.

4   Related Work

There are several tools designed for similar purposes, although to our knowledge none are designed specifically for non-speaker annotations. Many of the following tools are powerful and flexible, but would require significant refactoring to accommodate non-speakers.

The most prominent and popular is brat: rapid annotation tool (brat) (Stenetorp et al., 2012), a web-based general purpose annotation tool capable of a handling a wide variety of annotation tasks, including span annotations, and relations between spans. brat is open source, reliable, and available to download and run.

There are a number of tools with similar functionality. Sapient (Liakata et al., 2009) is a web-based system for annotating sentences in scientific documents. WebAnno (de Castilho et al., 2016) uses the frontend visualization from brat with a new backend designed to make large-scale project management easier. EasyTree (Little and Tratz, 2016) is a simple web-based tool for annotating dependency trees. Callisto[2] is a desktop tool for rich linguistic annotation.

---

[2]http://mitre.github.io/callisto/

SAWT (Samih et al., 2016) is a sequence annotation tool with a focus on being simple and lightweight, which is also a focus of ours. One key difference is that this expects that annotators will want to provide a tag for every word. This is inefficient for NER, where many tokens should take the default non-name label.

5 Experiment: Compare to brat

The brat rapid annotation tool (brat) (Stenetorp et al., 2012) is a popular and well-featured annotation tool, which makes for a natural comparison to TALEN. In this experiment, we compare tools qualitatively and quantitatively by hiring a group of annotators. We can compare performance between TALEN and brat by measuring the results after having annotators use both tools.

We chose to annotate Amharic, a language from Ethiopia. We have gold training and test data for this language from the Linguistic Data Consortium (LDC2016E87). The corpus is composed of several different genres, including newswire, discussion forums, web blogs, and social network (Twitter). In the interest of controlling for the domain, we chose only 125 newswire documents (NW) from the gold data, and removed all annotations before distribution. Since Amharic is written in Ge'ez script, we romanized it, so it can be read by English speakers. We partitioned the newswire documents into 12 (roughly even) groups of documents, and assigned each annotator 2 groups: one to be annotated in brat, the other with TALEN. This way, every annotator will use both interfaces, and every document will be annotated by both interfaces. We chose one fully annotated gold document and copied it into each group, so that the annotators have an annotation example.

We employed 12 annotators chosen from our NLP research group. Before the annotation period, all participants were given a survey about tool usage and language fluency. No users had familiarity with TALEN, and only one had any familiarity with brat. Of the annotators, none spoke Amharic or any related language, although one annotator had some familiarity with Hebrew, which shares a common ancestry with Amharic, and one annotator was from West Africa.[3]

Immediately prior to the annotation period, we gave a 15 minute presentation with instructions on tool usage, annotation guidelines, and annotation

---

[3]Ethiopia is in East Africa.

DATASET	PRECISION	RECALL	F1
brat	51.4	8.7	14.2
TALEN	53.6	12.6	20.0

DATASET	TOTAL NAMES	UNIQUE NAMES
Gold	2260	1154
brat	405	189
TALEN	457	174

Figure 4: Performance results. The precision, recall, and F1 are measured against the gold standard Amharic training data. When counting *Unique Names*, each unique surface form is counted once. We emphasize that these results are calculated over a *very* small amount of data annotated over a half-hour period by annotators with no experience with TALEN or Amharic. These only show a quick and dirty comparison to brat, and are not intended to demonstrate high-quality performance.

strategies. The tags used were Person, Organization, Location, and Geo-Political Entity. As for strategy, we instructed them to move quickly, annotating names only if they are confident (e.g. if they know the English version of that name), and to prioritize diversity of discovered surface forms over exhaustiveness of annotation. When using TALEN, we encouraged them to make heavy use of the lexicon. We provided a short list (less than 20 names) of English names that are likely to be found in documents from Ethiopia: local politicians, cities in the region, etc.

The annotation period lasted 1 hour, and consisted of two half hour sessions. For the first session, we randomly assigned half the annotators to use brat, and the other half to use TALEN. When this 30 minute period was over, all annotators switched tools. Those who had used brat use ours, and vice versa. We did this because users are likely to get better at annotating over time, so the second tool presented should give better results. Our switching procedure mitigates this effect.

At the end of the second session, each document group had been annotated twice: once by some annotator using brat, and once by some annotator using TALEN. These annotations were separate, so each tool started with a fresh copy of the data.

We report results in two ways: first, annotation quality as measured against a gold standard, and second, annotator feedback. Figure 4 shows basic statistics on the datasets. Since the documents we gave to the annotators came from a gold annotated set, we calculated precision, recall, and F1 with respect to the gold labels. First, we see that TALEN gives a 5.8 point F1 improvement over brat. This comes mostly from the recall, which improves by 3.9 points. This may be due to the automatic propagation, or it may be that having a lexicon helped users discover more names by proximity to known translations like *president*. In a less time-constrained environment, users of brat might be more likely select and annotate all surfaces of a name, but the reality is that all annotation projects are time-constrained, and any help is valuable.

The bottom part of the table shows the annotation statistics from TALEN compared with brat. TALEN yielded more name spans than brat, but fewer unique names, meaning that many of the names from TALEN are copies. This is also likely a product of the name propagation feature.

We gathered qualitative results from a feedback form filled out by each annotator after the evaluation. All but one of the annotators preferred TALEN for this task. In another question, they were asked to select an option for 3 qualities of each tool: efficiency, ease of use, and presentation. Each quality could take the options *Bad, Neutral, or Good*. On each of these qualities, brat had a majority of *Neutral*, and TALEN had a majority of *Good*. For TALEN, *Efficiency* was the highest rated quality, with 10 respondents choosing *Good*.

We also presented respondents with the 4 major features of TALEN (TF-IDF box, lexicon, entity propagation, Internet search), and asked them to rate them as *Useful* or *Not useful* in their experience. Only 4 people found the TF-IDF box useful; 10 people found the lexicon useful; all 12 people found the entity propagation useful; 7 people found the Internet search useful. These results are also reflected in the free text feedback. Most respondents were favorable towards the lexicon, and some respondents wrote that the TF-IDF box would be useful with more exposure, or with better integration (e.g. highlight on hover).

6 Technical Details

The interface is web-based, with a Java backend server. The frontend is built using Twitter bootstrap framework,[4] and a custom javascript library called `annotate.js`. The backend is built with the Spring Framework, written in Java, using the

TextAnnotation data structure from the CogComp NLP library (Khashabi et al., 2018) to represent and process text.

In cases where it is not practical to run a backend server (for example, Amazon Mechanical Turk[5]), we include a version written entirely in javascript, called `annotate-local.js`.

We allow a number of standard input file formats, and attempt to automatically discover the format. The formats we allow are: column, in which each *(word, tag)* pair is on a single line, serialized TextAnnotation format (from CogComp NLP (Khashabi et al., 2018)) in both Java serialization and JSON, and CoNLL column format, in which the tag and word are in columns 0 and 5, respectively.

When a user logs in and chooses a dataset to annotate, a new folder is created automatically with the username in the path. When that user logs in again, the user folder is reloaded on top of the original data folder. This means that multiple users can annotate the same corpus, and their annotations are saved in separate folders. This is in contrast to brat, where each dataset is modified in place.

7 Conclusions and Future Work

We have presented TALEN, a powerful interface for annotation of named entities in low-resource languages. We have explained the usage with screenshots and descriptions, and outlined a short user study showing that TALEN outperforms brat in a low-resource task in both qualitative and quantitative measures.

Acknowledgements

We would like to thank our annotators for their time and help in the small annotation project.

This material is based on research sponsored by the US Defense Advanced Research Projects Agency (DARPA) under agreement numbers FA8750-13-2-0008 and HR0011-15-2-0025. The U.S. Government is authorized to reproduce and distribute reprints for Governmental purposes notwithstanding any copyright notation thereon. The views and conclusions contained herein are those of the authors and should not be interpreted as necessarily representing the official policies or endorsements, either expressed or implied, of DARPA or the U.S. Government.

---

[4] `https://getbootstrap.com/`

[5] `mturk.com`

References

Richard Eckart de Castilho, Eva Mujdricza-Maydt, Muhie Seid Yimam, Silvana Hartmann, Iryna Gurevych, Anette Frank, and Chris Biemann. 2016. A web-based tool for the integrated annotation of semantic and syntactic structures. In *Proceedings of the Workshop on Language Technology Resources and Tools for Digital Humanities (LT4DH)*. pages 76–84.

David Kamholz, Jonathan Pool, and Susan M Colowick. 2014. Panlex: Building a resource for panlingual lexical translation. In *LREC*. pages 3145–3150.

Daniel Khashabi, Mark Sammons, Ben Zhou, Tom Redman, Christos Christodoulopoulos, Vivek Srikumar, Nicholas Rizzolo, Lev Ratinov, Guanheng Luo, Quang Do, Chen-Tse Tsai, Subhro Roy, Stephen Mayhew, Zhilli Feng, John Wieting, Xiaodong Yu, Yangqiu Song, Shashank Gupta, Shyam Upadhyay, Naveen Arivazhagan, Qiang Ning, Shaoshi Ling, and Dan Roth. 2018. Cogcompnlp: Your swiss army knife for nlp. In *11th Language Resources and Evaluation Conference*.

Maria Liakata, Claire Q, and Larisa N. Soldatova. 2009. Semantic annotation of papers: Interface & enrichment tool (sapient). In *BioNLP@HLT-NAACL*.

Alexa Little and Stephen Tratz. 2016. Easytree: A graphical tool for dependency tree annotation. In Nicoletta Calzolari (Conference Chair), Khalid Choukri, Thierry Declerck, Sara Goggi, Marko Grobelnik, Bente Maegaard, Joseph Mariani, Helene Mazo, Asuncion Moreno, Jan Odijk, and Stelios Piperidis, editors, *Proceedings of the Tenth International Conference on Language Resources and Evaluation (LREC 2016)*. European Language Resources Association (ELRA), Paris, France.

Stephen Mayhew, Chen-Tse Tsai, and Dan Roth. 2017. Cheap translation for cross-lingual named entity recognition. In *EMNLP*. http://cogcomp.org/papers/MayhewTsRo17.pdf.

Younes Samih, Wolfgang Maier, Laura Kallmeyer, and Heinrich Heine. 2016. Sawt: Sequence annotation web tool.

Rion Snow, Brendan T. O'Connor, Daniel Jurafsky, and Andrew Y. Ng. 2008. Cheap and fast - but is it good? evaluating non-expert annotations for natural language tasks. In *EMNLP*.

Pontus Stenetorp, Sampo Pyysalo, Goran Topić, Tomoko Ohta, Sophia Ananiadou, and Jun'ichi Tsujii. 2012. brat: a web-based tool for NLP-assisted text annotation. In *Proceedings of the Demonstrations Session at EACL 2012*. Association for Computational Linguistics, Avignon, France.

Chen-Tse Tsai, Stephen Mayhew, and Dan Roth. 2016. Cross-lingual named entity recognition via wikification. In *Proc. of the Conference on Computational Natural Language Learning (CoNLL)*. http://cogcomp.org/papers/TsaiMaRo16.pdf.

Boliang Zhang, Xiaoman Pan, Tianlu Wang, Ashish Vaswani, Heng Ji, Kevin Knight, and Daniel Marcu. 2016. Name tagging for low-resource incident languages based on expectation-driven learning. In *NAACL*.

A Web-scale system for scientific knowledge exploration

Zhihong Shen
Microsoft Research
Redmond, WA, USA

Hao Ma
Microsoft Research
Redmond, WA, USA

Kuansan Wang
Microsoft Research
Redmond, WA, USA

{zhihosh,haoma,kuansanw}@microsoft.com

Abstract

To enable efficient exploration of Web-scale scientific knowledge, it is necessary to organize scientific publications into a hierarchical concept structure. In this work, we present a large-scale system to (1) identify hundreds of thousands of scientific concepts, (2) tag these identified concepts to hundreds of millions of scientific publications by leveraging both text and graph structure, and (3) build a six-level concept hierarchy with a subsumption-based model. The system builds the most comprehensive cross-domain scientific concept ontology published to date, with more than 200 thousand concepts and over one million relationships.

1 Introduction

Scientific literature has grown exponentially over the past centuries, with a two-fold increase every 12 years (Dong et al., 2017), and millions of new publications are added every month. Efficiently identifying relevant research has become an ever increasing challenge due to the unprecedented growth of scientific knowledge. In order to assist researchers to navigate the entirety of scientific information, we present a deployed system that organizes scientific knowledge in a hierarchical manner.

To enable a streamlined and satisfactory semantic exploration experience of scientific knowledge, three criteria must be met:

- a comprehensive coverage on the broad spectrum of academic disciplines and concepts (we call them *concepts* or *fields-of-study*, abbreviated as *FoS*, in this paper);

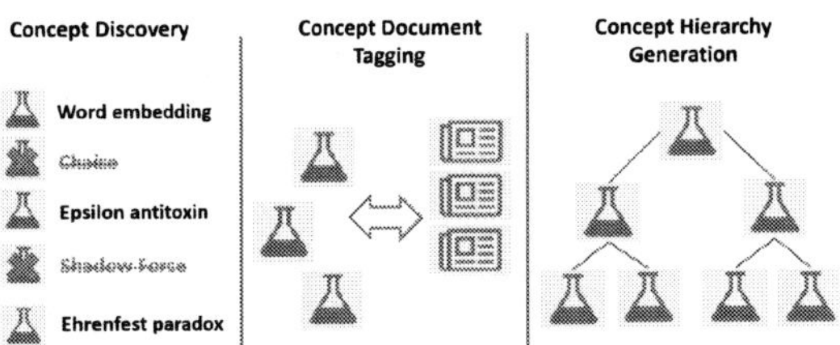

Figure 1: Three modules of the system: *concept discovery*, *concept-document tagging*, and *concept hierarchy generation*.

- a well-organized hierarchical structure of scientific *concepts*;

- an accurate mapping between these *concepts* and all forms of academic *publications*, including books, journal articles, conference papers, pre-prints, etc.

To build such a system on Web-scale, the following challenges need to be tackled:

- **Scalability:** Traditionally, academic discipline and concept taxonomies have been curated manually on a scale of hundreds or thousands, which is insufficient in modeling the richness of academic concepts across all domains. Consequently, the low concept coverage also limits the exploration experience of hundreds of millions of scientific publications.

- **Trustworthy representation:** Traditional concept hierarchy construction approaches extract concepts from unstructured documents, select representative terms to denote a concept, and build the hierarchy on top of them (Sanderson and Croft, 1999; Liu et al., 2012). The concepts extracted this way not only lack authoritative definition, but also

Proceedings of the 56th Annual Meeting of the Association for Computational Linguistics-System Demonstrations, pages 87–92
Melbourne, Australia, July 15 - 20, 2018. ©2018 Association for Computational Linguistics

	Concept discovery	Concept tagging	Hierarchy building
Main challenges	scalability / trustworthy representation	scalability / coverage	stability / accuracy
Problem formulation	knowledge base type prediction	multi-label text classification	topic hierarchy construction
Solution / model(s)	Wikipedia / KB / graph link analysis	word embedding / text + graph structure	extended subsumption
Data scale	$10^5 - 10^6$	$10^9 - 10^{10}$	$10^6 - 10^7$
Data update frequency	monthly	weekly	monthly

Table 1: System key features at a glance.

contain erroneous topics with subpar quality which is not suitable for a production system.

- **Temporal dynamics:** Academic publications are growing at an unprecedented pace (about 70K more papers per day according to our system) and new concepts are emerging faster than ever. This requires frequent inclusion on latest publications and re-evaluation in tagging and hierarchy-building results.

In this work, we present a Web-scale system with three modules—concept discovery, concept-document tagging, and concept-hierarchy generation—to facilitate scientific knowledge exploration (see Figure 1). This is one of the core components in constructing the Microsoft Academic Graph (MAG), which enables a semantic search experience in the academic domain[1]. MAG is a scientific knowledge base and a heterogeneous graph with six types of academic entities: publication, author, institution, journal, conference, and field-of-study (i.e., *concept* or *FoS*). As of March 2018, it contains more than 170 million publications with over one billion paper citation relationships, and is the largest publicly available academic dataset to date[2].

To generate high-quality *concepts* with comprehensive coverage, we leverage Wikipedia articles as the source of concept discovery. Each Wikipedia article is an *entity* in a general knowledge base (*KB*). A *KB* entity associated with a Wikipedia article is referred to as a Wikipedia entity. We formulate concept discovery as a knowledge base type prediction problem (Neelakantan

and Chang, 2015) and use graph link analysis to guide the process. In total, 228K academic concepts are identified from over five million English Wikipedia entities.

During the tagging stage, both textual information and graph structure are considered. The text from Wikipedia articles and papers' meta information (e.g., titles, keywords, and abstracts) are used as the *concept*'s and *publication*'s textual representations respectively. Graph structural information is leveraged by using text from a *publication*'s neighboring nodes in MAG (its citations, references, and publishing venue) as part of the *publication*'s representation with a discounting factor. We limit the search space for each publication to a constant range, reduce the complexity to $O(N)$ for scalability, where N is the number of publications. Close to one billion concept-publication pairs are established with associated confidence scores.

Together with the notion of subsumption (Sanderson and Croft, 1999), this confidence score is then used to construct a six-level directed acyclic graph (DAG) hierarchy with over 200K nodes and more than one million edges.

Our system is a deployed product with regular data refreshment and algorithm improvement. Key features of the system are summarized in Table 1. The system is updated weekly or monthly to include fresh content on the Web. Various document and language understanding techniques are experimented with and incorporated to incrementally improve the performance over time.

2 System Description

2.1 Concept Discovery

As top level disciplines are extremely important and highly visible to system end users, we man-

---

[1]The details about where and how we obtain, aggregate, and ingest academic publication information into the system is out-of-scope for this paper and for more information please refer to (Sinha et al., 2015).

[2]https://www.openacademic.ai/oag/

ually define 19 top level ("L0") disciplines (such as *physics*, *medicine*) and 294 second level ("L1") sub-domains (examples are *machine learning*, *algebra*) by referencing existing classification[3] and get their correspondent Wikipedia entities in a general in-house knowledge base (*KB*).

It is well understood that entity types in a general *KB* are limited and far from complete. Entities labeled with *FoS* type in *KB* are in the lower thousands and noisy for both in-house *KB* and latest Freebase dump[4]. The goal is to identify more *FoS* type entities from over 5 million English Wikipedia entities in an in-house KB. We formulate this task as a knowledge base type prediction problem, and focus on predicting only one specific type—*FoS*.

In addition to the above-mentioned "L0" and "L1" FoS, we manually review and identify over 2000 high-quality ones as initial seed FoS. We iterate a few rounds between a *graph link analysis* step for candidate exploration and an *entity type based filtering and enrichment* step for candidate fine-tuning based on *KB* types.

Graph link analysis: To drive the process of exploring new FoS candidates, we apply the intuition that if the majority of an entity's nearest neighbours are FoS, then it is highly likely an FoS as well. To calculate nearest neighbours, a distance measure between two Wikipedia entities is required. We use an effective and low-cost approach based on Wikipedia link analysis to compute the semantic closeness (Milne and Witten, 2008). We label a Wikipedia entity as an FoS candidate if there are more than K neighbours in its top N nearest ones are in a current FoS set. Empirically, N is set to 100 and K is in [35, 45] range for best results.

Entity type based filtering and enrichment: The candidate set generated in the above step contains various types of entities, such as *person*, *event*, *protein*, *book topic*, etc.[5] Entities with obvious invalid types are eliminated (e.g. *person*) and entities with good types are further included (e.g. *protein*, such that all Wikipedia entities which have labeled type as *protein* are added).

The results of this step are used as the input for *graph link analysis* in the next iteration.

More than 228K FoS have been identified with this iterative approach, based on over 2000 initial seed FoS.

2.2 Tagging Concepts to Publications

We formulate the concept tagging as a multi-label classification problem; i.e. each publication could be tagged with multiple FoS as appropriate. In a naive approach, the complexity could reach $M \cdot N$ to exhaust all possible pairs, where M is 200K+ for FoS and N is close to 200M for publications. Such a naive solution is computationally expensive and wasteful, since most scientific publications cover no more than 20 FoS based on empirical observation.

We apply heuristics to cut candidate pairs aggressively to address the scalability challenge, to a level of 300–400 FoS per publication[6]. Graph structural information is incorporated in addition to textual information to improve the accuracy and coverage when limited or inadequate text of a *concept* or *publication* is accessible.

We first define ***simple** representing text* (or *SRT*) and ***extended** representing text* (or *ERT*). *SRT* is the text used to describe the academic entity itself. *ERT* is the extension of *SRT* and leverages the graph structural information to include textual information from its neighbouring nodes in MAG.

A publishing venue's full name (i.e. the journal name or the conference name) is its *SRT*. The first paragraph of a concept's Wikipedia article is used as its *SRT*. Textual meta data, such as title, keywords, and abstract is a publication's *SRT*.

We sample a subset of publications from a given venue and concatenate their *SRT*. This is used as this venue's *ERT*. For broad disciplines or domains (e.g. L0 and L1 FoS), Wikipedia text becomes too vague and general to best represent its academic meanings. We manually curate such concept-venue pairs and aggregate *ERT* of venues associated with a given concept to obtain the *ERT* for the concept. For example, *SRT* of a subset of papers from *ACL* are used to construct *ERT* for *ACL*, and subsequently be part of the *ERT* for *natural language processing* concept. A *publication*'s *ERT* includes *SRT* from its citations, references and *ERT* of its linked publishing *venue*.

---

[3]http://science-metrix.com/en/classification

[4]https://developers.google.com/freebase/

[5]Entity types are obtained from the in-house KB, which has higher type coverage compared with Freebase, details on how the in-house KB produces entity types is out-of-scope and not discussed in this paper.

[6]We include all L0s and L1s and FoS entities spotted in a publication's *extended representing text*, which is defined later in this section

We use h_s^p and h_e^p to denote the representation of a *publication* (p)'s *SRT* and *ERT*, h_s^v and h_e^v for a *venue* (v)'s *SRT* and *ERT*. Weight w is used to discount different neighbours' impact as appropriate. Equation 1 and 2 formally define publication *ERT* and venue *ERT* calculation.

$$h_e^p = h_s^p + \sum_{i \in Cit} w_i h_s^p(i) + \sum_{j \in Ref} w_j h_s^p(j) + w_v h_e^v \tag{1}$$

$$h_e^v = \sum_{i \in V} h_s^p(i) + h_s^v \tag{2}$$

Four types of features are extracted from the text: bag-of-words (BoW), bag-of-entities (BoE), embedding-of-words (EoW), and embedding-of-entities (EoE). These features are concatenated for the vector representation h used in Equation 1 and 2. The *confidence score* of a concept-publication pair is the cosine similarity between these vector representations.

We pre-train the word embeddings by using the skip-gram (Mikolov et al., 2013) on the academic corpus, with 13B words based on 130M titles and 80M abstracts from English scientific publications. The resulting model contains 250-dimensional vectors for 2 million words and phrases. We compare our model with pre-trained embeddings based on general text (such as Google News[7] and Wikipedia[8]) and observe that the model trained from academic corpus performs better with higher accuracy on the concept-tagging task with more than 10% margin.

Conceptually, the calculation of publication and venue's *ERT* is to leverage neighbours' information to represent itself. The MAG contains hundreds of millions of nodes with billions of edges, hence it is computationally prohibitive by optimizing the node latent vector and weights simultaneously. Therefore, in Equation 1 and 2, we initialize h_s^p and h_s^v based on textual feature vectors defined above and adopt empirical weight values to directly compute h_e^p and h_e^v to make it scalable.

After calculating the similarity for about 50 billion pairs, close to 1 billion are finally picked based on the threshold set by the confidence score.

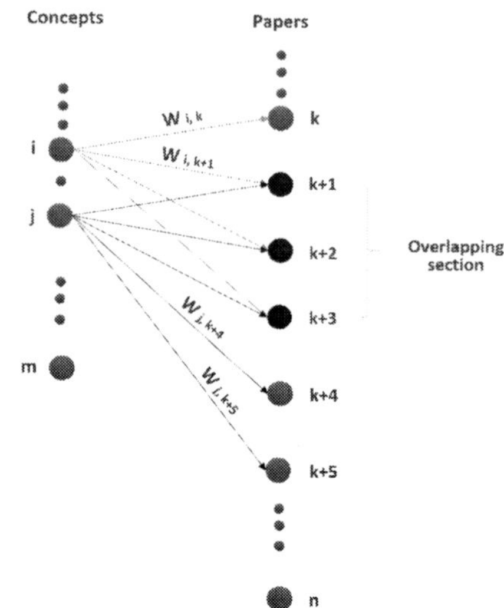

Figure 2: Extended subsumption for hierarchy generation.

2.3 Concept Hierarchy Building

In this subsection, we describe how to build a concept hierarchy based on concept-document tagging results. We extend Sanderson and Croft's early work (1999) which uses the notion of subsumption—a form of co-occurrence—to associate related terms. We say term x subsumes y if y occurs only in a subset of the documents that x occurs in. In the hierarchy, x is the parent of y. In reality, it is hard for y to be a strict subset of x. Sanderson and Croft's work relaxed the subsumption to 80% (e.g. $P(x|y) \geq 0.8, P(y|x) < 1$).

In our work, we extend the concept co-occurrence calculation weighted with the concept-document pair's confidence score from previous step. More formally, we define a *weighted relative coverage* score between two concepts i and j as below and illustrate in Figure 2.

$$RC(i,j) = \frac{\sum_{k \in (I \cap J)} w_{i,k}}{\sum_{k \in I} w_{i,k}} - \frac{\sum_{k \in (I \cap J)} w_{j,k}}{\sum_{k \in J} w_{j,k}} \tag{3}$$

Set I and J are documents tagged with concepts i and j respectively. $I \cap J$ is the overlapping set of documents that are tagged with both i and j. $w_{i,k}$ denotes the confidence score (or weights) between concept i and document k, which is the final *confidence score* in the previous concept-publication tagging stage. When $RC(i,j)$ is greater than a given positive threshold[9], i is the child of j. Since

---

[7]https://code.google.com/archive/p/word2vec/

[8]https://fasttext.cc/docs/en/pretrained-vectors.html

[9]It is usually in [0.2, 0.5] based on empirical observation.

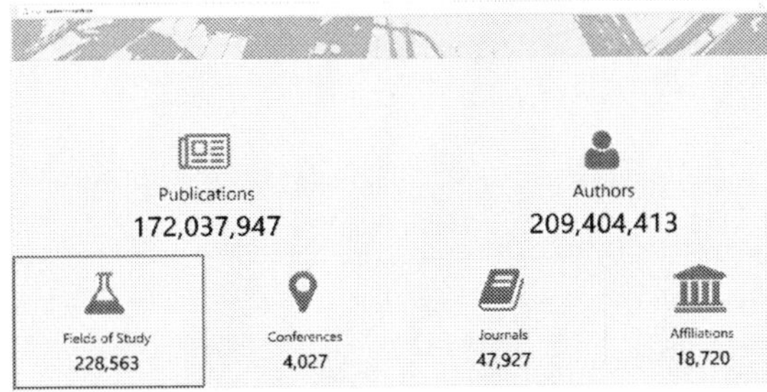

Figure 3: Deployed system homepage at March 2018, with all six types of entities statistics: over 228K *fields-of-study*.

Step	Accuracy
1. Concept discovery	94.75%
2. Concept tagging	81.20%
3. Build hierarchy	78.00%

Table 2: Accuracy results for each step.

this approach does not enforce single parent for any FoS, it results in a directed acyclic graph (DAG) hierarchy.

With the proposed model, we construct a six level FoS hierarchy (from L0 and L5) on over 200K concepts with more than 1M parent-child pairs. Due to the high visibility, high impact and small size, the hierarchical relationships between L0 and L1 are manually inspected and adjusted if necessary. The remaining L2 to L5 hierarchical structures are produced completely automatically by the extended subsumption model.

One limitation of subsumption-based models is the intransitiveness of parent-child relationships. This model also lacks a type-consistency check between parents and children. More discussions on such limitations with examples will be in evaluation section 3.2.

3 Deployment and Evaluation

3.1 Deployment

The work described in this paper has been deployed in the production system of Microsoft Academic Service[10]. Figure 3 shows the website homepage with entity statistics. The contents of MAG, including the full list of FoS, FoS hierarchy structure, and FoS tagging to papers, are accessible via API, website, and full graph dump from *Open Academic Society*[11].

Figure 4 shows the example for *word2vec* concept. Concept definition with linked Wikipedia page, its immediate parents (*machine learning, artificial intelligence, natural language processing*) in the hierarchical structure and its related concepts[12] (*word embedding, artificial neural network, deep learning*, etc.) are shown on the right rail pane. Top tagged publications (without *word2vec* explicitly stated in their text) are recognized via graph structure information based on citation relationship.

3.2 Evaluation

For this deployed system, we evaluate the accuracy on three steps (*concept discovery, concept tagging*, and *hierarchy building*) separately.

For each step, 500 data points are randomly sampled and divided into five groups with 100 data points each. On *concept discovery*, a data point is an FoS; on *concept tagging*, a data point is a concept-publication pair; and on *hierarchy building*, a data point is a parent-child pair between two concepts. For the first two steps, each 100-data-points group is assigned to one human judge. The concept hierarchy results are by nature more controversial and prone to individual subjective bias, hence we assign each group of data to three judges and use majority voting to decide final results.

The accuracy is calculated by counting positive labels in each 100-data-points group and averaging over 5 groups for each step. The overall accuracy is shown in Table 2 and some sampled hierarchical results are listed in Table 3.

Most hierarchy dissatisfaction is due to the intransitiveness and type-inconsistent limitations of the subsumption model. For example, most publications that discuss the *polycystic kidney disease* also mention *kidney*; however, for all publications that mentioned *kidney*, only a small subset would mention *polycystic kidney disease*. According to the subsumption model, *polycystic kidney disease* is the child of *kidney*. It is not legitimate for a *disease* as the child of an *organ*. Leveraging the entity type information to fine-tune hierarchy results is in our plan to improve the quality.

---

[10]https://academic.microsoft.com/
[11]https://www.openacademic.ai/oag/

[12]Details about how to generate related entities are out-of-scope and not included in this paper.

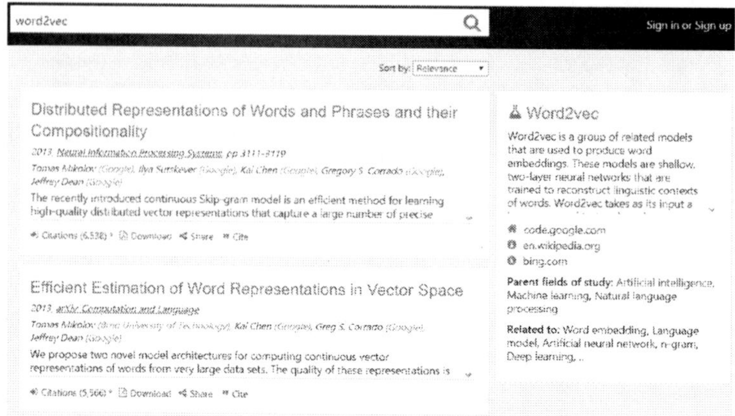

Figure 4: *Word2vec* example, with its parent *FoS*, related *FoS* and top tagged publications.

L5	L4	L3	L2	L1	L0
Convolutional Deep Belief Networks	Deep belief network	Deep learning	Artificial neural network	Machine learning	Computer Science
(Methionine synthase) reductase	Methionine synthase	Methionine	Amino acid	Biochemistry / Molecular biology	Chemistry / Biology
(glycogen-synthase-D) phosphatase	Phosphorylase kinase	Glycogen synthase	Glycogen	Biochemistry	Chemistry
	Fréchet distribution	Generalized extreme value distribution	Extreme value theory	Statistics	Mathematics
Hermite's problem	Hermite spline	Spline interpolation	Interpolation	Mathematical analysis	Mathematics

Table 3: Sample results for *FoS* hierarchy.

4 Conclusion

In this work, we demonstrated a Web-scale production system that enables an easy exploration of scientific knowledge. We designed a system with three modules: concept discovery, concept tagging to publications, and concept hierarchy construction. The system is able to cover latest scientific knowledge from the Web and allows fast iterations on new algorithms for document and language understanding.

The system shown in this paper builds the largest cross-domain scientific concept ontology published to date, and it is one of the core components in the construction of the Microsoft Academic Graph, which is a publicly available academic knowledge graph—a data asset with tremendous value that can be used for many tasks in domains like data mining, natural language understanding, science of science, and network science.

References

Yuxiao Dong, Hao Ma, Zhihong Shen, and Kuansan Wang. 2017. A century of science: Globalization of scientific collaborations, citations, and innovations. In *KDD*, pages 1437–1446.

Xueqing Liu, Yangqiu Song, Shixia Liu, and Haixun Wang. 2012. Automatic taxonomy construction from keywords. In *KDD*, pages 1433–1441.

Tomas Mikolov, Ilya Sutskever, Kai Chen, Gregory S. Corrado, and Jeffrey Dean. 2013. Distributed representations of words and phrases and their compositionality. In *NIPS*, pages 3111–3119.

David Milne and Ian H. Witten. 2008. An effective, low-cost measure of semantic relatedness obtained from wikipedia links. *WIKIAI*, pages 25–30.

Arvind Neelakantan and Ming-Wei Chang. 2015. Inferring missing entity type instances for knowledge base completion: New dataset and methods. In *NAACL*, pages 515–525.

Mark Sanderson and W. Bruce Croft. 1999. Deriving concept hierarchies from text. In *SIGIR*, pages 206–213.

Arnab Sinha, Zhihong Shen, Yang Song, Hao Ma, Darrin Eide, Bo-June Paul Hsu, and Kuansan Wang. 2015. An overview of microsoft academic service (mas) and applications. In *WWW*, pages 243–246.

ScoutBot: A Dialogue System for Collaborative Navigation

Stephanie M. Lukin[1], Felix Gervits[2*], Cory J. Hayes[1], Anton Leuski[3], Pooja Moolchandani[1],
John G. Rogers III[1], Carlos Sanchez Amaro[1], Matthew Marge[1], Clare R. Voss[1], David Traum[3]

[1] U.S. Army Research Laboratory, Adelphi, MD 20783
[2] Tufts University, Medford MA 02155
[3] USC Institute for Creative Technologies, Playa Vista, CA 90094
stephanie.m.lukin.civ@mail.mil, felix.gervits@tufts.edu, traum@ict.usc.edu

Abstract

ScoutBot is a dialogue interface to physical and simulated robots that supports collaborative exploration of environments. The demonstration will allow users to issue unconstrained spoken language commands to ScoutBot. ScoutBot will prompt for clarification if the user's instruction needs additional input. It is trained on human-robot dialogue collected from Wizard-of-Oz experiments, where robot responses were initiated by a human wizard in previous interactions. The demonstration will show a simulated ground robot (Clearpath Jackal) in a simulated environment supported by ROS (Robot Operating System).

1 Introduction

We are engaged in a long-term project to create an intelligent, autonomous robot that can collaborate with people in remote locations to explore the robot's surroundings. The robot's capabilities will enable it to effectively use language and other modalities in a natural manner for dialogue with a human teammate. This demo highlights the current stage of the project: a data-driven, automated system, ScoutBot, that can control a simulated robot with verbally issued, natural language instructions within a simulated environment, and can communicate in a manner similar to the interactions observed in prior Wizard-of-Oz experiments. We used a Clearpath Jackal robot (shown in Figure 1a), a small, four-wheeled unmanned ground vehicle with an onboard CPU and inertial measurement unit, equipped with a camera and light detection and ranging (LIDAR) mapping that

readily allows for automation. The robot's task is to navigate through an urban environment (e.g., rooms in an apartment or an alleyway between apartments), and communicate discoveries to a human collaborator (the Commander). The Commander verbally provides instructions and guidance for the robot to navigate the space.

The reasons for an intelligent robot collaborator, rather than one teleoperated by a human, are twofold. First, the human resources needed for completely controlling every aspect of robot motion (including low-level path-planning and navigation) may not be available. Natural language allows for high-level tasking, specifying a desired plan or end-point, such that the robot can figure out the details of how to execute these natural language commands in the given context and report back to the human as appropriate, requiring less time and cognitive load on humans. Second, the interaction should be robust to low-bandwidth and unreliable communication situations (common in disaster relief and search-and-rescue scenarios), where it may be impossible or impractical to exercise real-time control or see full video streams. Natural language interaction coupled with low-bandwidth, multimodal updates addresses both of these issues and provides less need for high-bandwidth, reliable communication and full attention of a human controller.

We have planned the research for developing ScoutBot as consisting of five conceptual phases, each culminating in an experiment to validate the approach and collect evaluation data to inform the development of the subsequent phase. These phases are:

1. Typed wizard interaction in real-world environment
2. Structured wizard interaction in real environment
3. Structured wizard interaction in simulated environment
4. Automated interaction in simulated environment
5. Automated interaction in real environment

---

*Contributions were primarily performed during an internship at the Institute for Creative Technologies.

Proceedings of the 56th Annual Meeting of the Association for Computational Linguistics-System Demonstrations, pages 93–98
Melbourne, Australia, July 15 - 20, 2018. ©2018 Association for Computational Linguistics

(a) Real-World Jackal   (b) Simulated Jackal

Figure 1: Jackal Robot

The first two phases are described in Marge et al. (2016) and Bonial et al. (2017), respectively. Both consist of Wizard-of-Oz settings in which participants believe that they are interacting with an autonomous robot, a common tool in Human-Robot Interaction for supporting not-yet fully realized algorithms (Riek, 2012). In our two-wizard design, one wizard (the Dialogue Manager or DM-Wizard) handles the communication aspects, while another (the Robot Navigator or RN-Wizard) handles robot navigation. The DM-Wizard acts as an interpreter between the Commander and robot, passing simple and full instructions to the RN-Wizard for execution based on the Commander instruction (e.g., the Commander instruction, *Now go and make a right um 45 degrees* is passed to the RN-Wizard for execution as, *Turn right 45 degrees*). In turn, the DM-Wizard informs the Commander of instructions the RN-Wizard successfully executes or of problems that arise during execution. Unclear instructions from the Commander are clarified through dialogue with the DM-Wizard (e.g., *How far should I turn?*). Additional discussion between Commander and DM-Wizard is allowed at any time. Note that because of the aforementioned bandwidth and reliability issues, it is not feasible for the robot to start turning or moving and wait for the Commander to tell it when to stop - this may cause the robot to move too far, which could be dangerous in some circumstances and confusing in others. In the first phase, the DM-Wizard uses unconstrained texting to send messages to both the Commander and RN-Wizard. In the second phase, the DM-Wizard uses a click-button interface that facilitates faster messaging. The set of DM-Wizard messages in this phase were constrained based on the messages from the first phase.

This demo introduces ScoutBot automation of the robot to be used in the upcoming phases: a simulated robot and simulated environment to support the third and fourth project phases, and initial automation of DM and RN roles, to be used in the fourth and fifth phases. Simulation and automation were based on analyses from data collected in the first two phases. Together, the simulated environment and robot allow us to test the automated system in a safe environment, where people, the physical robot, and the real-world environment are not at risk due to communication or navigation errors.

2   System Capabilities

ScoutBot engages in collaborative exploration dialogues with a human Commander, and controls a robot to execute instructions and navigate through and observe an environment. The real-world Jackal robot measures 20in x 17in x 10in, and weights about 37lbs (pictured in Figure 1a). Both it and its simulated counterpart (as seen in Figure 1b) can drive around the environment, but cannot manipulate objects or otherwise interact with the environment. While navigating, the robot uses LIDAR to construct a map of its surroundings as well as to indicate its position in the map. The Commander is shown this information, as well as static photographs of the robot's frontal view in the environment (per request) and dialogue responses in a text interface.

Interactions with ScoutBot are collaborative in that ScoutBot and the Commander exchange information through dialogue. Commanders issue spoken navigation commands to the robot, request photos, or ask questions about its knowledge and perception. ScoutBot responds to indicate when commands are actionable, and gives status feedback on its processing, action, or inability to act. When ScoutBot accepts a command, it is carried out in the world.

Figure 2 shows a dialogue between a Commander and ScoutBot. The right two columns show how the Commander's language was interpreted, and the action the robot takes. In this dialogue, the Commander begins by issuing a single instruction, *Move forward* (utterance #1), but the end-point is underspecified, so ScoutBot responds by requesting additional information (#2). The Commander supplies the information in #3, and the utterance is understood as an instruction to move forward 3 feet. ScoutBot provides feedback to the Commander as the action is begins (#4) and upon completion (#5). Another successful action is executed in #6-8. Finally, the Commander's request to know what the robot sees in #9 is interpreted as a re-

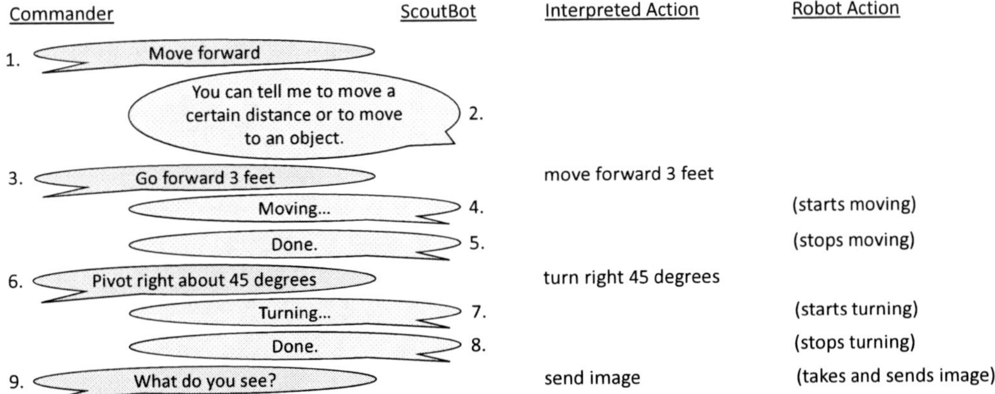

Figure 2: Dialogue between a Commander and ScoutBot

quest for a picture from the robot's camera, which is taken and sent to the Commander.

ScoutBot accepts unconstrained spoken language, and uses a statistical text classifier trained on annotated data from the first two phases of the project for interpreting Commander instructions. Dialogue management policies are used to generate messages to both the Commander and interpreted actions for automated robot navigation. Our initial dialogue management policies are fairly simple, yet are able to handle a wide range of phenomena seen in our domain.

3 System Overview

ScoutBot consists of several software systems, running on multiple machines and operating systems, using two distributed agent platforms. The architecture utilized in simulation is shown in Figure 3. A parallel architecture exists for a real-world robot and environment. Components primarily involving language processing use parts of the Virtual Human (VH) architecture (Hartholt et al., 2013), and communicate using the Virtual Human Messaging (VHMSG), a thin layer on top of the publicly available ActiveMQ message protocol[1]. Components primarily involving the real or simulated world, robot locomotion, and sensing are embedded in ROS[2]. To allow the VHMSG and ROS modules to interact with each other, we created ros2vhmsg, software that bridges the two messaging architectures. The components are described in the remainder of this section.

The system includes several distinct worksta-

---

[1] http://activemq.apache.org
[2] http://www.ros.org

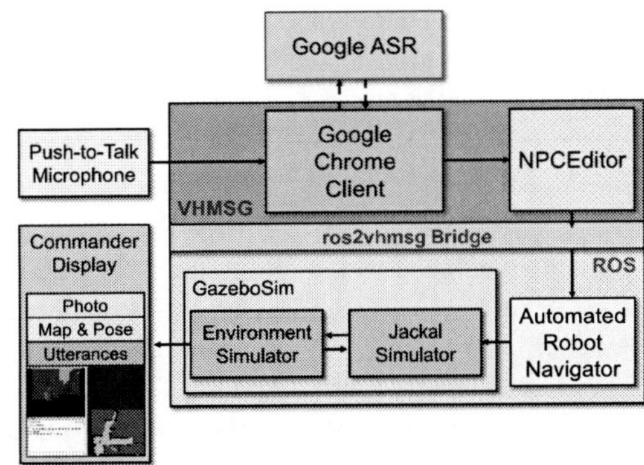

Figure 3: ScoutBot architecture interfacing with a simulated robot and environment: Solid arrows represent communications over a local network; dashed arrows indicate connections with external resources. Messaging for the spoken language interface is handled via VHMSG, while robot messages are facilitated by ROS. A messaging bridge, ros2vhmsg, connects the components.

tion displays for human participants. The Commander display is the view of the collaborative partner for the robot (lower left corner of Figure 3). This display shows a map of the robot's local surroundings, the most recent photo the robot has sent, and a chat log showing text utterances from the robot. The map is augmented as new areas are explored, and updated according to the robot's position and orientation. There are also displays for experimenters to monitor (and in the case of Wizards-of-Oz, engage in) the interaction. These displays show real-time video updates of what the robot can see, as well as internal communication and navigation aids.

3.1 VHMSG Components

VHMSG includes several protocols that implement parts of the Virtual Human architecture. We use the protocols for speech recognition, as well as component monitoring and logging. The NPCEditor and other components that use these protocols are available as part of the ICT Virtual Human Toolkit (Hartholt et al., 2013). These protocols have also been used in systems, as reported by Hill et al. (2003) and Traum et al. (2012, 2015). In particular, we used the adaptation of Google's Automated Speech Recognition (ASR) API used in Traum et al. (2015). The NPCEditor (Leuski and Traum, 2011) was used for Natural Language Understanding (NLU) and dialogue management. The new ros2vhmsg component for bridging the messages was used to send instructions from the NPCEditor to the automated RN.

3.1.1 NPCEditor

We implemented NLU using the statistical text classifier included in the NPCEditor. The classifier learns a mapping from inputs to outputs from training data using cross-language retrieval models (Leuski and Traum, 2011). The dialogues collected from our first two experimental phases served as training data, and consisted of 1,500 pairs of Commander (user) utterances and the DM-Wizard's responses. While this approach limits responses to the set that were seen in the training data, in practice it works well in our domain, achieving accuracy on a held out test set of 86%. The system is particularly effective at translating actionable commands to the RN for execution (e.g., *Take a picture*). It is robust at handling commands that include pauses, fillers, and other disfluent features (e.g., *Uh move um 10 feet*). It can also handle simple metric-based motion commands (e.g., *Turn right 45 degrees*, *Move forward 10 feet*) as well as action sequences (e.g., *Turn 180 degrees and take a picture every 45*). The system can interpret some landmark-based instructions requiring knowledge of the environment (e.g., *Go to the orange cone*), but the automated RN component does not yet have the capability to generate the low-level, landmark-based instructions for the robot.

Although the NPCEditor supports simultaneous participation in multiple conversations, extensions were needed for ScoutBot to support multi-floor interaction (Traum et al., 2018), in which two conversations are linked together. Rather than just responding to input in a single conversation, the DM-Wizard in our first project phases often translates input from one conversational floor to another (e.g., from the Commander to the RN-Wizard, or visa versa), or responds to input with messages to both the Commander and the RN. These responses need to be consistent (e.g. translating a command to the RN should be accompanied by positive feedback to the Commander, while a clarification to the commander should not include an RN action command). Using the dialogue relation annotations described in Traum et al. (2018), we trained a hybrid classifier, including translations to RN if they existed, and negative feedback to the Commander where they did not. We also created a new dialogue manager policy that would accompany RN commands with appropriate positive feedback to the commander, e.g., response of "Moving.." vs "Turning..." as seen in #4 and #7 in Figure 2.

3.1.2 ros2vhmsg

ros2vhmsg is a macOS application to bridge the VHMSG and ROS components of ScoutBot. It can be run from a command line or using a graphical user interface that simplifies the configuration of the application. Both VHMSG and ROS are publisher-subscriber architectures with a central broker software. Each component connects to the broker. They publish messages by delivering them to the broker and receive messages by telling the broker which messages they want to receive. When the broker receives a relevant message, it is delivered to the subscribers.

ros2vhmsg registers itself as a client for both VHMSG and ROS brokers, translating and reissuing the messages. For example, when ros2vhmsg receives a message from the ROS broker, it converts the message into a compatible VHMSG format and publishes it with the VHMSG broker. Within ros2vhmsg, the message names to translate along with the corresponding ROS message types must be specified. Currently, the application supports translation for messages carrying either text or robot navigation commands. The application is flexible and easily extendable with additional message conversion rules. ros2vhmsg annotates its messages with a special metadata symbol and uses that information to avoid processing messages that it already published.

Figure 4: Real-world and simulated instances of the same environment.

3.2 ROS Components

ROS provides backend support for robots to operate in both real-world and simulated environments. Here, we describe our simulated testbed and automated navigation components. Developing automated components in simulation allows for a safe test space before software is transitioned to the real-world on a physical robot.

3.2.1 Environment Simulator

Running operations under ROS makes the transition between real-world and simulated testing straightforward. Gazebo[3] is a software package compatible with ROS for rendering high-fidelity virtual simulations, and supports communications in the same manner as one would in real-world environments. Simulated environments were modeled in Gazebo after their real-world counterparts as shown in Figure 4. Replication took into consideration the general dimensions of the physical space, and the location and size of objects that populate the space. Matching the realism and fidelity of the real-world environment in simulation comes with a rendering trade-off: objects requiring a higher polygon count due to their natural geometries results in slower rendering in Gazebo and a lag when the robot moves in the simulation. As a partial solution, objects were constructed starting from their basic geometric representations, which could be optimized accordingly, e.g., the illusion of depth was added with detailed textures or shading on flat-surfaced objects. Environments rendered in Gazebo undergo a complex workflow to support the aforementioned requirements. Objects and their vertices are placed in an environment, and properties about collisions and gravity are encoded in the simulated environment.

3.2.2 Jackal Simulator

Clearpath provides a ROS package with a simulated model of the Jackal robot (Figure 1b) and customizable features to create different simulated configurations. We configured our simulated Jackal to have the default inertial measurement unit, a generic camera, and a Hokuyo LIDAR laser scanner.

As the simulated Jackal navigates through the Gazebo environment, data from the sensors is relayed to the workstation views through rviz[4], a visualization tool included with ROS that reads and displays sensor data in real-time. Developers can select the data to display by adding a panel, selecting the data type, and then selecting the specific ROS data stream. Both physical and simulated robot sensors are supported by the same rviz configuration, since rviz only processes the data sent from these sensors; this means that an rviz configuration created for data from a simulated robot will also work for a physical robot if the data stream types remain the same.

3.2.3 Automated Robot Navigator

Automated robot navigation is implemented with a python script and the ROSPY package[5]. The script runs on a ROS-enabled machine running the simulation. The script subscribes to messages from NPCEditor, which are routed through ros2vhmsg. These messages contain text output from the NLU classifier that issue instructions to the robot based on the user's unconstrained speech.

A mapping of pre-defined instructions was created, with keys matching the strings passed from NPCEditor via ros2vhmsg (e.g., *Turn left 90 degrees*). For movement, the map values are a ROS TWIST message that specifies the linear motion and angular rotation payload for navigation. These TWIST messages are the only way to manipulate the robot; measures in units of feet and degrees cannot be directly translated. The mapping is straightforward to define for metric instructions. Included is basic coverage of moving forward or backward between 1 and 10 feet, and turning right and left 45, 90, 180, or 360 degrees. Pictures from the robot's simulated camera can be requested by sending a ROS IMAGE message. The current mapping does not yet support collision avoidance or landmark-based instructions that require knowledge of the surrounding environment (e.g., *Go to the nearby chair*).

---

[3]http://gazebosim.org/

[4]http://wiki.ros.org/rviz
[5]http://wiki.ros.org/rospy

4 Demo Summary

In the demo, visitors will see the simulated robot dynamically move in the simulated environment, guided by natural language interaction. Visitors will be able to speak instructions to the robot to move in the environment. Commands can be given in metric terms (e.g., #3 and #6 in Figure 2), and images requested (e.g., #9). Undecipherable or incomplete instructions will result in clarification subdialogues rather than robot motion (e.g., #1). A variety of command formulations can be accommodated by the NLU classifier based on the training data from our experiments. Visualizations of different components can be seen in: `http://people.ict.usc.edu/~traum/Movies/scoutbot-acl2018demo.wmv`.

5 Summary and Future Work

ScoutBot serves as a research platform to support experimentation. ScoutBot components will be used in our upcoming third through fifth development phases. We are currently piloting phase 3 using ScoutBot's simulated environment, with human wizards. Meanwhile, we are extending the automated dialogue and navigation capabilities.

This navigation task holds potential for collaboration policies to be studied, such as the amount and type of feedback given, how to negotiate to successful outcomes when an initial request was underspecified or impossible to carry out, and the impact of miscommunication. More sophisticated NLU methodologies can be tested, including those that recognize specific slots and values or more detailed semantics of spatial language descriptions. The use of context, particularly references to relative landmarks, can be tested by either using the assumed context as part of the input to the NLU classifier, transforming the input before classifying, or deferring the resolution and requiring the action interpreter to handle situated context-dependent instructions (Kruijff et al., 2007).

Some components of the ScoutBot architecture may be substituted for different needs, such as different physical or simulated environments, robots, or tasks. Training new DM and RN components can make use of this general architecture, and the resulting components aligned back with ScoutBot.

Acknowledgments

This work was supported by the U.S. Army.

References

Claire Bonial, Matthew Marge, Ashley Foots, Felix Gervits, Cory J Hayes, Cassidy Henry, Susan G Hill, Anton Leuski, Stephanie M Lukin, Pooja Moolchandani, Kimberly A. Pollard, David Traum, and Clare R. Voss. 2017. Laying Down the Yellow Brick Road: Development of a Wizard-of-Oz Interface for Collecting Human-Robot Dialogue. *Proc. of AAAI Fall Symposium Series*.

Arno Hartholt, David Traum, Stacy C Marsella, Ari Shapiro, Giota Stratou, Anton Leuski, Louis-Philippe Morency, and Jonathan Gratch. 2013. All Together Now Introducing the Virtual Human Toolkit. In *Proc. of Intelligent Virtual Agents*, pages 368–381. Springer.

Randall Hill, Jr., Jonathan Gratch, Stacy Marsella, Jeff Rickel, William Swartout, and David Traum. 2003. Virtual Humans in the Mission Rehearsal Exercise System. *KI Embodied Conversational Agents*, 17:32–38.

Geert-Jan M Kruijff, Pierre Lison, Trevor Benjamin, Henrik Jacobsson, and Nick Hawes. 2007. Incremental, Multi-Level Processing for Comprehending Situated Dialogue in Human-Robot Interaction. In *Symposium on Language and Robots*.

Anton Leuski and David Traum. 2011. NPCEditor: Creating virtual human dialogue using information retrieval techniques. *AI Magazine*, 32(2):42–56.

Matthew Marge, Claire Bonial, Kimberly A Pollard, Ron Artstein, Brendan Byrne, Susan G Hill, Clare Voss, and David Traum. 2016. Assessing Agreement in Human-Robot Dialogue Strategies: A Tale of Two Wizards. In *Proc. of Intelligent Virtual Agents*, pages 484–488. Springer.

Laurel Riek. 2012. Wizard of Oz Studies in HRI: A Systematic Review and New Reporting Guidelines. *Journal of Human-Robot Interaction*, 1(1).

David Traum, Priti Aggarwal, Ron Artstein, Susan Foutz, Jillian Gerten, Athanasios Katsamanis, Anton Leuski, Dan Noren, and William Swartout. 2012. Ada and Grace: Direct Interaction with Museum Visitors. In *Proc. of Intelligent Virtual Agents*.

David Traum, Kallirroi Georgila, Ron Artstein, and Anton Leuski. 2015. Evaluating Spoken Dialogue Processing for Time-Offset Interaction. In *Proc. of Special Interest Group on Discourse and Dialogue*, pages 199–208. Association for Computational Linguistics.

David Traum, Cassidy Henry, Stephanie Lukin, Ron Artstein, Felix Gervits, Kimberly Pollard, Claire Bonial, Su Lei, Clare Voss, Matthew Marge, Cory Hayes, and Susan Hill. 2018. Dialogue Structure Annotation for Multi-Floor Interaction. In *Proc. of Language Resources and Evaluation Conference*.

The SUMMA Platform: A Scalable Infrastructure for Multi-lingual Multi-media Monitoring

Ulrich Germann
University of Edinburgh
ugermann@ed.ac.uk

Renārs Liepiņš
LETA
renars.liepins@leta.lv

Guntis Barzdins
University of Latvia
guntis.barzdins@lu.lv

Didzis Gosko
LETA
didzis.gosko@leta.lv

Sebastião Miranda
Priberam Labs
Sebastiao.Miranda@priberam.pt

David Nogueira
Priberam Labs
David.Nogueira@priberam.pt

Abstract

The open-source SUMMA Platform is a highly scalable distributed architecture for monitoring a large number of media broadcasts in parallel, with a lag behind actual broadcast time of at most a few minutes.

The Platform offers a fully automated media ingestion pipeline capable of recording live broadcasts, detection and transcription of spoken content, translation of all text (original or transcribed) into English, recognition and linking of Named Entities, topic detection, clustering and cross-lingual multi-document summarization of related media items, and last but not least, extraction and storage of factual claims in these news items. Browser-based graphical user interfaces provide humans with aggregated information as well as structured access to individual news items stored in the Platform's database.

This paper describes the intended use cases and provides an overview over the system's implementation.

1 Introduction

SUMMA ("Scalable Understanding of Multilingual Media") is an EU-funded *Research and Innovation Action* that aims to assemble state-of-the-art NLP technologies into a functional media processing pipeline to support large news organizations in their daily work. The project consortium consists of the University of Edinburgh, the Lativan Information Agency (LETA), Idiap Research Institute, Priberam Labs, Qatar Computing Research Institute, University College London, and Sheffield University as technical partners, and BBC Monitoring and Deutsche Welle as use case partners.

1.1 Use Cases

Three use cases drive the technology integration efforts.

1.1.1 External Media Monitoring

BBC Monitoring[1] is a business unit within the British Broadcasting Corporation (BBC). In operation since 1939 and with a staff of currently ca. 300 regional expert journalists, it provides media monitoring and analysis services to the BBC's own news rooms, the British government, and other subscribers.

Each staff journalist monitors up to four live broadcasts in parallel, plus several other information sources such as social media feeds. Assuming work distributed around the clock in three shifts,[2] BBC Monitoring currently has, on average, the capacity to actively monitor about 400 live broadcasts at any given time. At the same time, it has access to over 1,500 TV stations and ca. 1,350 radio stations world-wide via broadcast reception, as well as a myriad of information sources on the internet. The main limiting factor in maintaining (or even extending) monitoring coverage is the cost and availability of the staff required to do so.

Continuous live monitoring of broadcast channels by humans is not the most effective use of their time. Entertainment programming such as movies and sitcoms, commercial breaks, and repetitions of content (e.g., on 24/7 news channels), for example, are of limited interest to monitoring operations. What is of interest are emerging stories, new developments, and shifts in reporting. By automatically recording, monitoring, and indexing media content from a large number of media streams, and storing it in a database within a very short period of time after it has been published, the Platform allows analysts to focus on media content that is most relevant to their work and alleviates them from the tedious task of just monitoring broadcast streams in search of such relevant content.

1.1.2 Internal Monitoring

Deutsche Welle,[3] headquartered in Germany, is an international public broadcaster covering world-

---

[1] https://monitoring.bbc.co.uk/
[2] Actual staff allocation and thus the amount of media monitoring may vary over the course of the day.
[3] http://www.dw.com

Proceedings of the 56th Annual Meeting of the Association for Computational Linguistics-System Demonstrations, pages 99–104
Melbourne, Australia, July 15 - 20, 2018. ©2018 Association for Computational Linguistics

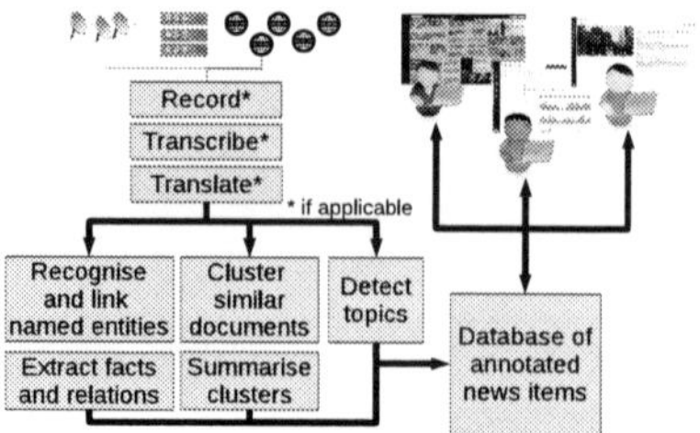

Figure 1: Overview of the SUMMA architecture.

wide news in 30 different languages. Regional news rooms produce and broadcast content independently; journalistic and programming decisions are *not* made by a central authority within Deutsche Welle. This means that it is difficult for the organization at large, from regional managers in charge of several news rooms to top management, to maintain an accurate and up-to-date overview of what is being broadcast, what stories have been covered, and where there is potential for synergies, for example by using journalistic background work that was performed for one story to produce similar content for a different audience in a different broadcast region and language.

The SUMMA Platform's cross-lingual story clustering and summarization module with the corresponding online visualization tool addresses this need. It provides an aggregate view of recent captured broadcasts, with easy access to individual broadcast segments in each cluster.

1.1.3 Data Journalism

The third use case is the use of the platform (or more specifically, it's database API) by journalists and researchers (e.g., political scientists) who want to perform data analyses based on large amounts of news reports. Potential uses are the plotting of events or time series of events on maps, analysis of bias or political slant in news reporting, etc. This use case is the most open-ended and, unlike the other two, has not been a major driving force in the actual design and implementation of the Platform so far.

2 System Architecture

2.1 Design

Figure 1 shows a schematic overview over the Platform's workflow. The Platform comprises three major parts: a data ingestion pipeline build mostly upon existing state-of-the-art NLP technology; a web-based user front-end specifically developed with the intended use cases in mind, and a database at the center that is continuously updated by the data ingestion pipeline and accessed by end users through the web-based GUI, or through a REST API by downstream applications.

Services within the Platform — technical such as the database server or the message queue, and services performing natural language processing tasks — run independently in individual Docker[4] application containers. This encapsulation allows for mostly independent development of the components by the consortium partners responsible for them.

Each NLP service augments incoming media items (represented as `json` structures) with additional information: automatic speech recognition (ASR) services add transcriptions, machine translation (MT) engines add translations, and so forth.

The flow of information within the Platform is realized via a message queues[5]. Each type of task (e.g., speech recognition in a specific language, machine translation from a specific language into English, etc.) has a queue for pending tasks and another queue for completed tasks; task workers pop a message off the input queue, acknowledge it upon successful completion, and push the output of the completed task onto the output queue. A task scheduler (the only component that needs to "know" about the overall structure of the processing pipeline) orchestrates the communication.

The use of a message queues allows for easy scalability of the Platform — if we need more throughput, we add more workers, which all share the same queues.

The central database for orchestration of media item processing is an instance of RethinkDB,[6] a document-oriented database that allows clients to subscribe to a continuous stream of notifications about changes in the database. Each document consists of several fields, such as the URL of the original news item, a transcript for audio sources, or the original text, a translation into English if applicable, entities such as persons, organisations or locations mentioned in the news items, etc.

For the user-facing front end, we use an instance of PostgreSQL[7] that pulls in new arrivals periodically from the RethinkDB. The PostgreSQL database was not part of the original platform design. It was introduced out of performance concerns, when we noticed at at some point that RethinkDB's reponsiveness was deteriorating rapidly as the database grew. We ultimately determined that this was due to an error in our set-up of the database — we had failed to set up indexing for certain fields in the database, resulting in linear searches through the database that grew longer and longer as the number of items in the database increased. However, we did not realise this until after we had migrated the user front-ends to interact

---

[4] `www.docker.com`

[5] `www.rabbitmq.com`

[6] `www.rethinkdb.com`

[7] `www.postgresql.org`

with a PostgreSQL database. The Platform also provides an export mechanism into ElasticSearch[8] databases.

The web-based graphical user front-end was developed specifically for SUMMA, based on wireframe designs from our use case partners. It is implemented in the Aurelia JavaScript Client Framework[9].

In the following section, we briefly present the individual components of the data ingestion pipeline.

3 Data Ingestion Pipeline Components

3.1 Live Stream Recorder and Chunker

The recorder and chunker monitors one or more live streams via their respective URLs. Broadcast signals received via satellite are converted into transport streams suitable for streaming via the internet and provided via a web interface. All data received by the Recorder is recorded to disk und chunked into 5-minutes segments for further processing. Within the Platform infrastructure, the recorder and chunker also serves as the internal video server for recorded transitory material.

Once downloaded and chunked, a document stub with the internal video URL is entered into the database, which then schedules them for downstream processing.

Video and audio files that are not transitory but provided by the original sources in more persistent forms (i.e., served from a permanent location), are currently not recorded but retrieved from the original source when needed.

3.2 Other Data Feeds

Text-based data is retrieved by data feed modules that poll the providing source at regular intervals for new data. The data is downloaded and entered into the database, which then schedules the new arrivals for downstream processing.

In addition to a generic RSS feed monitor, we use custom data monitors that are tailored to specific data sources, e.g. the specific APIs that broadcaster-specific news apps use for updates. The main task of these specialized modules is to map between data fields of the source API's specific (json) response and the data fields used within the Platform.

3.3 Automatic Speech Recognition

The ASR modules within the Platform are built on top of CloudASR (Klejch et al., 2015); the underlying speech recognition models are trained with the Kaldi toolkit (Povey et al., 2011). Punctuation is added using a neural MT engine that was trained to translate from un-punctuated text to punctuation. The training data for the punctuation module is created by stripping punctuation from an existing corpus of news texts. The MT engine used for punctuation insertion uses the same software components as the MT engines used for language translation. Currently, the Platform supports ASR of English, German, Arabic, Russian, Spanish, and Latvian; systems for Farsi, Portuguese and Ukranian are planned.

3.4 Machine Translation

The machine translation engines for language translation use the Marian decoder (Junczys-Dowmunt et al., 2016) for translation, with neural models trained with the Nematus toolkit (Sennrich et al., 2017). In the near future, we plan to switch to Marian entirely for training and translation. Currently supported translation directions are from German, Arabic, Russian, Spanish, and Latvian into English. Systems for translation from Farsi, Portuguese and Ukranian into English are planned.

3.5 Topic Classification

The topic classifier uses a hierarchical attention model for document classification (Yang et al., 2016) trained on nearly 600K manually annotated documents in 8 languages.[10]

3.6 Storyline Clustering and Cluster Summarization

Incoming stories are clustered into storylines with the online clustering algorithm by Aggarwal and Yu (2006). The resulting storylines are summarized with the extractive summarization algorithm by Almeida and Martins (2013).

3.7 Named Entity Recognition and Linking

For Named Entity Recognition, we use TurboEntityRecognizer, a component within TurboParser[11] (Martins et al., 2009). Recognized entities and relations between them (or propositions about them) are linked to a knowledge base of facts using AMR techniques developed by Paikens et al. (2016).

3.8 Trained systems and their performance

Space contraints prevent us from discussing the NLP components in more detail here. Detailed information about the various components can be found in the project deliverables 3.1, 4.1, and 5.1,

---

[8] www.elastic.co

[9] aurelia.io

[10] The Platform currently is designed to handle 9 languages: English, Arabic, Farsi, German, Latvian, Portuguese, Russian, Spanish, and Ukrainian.

[11] https://github.com/andre-martins/TurboParser

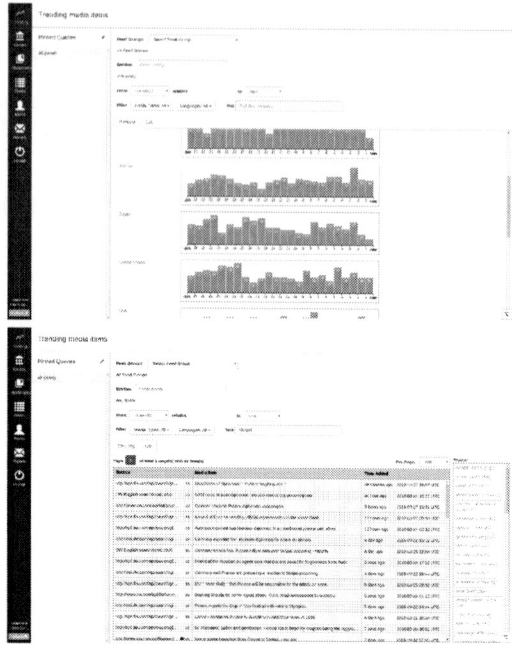

Figure 2: Trending media item views: histogram (top), and list (bottom)

which are available from the SUMMA project's web page.[12]

4   User Interfaces

The platform provides several user interfaces ("views"), to accommodate different user's needs.

The trending media item views (Fig 2) rely on recognised Named Entities. For each entity recognized by the Named Entity recognizer, the histogram view (top) shows a bar chart with the number of media items that mention said entity within each hour for the past n hours. The order of the list of histograms corresponds to the recent prominence of the respective entity. In the list view (bottom), recent arrivals for a specific Named Entity are sorted most-recent-first. The screenshot shows the result of a full text search.

Figure 3 shows the view of a recorded video segment. The video player panel is on the left. On the right, we see topic labels (top), a summary of the transcript (middle), and the original transcript. The transcript is synchronized with the video, so that recognized speech is automatically highlighted in the transcript as the video is played, and a click into the transcript takes the user to the corresponding position in the video.

The document cluster view (Fig. 4) gives a bird eye's view of the clustered media items; the area occupied by each cluster corresponding to the number of items within the cluster. A click on the respective tile shows a multi-document summary of the cluster and a list of related media items.

The trending media item views correspond most to our first use case: journalists keeping track of specific stories linked to specific entities and identifying emerging topics.

The document cluster ciew corresponds best to the needs of our second use case: internal monitoring of a media organisation's output.

In addition to these visual user interfaces, the platform can also expose a database API, so that users wishing to access the database directly with their own analysis or visualisation tools can do so. A number of ideas for such tools were explored recently at BBC's SUMMA-related #NewsHack event in London in November 2017.[13] They include a slackbot that allows journalists to query the database in natural language via a chat interface, automatic generation of short videos capturing and summarizing the news of the days in a series of captioned images, or contrasting the coverage by a specific media outlet against a larger pool of information sources.

5   Hardware Requirements and Performance Analysis

When designing the system, we made a deliberate decision to avoid reliance on GPUs for processing, due to the high cost of the hardware, especially when rented from cloud computing services. This constraint does not apply to the training of the underlying models, which we assume to be done offline. For most components, pre-trained models are available for download.

5.1   Disk Space

A basic installation of the platform with models for 6 languages / 5 translation directions currently requires about 150GB of disk space. Recording of live video streams requires approximately 10–25 GB per stream per day, depending on the resolution of the underlying video. We do not transcode incoming videos to a lower resolution, due to the high processing cost of transcoding.

5.2   CPU Usage and Memory Requirements

Table 1 shows a snapshot of performance monitoring on a singe-host deployment of the Platform that we use for user interface testing and user experience evaluation, measured over a period of about 20 minutes. The deployment's host is a large server

---

[13] http://bbcnewslabs.co.uk/2017/11/24/ summa-roundup. The event attracted 63 registrations; subtracting no-shows, the event had ca. 50 attendees.

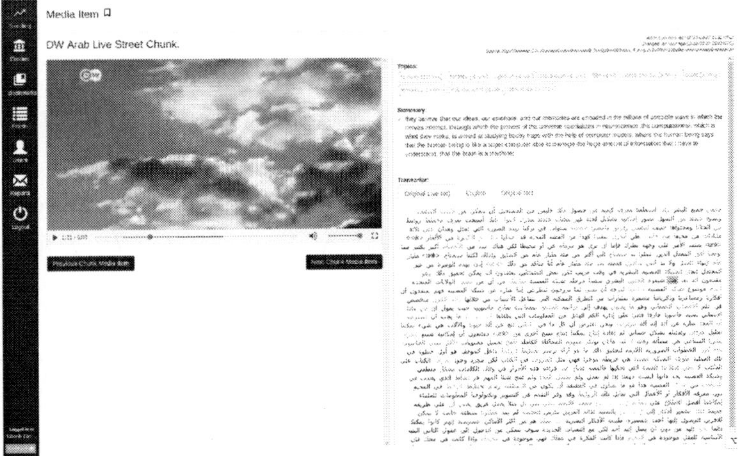

Figure 3: Single media item view

Figure 4: Document cluster view

with 32 CPU cores and 287 GB of memory, of which ca. 120GB are currently used by the Platform, supporting transcription in 6 languages and translation from 5 into English. Not shown in the table are the ASR, Punctuation and MT components for Latvian and German, as they were idle at the time.

Notice that except for the Named Entity recognizer, no component has a peak memory use of more than 4 GB, so that individual components can be run on much smaller machines in a distributed set-up.

Speech recognition is clearly the bottleneck and resource hog in the pipeline. The ASR engine currently is a single-threaded process that can transcribe speech at about half the "natural" speaking rate.[14] Each segment is transcribed in one chunk; we use multiple workers (2-3) per channel to keep up with the speed of data arrival.

The multi-threaded MT engines use all available cores to translate in parallel and are able to translate some 500 words per minute per thread.[15] For comparison: the typical speaking rate of an English-speaking news speaker is about 160 words per minute. A single MT engine can thus easily accommodate transcripts from multiple transcribed live streams.

---

[14] For segments without speech, the processing speed may be about 8 times real time, as the speech recognizer gets confused and explores a much larger search space.

[15] Junczys-Dowmunt et al. (2016) report 141 words per second on a 16-thread machine; this means ca. 528 words per minute per thread.

Table 1: Relative use of CPU time and peak memory use (per container) for various tasks in the NLP processing pipeline.

Task	CPU	RAM
ASR (ar)	27.26%	1359 MiB
ASR (en)	26.53%	2594 MiB
ASR (ru)	22.40%	2044 MiB
ASR (es)	13.44%	2800 MiB
MT (ar)	3.34%	926 MiB
MT (ru)	3.14%	1242 MiB
Summarization	1.21%	3609 MiB
Semantic parsing	0.97%	3290 MiB
MT (es)	0.34%	1801 MiB
Job queue	0.30%	326 MiB
Topic identification	0.27%	1418 MiB
Named entity recognition	0.18%	12625 MiB
Punctuation (en)	0.16%	362 MiB
Database	0.16%	3021 MiB
Recording and chunking	0.15%	337 MiB
Punctuation (ru)	0.04%	285 MiB
Punctuation (ar)	0.03%	276 MiB
DB REST interface	0.02%	153 MiB
Clustering	0.01%	1262 MiB
Data feed (not streamed)	0.01%	141 MiB
Punctuation (es)	0.01%	240 MiB
Task creation	0.01%	1076 MiB
Result writer (msg. queue to DB)	0.01%	1003 MiB

In a successful scalability test with docker swarm in January 2018 we were able to ingest 400 TV streams simultaneously on Amazon's AWS EC2 service, allocating 2 t2.2xlarge virtual machines (8 CPUs, 32GB RAM) per stream, although 1 machine per stream probably would have be sufficient. For this test, we deployed several clones of the entire platform for data ingestion, all feeding into a single user-facing PostgreSQL database instance.

6   Conclusion

The SUMMA Platform successfully integrates a multitude of state-of-the-art NLP components to provide an integrated platform for multi-lingual media monitoring and analysis. The Platform design provides for easy scalability and facilitates the integration of additional NLP analysis modules that augment existing data.

Availability

The Platform infrastructure and most of its components are currently scheduled to be released as open-source software in late August 2018 and will available through the project home page at

`http://www.summa-project.eu`

Acknowledgements

This work was conducted within the scope of the Research and Innovation Action *SUMMA*, which has received funding from the European Union's Horizon 2020 research and innovation programme under grant agreement No 688139.

References

Aggarwal, Charu C and Philip S Yu. 2006. "A framework for clustering massive text and categorical data streams." *SIAM Int'l. Conf. on Data Mining*, 479–483. Boston, MA, USA.

Almeida, Miguel B and Andre FT Martins. 2013. "Fast and robust compressive summarization with dual decomposition and multi-task learning." *ACL*, 196–206. Sofia, Bulgaria.

Junczys-Dowmunt, Marcin, Tomasz Dwojak, and Hieu Hoang. 2016. "Is neural machine translation ready for deployment? A case study on 30 translation directions." *International Workshop on Spoken Language Translation*. Seattle, WA, USA.

Klejch, Ondřej, Ondřej Plátek, Lukáš Žilka, and Filip Jurčíček. 2015. "CloudASR: platform and service." *Int'l. Conf. on Text, Speech, and Dialogue*, 334–341. Pilsen, Czech Republic.

Martins, André FT, Noah A Smith, and Eric P Xing. 2009. "Concise integer linear programming formulations for dependency parsing." *ACL-IJCNLP*, 342–350. Singapore.

Paikens, Peteris, Guntis Barzdins, Afonso Mendes, Daniel Ferreira, Samuel Broscheit, Mariana S. C. Almeida, Sebastião Miranda, David Nogueira, Pedro Balage, and André F. T. Martins. 2016. "SUMMA at TAC knowledge base population task 2016." *TAC*. Gaithersburg, Maryland, USA.

Povey, Daniel, Arnab Ghoshal, Gilles Boulianne, Lukáš Burget, Ondřej Glembek, Nagendra Goel, Mirko Hannemann, Petr Motlíček, Yanmin Qian, Petr Schwarz, Jan Silovský, Georg Stemmer, and Karel Veselý. 2011. "The Kaldi speech recognition toolkit." *ASRU*. Waikoloa, HI, USA.

Sennrich, Rico, Orhan Firat, Kyunghyun Cho, Alexandra Birch, Barry Haddow, Julian Hitschler, Marcin Junczys-Dowmunt, Samuel Läubli, Antonio Valerio Miceli Barone, Jozef Mokry, and Maria Nadejde. 2017. "Nematus: a toolkit for neural machine translation." *EACL Demonstration Session*. Valencia, Spain.

Yang, Zichao, Diyi Yang, Chris Dyer, Xiaodong He, Alexander J. Smola, and Eduard H. Hovy. 2016. "Hierarchical attention networks for document classification." *NAACL*. San Diego, CA, USA.

CRUISE: Cold-Start New Skill Development via Iterative Utterance Generation

Yilin Shen, Avik Ray, Abhishek Patel, Hongxia Jin
Samsung Research America, Mountain View, CA, USA
`{yilin.shen,avik.r,abhisehek.p,hongxia.jin}@samsung.com`

Abstract

We present a system, CRUISE, that guides ordinary software developers to build a high quality natural language understanding (NLU) engine from scratch. This is the fundamental step of building a new skill for personal assistants. Unlike existing solutions that require either developers or crowdsourcing to manually generate and annotate a large number of utterances, we design a hybrid rule-based and data-driven approach with the capability to iteratively generate more and more utterances. Our system only requires light human workload to iteratively prune incorrect utterances. CRUISE outputs a well trained NLU engine and a large scale annotated utterance corpus that third parties can use to develop their custom skills. Using both benchmark dataset and custom datasets we collected in real-world settings, we validate the high quality of CRUISE generated utterances via both competitive NLU performance and human evaluation. We also show the largely reduced human workload in terms of both cognitive load and human pruning time consumption.

1 Introduction

Artificially intelligent voice-enabled personal assistants have been emerging in our daily life, such as Alexa, Google Assistant, Siri, Bixby, etc. Existing off-the-shelf personal assistants provide a large number of capabilities, referred to as *skills*, and the number of skills keeps growing rapidly. Thus, it is critically desirable to design an easy to use system that facilitates developers to quickly build high quality new skills.

The key of developing a new skill is to understand all varieties of user utterances and carry out the intent of users, referred to as *natural language understanding* (NLU) engine. Existing industrial personal assistant products or open source tools (e.g., API.ai, WIT.ai) require software developers themselves or via crowdsourcing to manually input various natural utterances and annotate the slots for each utterance. Recently, researches have been made to bootstrap the utterance generations. These approaches first generate canonical utterances based on either lexicon/grammar (Wang et al., 2015) or language/SQL templates (Iyer et al., 2017); then utilize crowdsourcing to create paraphrases and correct labels. Unfortunately, they require software developers to have natural language expertise and still heavily rely on costly crowdsourcing. Thus, it is significantly and crucially desirable to develop a system for helping *ordinary developers* quickly build a high quality skill for personal assistants.

In this paper, we present a system, called *Cold-start iteRative Utterance generatIon for Skill dEvelopment* (CRUISE). As the name suggests, CRUISE aims to guide software developers to build a new skill from scratch, a.k.a., *cold-start*. It is defined from two aspects: *cold-start software developers* which refer to the ordinary developers who do not have either linguistic expertise or complete functionalities of the new skill in mind; and *cold-start dataset* which means that there is zero or very few training samples available. Specifically, CRUISE initially takes the list of intents in a new skill as inputs from software developers and runs a hybrid rule-based and data-driven algorithm to automatically generate more and more new utterances for each intent. During the whole process, software developers only need to iteratively *prune* the incorrect samples. As

105

Proceedings of the 56th Annual Meeting of the Association for Computational Linguistics-System Demonstrations, pages 105–110
Melbourne, Australia, July 15 - 20, 2018. ©2018 Association for Computational Linguistics

such, CRUISE does not depend on crowdsourcing to conduct the heavy task of manually generating utterances and annotating slots.

2 Background and Related Work

Natural language understanding is a key component in skill development. In personal assistants, since users intend to use spoken language to interact with personal assistant agents, most industrial products are focused on spoken language understanding (SLU) in which it is sufficient to understand user query by classifying the intent and identifying a set of slots (Liu and Lane, 2016). One class of approaches is to paraphrase user utterances to increase the number of training set (Barzilay and Lee, 2003; Quirk et al., 2004; Kauchak and Barzilay, 2006; Zhao et al., 2009; Prakash et al., 2016). However, these approaches depend on the existence of large amount of dataset for training paraphrasing model. As discussed above, the most relevant works (Wang et al., 2015; Iyer et al., 2017) bootstrapped the utterances based on grammar and SQL templates respectively and then relied on crowdsourcing to increase the utterance varieties and correct the labels. Unfortunately, they require both linguistic expertise from software developers and heavy human workload. In this paper, we use NLU and SLU engines equivalently.

3 CRUISE System Overview

3.1 Our Settings

Settings for Software Developers: To build a new skill S, a software developer starts with providing a list of predefined intents in this skill S. For each intent, as shown in Figure 1, the software developer first reviews and prunes an automatically constructed knowledge base. Next, the only human labor of a developer is to iteratively prune incorrect generated utterances. In the end, CRUISE will automatically outputs both a well-trained NLU engine for skill S and a large number of annotated correct utterances that can be used directly by third parties to train their own NLU engines.

Offline Preprocessed Components: CRUISE also consists of the following components which have been preprocessed offline *without the involvement of software developers*: *(1) Publicly available InfoBox template* Ω *(InfoBox, 2017):* contains a subset of information/attributes about an object, i.e., a set of object-attribute pairs. For example, the object `food` has attributes such as `course`, `region`, etc. (2) *Language model*: pre-trained on a public corpus (e.g., Wikipedia). (3) *Pre-built concept hash table*: for each word in the language model vocabulary, we use MS term conceptualizer (Wang and Wang, 2016) to find its most likely concept/category. For example, the word *pizza* is considered as an instance of the concept `food`. Then a hash table is constructed to map each concept to its instances.

3.2 CRUISE Design

We discuss the goals of CRUISE system design and the key ideas to achieve them.

Cold start Support: As discussed in introduction, the first trade-off in CRUISE design is between cold start (lack of training data and expertise from developers) and a high quality NLU engine. In order to accommodate the developers who do not have any linguistic expertise and reduce their workload to manually generate various utterances, we design an *Iterative Utterance Generation* approach. It starts from an intent as a simplest natural language utterance and decomposes the complex utterance generation into small tasks to tackle them one by one iteratively.

Reduced Human Workload: Another trade-off in CRUISE design is between human workload minimization and high quality of generated utterances. To address this, we design CRUISE from two aspects: (1) *Human-in-the-loop Pruning* allows developers iteratively *prune* the incorrect generated utterances. In next iteration, more utterances are generated *only* based on the previously selected *correct* utterances. (2) *Automated Utterance Annotation* generates an utterance corpus that can be directly used to train NLU engine without extra human efforts. The idea is to generate *tagged utterances* in which each tag can be simply coupled with its corresponding instances to automatically annotate the slots. For example, a tagged utterance contains `@food` and `@size` tags rather than their instances such as *pizza* and *large* (in Figure 1).

3.3 CRUISE Components & Workflow

As the running example shows in Figure 1, CRUISE has two main steps, *knowledge base construction* and *iterative utterance generation*.

Step 1. Knowledge Base Construction: for each

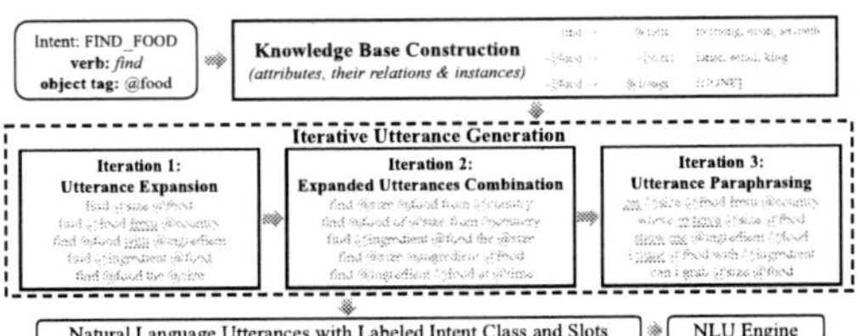

Figure 1: A running example of CRUISE system: it takes a new intent "FIND_FOOD" as input and outputs both annotated natural language utterances (each utterance with an intent label and slots labels) and a trained NLU engine. Each black box corresponds to a component in CRUISE, with both correct outputs (in green) and incorrect outputs (in red) to be pruned by developers. The underlined words are generated by the data-driven tagged sentence filler (Section 4.2) and the other words are generated by rules (Section 4.1).

intent (e.g., "FIND_FOOD" includes a verb *find* and an object tag @FOOD), CRUISE constructs *a knowledge base* with the following information: (1) identified list of attribute tags depending on object tag using Infobox template Ω (e.g. attribute tag @SIZE depends on object tag @FOOD); (2) the sample instances belong to each tag using pre-built concept hash table (e.g. instances "large", "small" for tag @SIZE). In addition, developers can also add or remove the tags and instances of each tag.

Step 2. Iterative Utterance Generation: CRUISE iteratively generates more and more utterances with human-in-the-loop pruning. CRUISE outputs the generated natural language utterances with both intent and slots annotations as well as a ready-to-use NLU engine trained on these utterances.

4 Iterative Utterance Generation

In this section, we describes the details of utterance generation in each iteration. *The key idea to generate utterances in each iteration is the hybrid of rule-based and data-driven approaches.* In brief, we utilize a small set of rules to derive a list of incomplete tagged utterances with blanks (word placeholders); then use data-driven tagged utterance filler algorithm to fill in the blanks. The rest of this section includes rule-based iteration design and data-driven tagged utterance filler algorithm respectively.

4.1 Rule-based Iteration Design

The key idea is to decompose the task of generating complex utterances into three subtasks and tackle each task in one iteration. Specifically, we divide the utterance generation task into the following subtasks in three iterations (idea

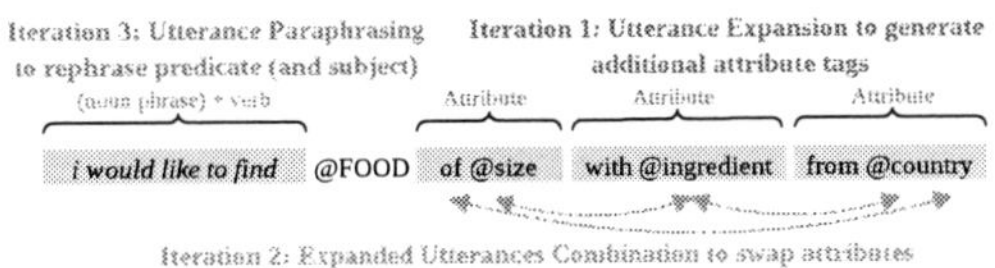

Figure 2: A running example to illustrate *subtasks* in each iteration towards generating a tagged utterance

illustration in Figure 2 and examples in Figure 1): *(1) Utterance Expansion:* generate attributives and adjuncts to expand an utterance into utterances with an additional new tag. *(2) Expanded Utterances Combination:* swap attributives and adjuncts to concatenate previously expanded utterances. *(3) Utterance Paraphrasing:* rephrase predicate (and subject) to paraphrase each utterance. At the end of each iteration i, we provide all generated utterances to the software developer for pruning such that only the selected *correct* utterances will be the input of next iteration. At last, we output the natural language utterances by substituting instances into tags with slot annotations.

Iteration 1. Utterance Expansion: Given an intent as a simplest verb phrase consisting of only a verb and its direct object (tag), the goal is to expand it into utterances such that each generated utterance has an additional attribute tag associated with the object tag. Thanks to the simple verb phrase, the expansion has no semantic ambiguity. Thus, for each new tag t, we expand the utterance by inserting t before and after the object tag. While it is straightforward to insert t directly before the object, the insertion of t after the object need joiner words where we introduce blanks. In the end, we fill out the blanks (usually 1-3) in tagged utterances as described in Section 4.2.

Iteration 2. Expanded Utterances Combination: The goal is to combine the previously generated correct utterances (two tags in each utterance) into long utterances with all combination of different tags in each utterance. We generate the permutations of attribute tags themselves (and with joiner words) before (after) the object. This iteration then outputs utterances these attribute tag permutations before and after the object with non-overlapping attribute tags. Thanks to the correct input utterances, most of combined utterances are surely correct, which saves a lot of pruning efforts.

Iteration 3. Utterance Paraphrasing: Since the previous iterations have covered the varieties for attributives phrases and clauses, the goal of iteration 3 is to increase the varieties of predicates. We generate different predicates for a tagged utterance as follows: (1) verb replacement, (2) wh-word question rephrasing, and (3) "I" started utterance rephrasing. Both (2) and (3) are motivated by the application of personal assistants that help the user who initiates the utterance. Likewise, we invoke tagged utterance filler to fill out the blanks (usually 3) for each predicate. In order to further reduce the human pruning workload, we group the same predicates for developers to prune them at once instead of pruning every single utterance again and again.

4.2 Data-driven Tagged Sentence Filler

As a key data-driven subroutine, this module takes a tagged utterance with blanks (i.e., word placeholders) u as the input and outputs the complete tagged utterance with all blanks filled by natural language words, called *filler words*. We first instantiate the attribute and object tags in u using their mapped instances in the pre-built concept hash table. Since all instances belong to the vocabulary of the pre-trained language model, we avoid tackling out of vocabulary problem. Based on the intuition that good filler words are usually generated repeatedly in many instantiated utterances, we fill out the blanks in all instantiated utterances and return the K_t (up to 20) filler words ranked by the frequency of their appearances.

To fill out the blanks in an incomplete natural language utterance, we use an efficient beam search algorithm via RNN based pre-trained language models. This returns a list of K_n (up to 30) best filler words, ranked according to their likelihood scores.

5 Experimental Evaluation

We implement the CRUISE system with an easy-to-use user interface (Figure 3) with the thumb up/down mechanism for efficient human pruning. We have internal developers to use and evaluate this real system in terms of both utterance quality and human workload.

5.1 Data Quality Evaluation

5.1.1 Objective Evaluation via NLU Engines

We validate our CRUISE system by first evaluating the performance of existing NLU engines trained using our generated utterances compared with using benchmark or manually

Figure 3: CRUISE User Interface

Table 1: Human NLU engine vs. CRUISE NLU engine results in benchmark and custom datasets

		Human NLU		CRUISE NLU	
Dataset	NLU Engine	Intent Accuracy	Slot Tagging F-1 Score	Intent Accuracy	Slot Tagging F-1 Score
ATIS	RASA	93.29%	90.84	83.33%	80.25
	RNN	97.96%	96.02	82.60%	84.70
Food	RASA	99.4%	91.92	**99.58%**	**93.91**
	RNN	99.31 %	92.28	**99.73%**	**94.70**
Hotel	RASA	-	92.22	-	89.92
	RNN	-	92.09	-	**94.85**

generated utterances. For simplicity, we refer to our CRUISE generated datasets as *CRUISE Dataset* in comparison of *Benchmark/Human Dataset*. Correspondingly, the NLU engines trained on CRUISE and benchmark human generated datasets are referred to as ***CRUISE NLU*** and ***Human NLU*** engines respectively. Both NLU engines are evaluated by testing on benchmark or user generated utterances.

NLU Engines & Performance Metrics: To maximally reduce the bias from NLU engines, we evaluate the performance using different existing NLU engines: open source *RASA* (RASA, 2017) and deep learning based *RNN* NLU engine with joint learning of intent classifier and slot tagger (Liu and Lane, 2016). Both NLU engines target on classifying the intent of each whole utterance and identifying tags/entities (a.k.a. slot tagging). Thus, we use the accuracy and F-1 score as the metrics for intent classifier and slot tagging respectively. We run RASA NLU engine using their default parameters.

Benchmark Dataset Evaluation: Although the benchmark NLU trained on crowdsourced data is expected to perform much better than CRUISE NLU trained on machine generated dataset from cold start, we show that CRUISE NLU still achieves a high accuracy and efficiently trades off NLU performance and human workload.

We evaluate our system on the ATIS (Airline Travel Information Systems) dataset (Hemphill

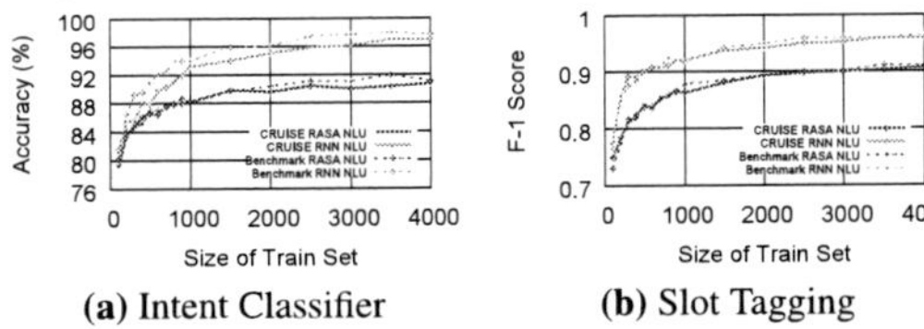

(a) Intent Classifier   (b) Slot Tagging

Figure 4: Mixed NLU results in ATIS Dataset

et al., 1990), a widely used dataset in SLU research. It contains 4,978 training utterances and 893 testing utterances with 127 distinct slot labels and 22 different intents. We generate 767,985 unique tagged utterances using CRUISE system. For a fair comparison, we randomly sample 5,000 utterances from CRUISE dataset as training set. Since ATIS is relatively larger, we select both word embedding and LSTM hidden dimension as 128 with 1 hidden layer in RNN NLU.

Table 1 reports the result of NLU performance comparison. As one can see, the performance of CRUISE NLU engine is roughly around 10-15% worse than benchmark NLU engine trained on crowdsourced benchmark data for both intent classification and slot tagging. After a detailed analysis, we find that CRUISE data has smaller vocabulary size (301 words) than the crowdsourced benchmark data (949 words) due to the selection of high likelihood words in beam search. Hence, we attribute a significant cause of errors because of the out-of-vocabulary words in test set. We further test CRUISE NLU on the subset of test set without out-of-vocabulary words and observe 5-6% improvement of NLU performance. Importantly, we observe that CRUISE NLU performs much better on more complex utterances, e.g., *"show me fares for round trip flights with first class of delta from miami into houston"*, where the benchmark NLU fail for both intent classification and slot tagging.

In addition to CRUISE NLU, we further test the performance of NLU engines which are trained by mixed CRUISE and benchmark datasets, named **Mixed NLU**. The benchmark data is treated as the manual entry data from developers such that we can better study another trade-off between additional human workload and NLU engine performance. Figure 4 reports the result of mixed NLU engine performance with half CRUISE data and half benchmark data. Both the mixed and benchmark NLU engines achieve similar performance for different sizes of training set on the costly crowdsourced ATIS dataset.

This implies that we can reduce nearly half human workload for developing a skill, given the negligible pruning effort (Section 5.2).

Real-World Setting Evaluation: We further evaluate CRUISE in a simulated real-world scenario when a software developer starts to develop a new skill. In order to do so, we create two custom datasets: (a) *Food* and (b) *Hotel*. Food data has three intents and hotel data has only one intent. Each intent is associated with six to eight different attributes/tags selected from InfoBox template or provided by internal developers. For each intent, we ask two developers to generate a list of tagged utterances manually and using our CRUISE system respectively. The total sizes of human and CRUISE generated utterances are 5,352 and 21,429 in food and hotel datasets respectively. For fairness, we randomly select a subset from human dataset as a standard test data to test both NLU engines. Table 1 shows that CRUISE NLU outperforms human NLU in most cases. This is because CRUISE dataset has a larger number and varieties of high quality utterances than human dataset.

5.1.2 Subjective Human Evaluation

We further evaluate the CRUISE dataset subjectively by soliciting judgments from Amazon Mechanical Turkers. Each turker was presented a task of rating utterances sampled from mixed CRUISE and human generated datasets. Turkers rate each question on a 5 point Likert scale (Likert, 1932) as to whether the utterance is *natural* and *grammatically correct*. Ratings range from 1 (worst) to 5 (best). Thus, our evaluation provides more detailed rating than what automatic metrics such as BLEU can provide (Papineni et al., 2002). In order to control the evaluation quality, we further judge the *trustworthiness* of each turker by scoring their performance on 20-30 gold-standard utterances that were internally rated by experts. Based on this trustworthiness score, we establish a group of *trusted turkers*. Then, we collect 10 ratings for each utterance from these trusted turkers. Finally, we compute the average score over all trusted ratings on 300-500 randomly sampled utterances in each dataset.

Table 2 reports human evaluation results between CRUISE and human generated data. We observe that CRUISE generated dataset achieves close performance in terms of both metrics in

109

Table 2: Human Evaluation Results

	Dataset	Naturalness	Grammar	Overall
ATIS	CRUISE	3.32	3.37	3.35
	Human	3.74	3.78	3.76
Custom	CRUISE	**3.60**	**3.41**	**3.50**
	Human	3.35	3.08	3.21

ATIS, which is collected via costly crowdsourcing. More importantly, for human data generated by only a single developer in custom datasets, the results show that CRUISE data has better quality than human data in terms of both metrics.

5.2 Human Workload Analysis

We analyze the cognitive load via preliminary qualitative analysis from internal developers. Specifically, we interview the participated developers regarding different types of cognitive load (Sweller et al., 1998). In terms of *intrinsic cognitive load* about the inherent difficulty level to use CRUISE system, the developers concluded CRUISE as a more easy-to-use system than both existing industrial tools and academic solutions. *Extraneous cognitive load* is also largely reduced since our design enables batch processing of human pruning by one-click marking of all utterances in each page. At last, the developers are also satisfied with the reduced *germane cognitive load* due to the iterative pruning design in CRUISE which dramatically minimize the whole pruning effort by generating more utterances only based on the correct ones in previous iteration.

Next, we report the time consumption of human pruning to evaluate the workload quantitatively. As shown in Figure 5, we observe that it takes less than 0.15s on average to prune each utterance, and as low as 0.01s for some intents. This is because iteration design in our CRUISE system enables the capability that each picked correct utterance can generate many utterances at one time. In comparison, we observe that human developers take around 30 seconds on average to generate and annotate an utterance in our custom dataset. In the example of ATIS dataset, it takes around 0.05s on average to prune each utterance. Thus, a developer only needs to spend less than 5 mins on average to prune incorrect utterances in order to find 5,000 correct utterance for training a competitive NLU engine. For frequent intents, it takes less time to prune as CRUISE intends to generate more correct utterances determined by a better language model.

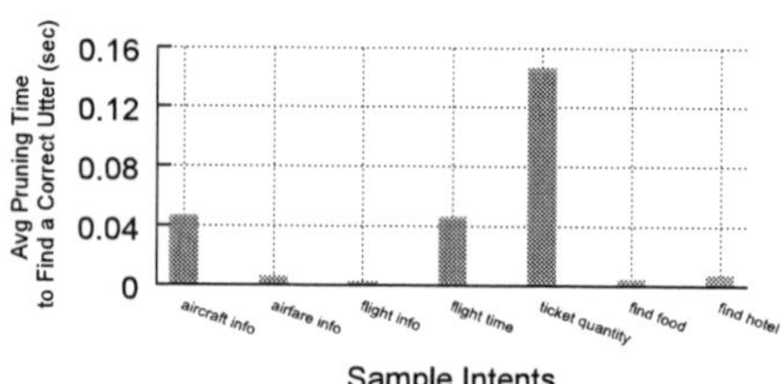

Figure 5: Time Consumption for Human Pruning (Green:ATIS, Blue:custom)

References

Regina Barzilay and Lillian Lee. 2003. Learning to paraphrase: an unsupervised approach using multiple-sequence alignment. In *NAACL-HLT*.

Charles T. Hemphill, John J. Godfrey, and George R. Doddington. 1990. The atis spoken language systems pilot corpus. In *HLT*.

InfoBox. 2017. https://en.wikipedia.org/wiki/Infobox.

Srinivasan Iyer, Ioannis Konstas, Alvin Cheung, Jayant Krishnamurthy, and Luke Zettlemoyer. 2017. Learning a neural semantic parser from user feedback. In *ACL*.

David Kauchak and Regina Barzilay. 2006. Paraphrasing for automatic evaluation. In *HLT–NAACL*.

Likert. 1932. https://en.wikipedia.org/wiki/Likert_scale.

Bing Liu and Ian Lane. 2016. Attention-based recurrent neural network models for joint intent detection and slot filling. In *INTERSPEECH*.

Kishore Papineni, Salim Roukos, Todd Ward, and Wei-Jing Zhu. 2002. Bleu: A method for automatic evaluation of machine translation. In *ACL*.

Aaditya Prakash, Sadid A. Hasan, Kathy Lee, Vivek V. Datla, Ashequl Qadir, Joey Liu, and Oladimeji Farri. 2016. Neural paraphrase generation with stacked residual LSTM networks. In *COLING*.

Chris Quirk, Chris Brockett, and William Dolan. 2004. Monolingual machine translation for paraphrase generation. In *EMNLP*.

RASA. 2017. https://rasa.ai/.

John Sweller, Jeroen J. G. Van Merrienboer, and Fred G. W. C. Paas. 1998. Cognitive architecture and instructional design. *Educational Psychology Review*.

Yushi Wang, Jonathan Berant, and Percy Liang. 2015. Building a semantic parser overnight. In *ACL*.

Zhongyuan Wang and Haixun Wang. 2016. Understanding short texts. In *ACL (Tutorial)*.

Shiqi Zhao, Xiang Lan, Ting Liu, and Sheng Li. 2009. Application-driven statistical paraphrase generation. In *ACL*.

Praaline: An Open-Source System for Managing, Annotating, Visualising and Analysing Speech Corpora

George Christodoulides
Metrology and Language Sciences Unit, University of Mons
Place du Parc 18, B-7000 Mons, Belgium
`george@mycontent.gr`

Abstract

In this system demonstration we present the latest developments of Praaline, an open-source software system for constituting and managing, manually and automatically annotating, visualising and analysing spoken language and multimodal corpora. We review the system's functionality and design architecture, present current use cases and directions for future development.

1 Introduction

In this system demonstration, we present *Praaline*. *Praaline* is an open-source application for creating and managing speech and multi-modal corpora, annotating them manually or automatically, visualising the speech signal and annotations, querying the data and creating concordances, and performing statistical analyses. The system was first presented in (Christodoulides, 2014). *Praaline* is a cross-platform standalone application that runs on Windows, Mac OSX and Linux. It is written in C++ using the Qt framework. The application is available for download at `https://www.praaline.org` and the source code is available on GitHub (`https://github.com/praaline`), under the GPL version 3 license.

Several tools are being used currently in spoken language research. In the phonetics and prosody domain, the most widely used tool is *Praat* (Boersma and Weenink, 2018); in the pragmatics and discourse studies community Exmaralda (Schmidt and Wörner, 2009) is appreciated for its concordancing functionality; for multimodal and signed language corpora, *ELAN* (Brugman and Russel, 2004) is often preferred; and large corpora have been transcribed using *TranscriberAG* (Barras et al., 1998).

We have focused on creating a tool that will cover the needs of researchers working simultaneously on speech (phonetics, phonology, prosody) and discourse (syntax, semantics, pragmatics). *Praaline* should help an individual researcher organise their data using the best practices in corpus design and data management, and allow them to work independently. At the same time, our system aims to facilitate depositing the corpus data to a central repository at the end of a research project, using a structure that will facilitate long-term storage and reuse. For these reasons, we have decided to use an SQL relational database for data storage: an SQLite database for local projects, or a MySQL or PostgreSQL database for using *Praaline* in a network environment. Furthermore the system provides extensive support for importing and exporting data between *Praaline* and other annotation tools (*Praat, Exmaralda, ELAN, TranscriberAG*, other formats), as well as support for importing and exporting annotation data in the XML and JSON formats.

In the following, we will present the main functionality of *Praaline*, describe its design architecture and conclude with our plans for future development.

2 Features

2.1 Corpus Management

A collection of recordings (audio and video) constitutes a Corpus, which can be stored in a Corpus Repository. A repository provides a common structure for metadata and annotations (see next section). A Corpus contains a collection of Communications and Speakers. Each Communication consists of one or more Recordings and corresponding Annotation documents. Speakers are linked to the Communications in which they are involved though Participation objects. The six ba-

111

Proceedings of the 56th Annual Meeting of the Association for Computational Linguistics-System Demonstrations, pages 111–115
Melbourne, Australia, July 15 - 20, 2018. ©2018 Association for Computational Linguistics

sic objects can all be described using a set of meta-data. *Praaline* does not impose any schema for metadata: the user can define their own metadata schema per Repository. The Corpus Explorer (see Figure 1) is used to constitute the corpus and to edit its metadata: corpus objects can be browsed in a tree (possibly grouped based on metadata information); the user can also edit metadata using a spreadsheet-like display.

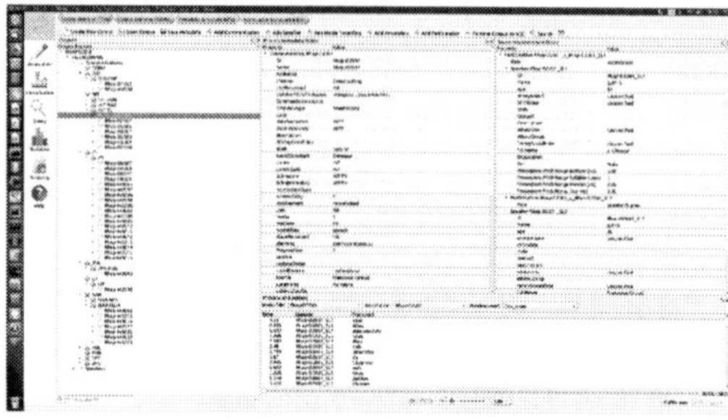

Figure 1: Corpus Explorer

2.2 Metadata and Annotation Structure

Each Corpus Repository will have a defined data structure for its metadata and annotations. Templates are provided to help individual researchers; it is also possible to standardise these structures when multiple users are accessing the same database. *Praaline* includes an editor for metadata and annotation structures: the editors perform data definition language (DDL) queries to change the SQL database structure. The metadata structure editor allows the user to define the fields that will be stored for each of the six main objects described in the previous section. Annotations are organised in Levels and Attributes: a Level describes a unit of linguistic analysis (e.g. a syllable, a token, an utterance etc) and contains a label and an arbitrary number of Attributes. Each Annotation Level corresponds to a table in the SQL database and Attributes correspond to columns. The data structure editor for annotations is shown in Figure 2).

The metadata and annotation structure editors allow the user to define fields having any of the standard SQL data types (integers, real numbers, strings, boolean values etc.). Furthermore, a system for defining and importing/exporting name-value lists is available. A name-value list (NVL) can be associated with any number of metadata fields or annotation attributes. The NVL subsystem can improve data quality by enforcing ref-

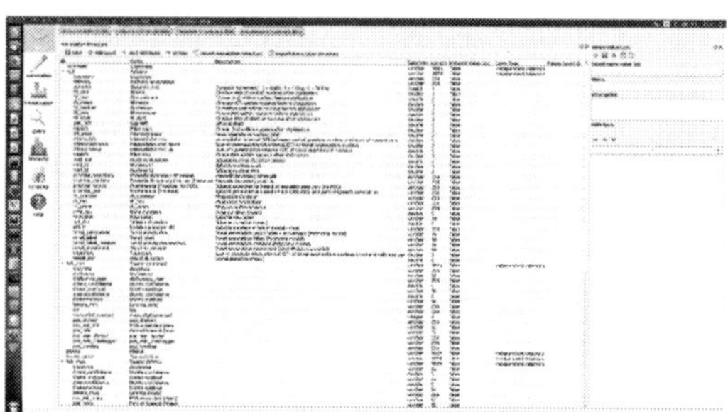

Figure 2: Annotation Structure and Vocabularies

erential integrity rules and help users in annotating data based on a closed vocabulary (e.g. a defined set of part-of-speech tags, dependency relations, discourse relations, phoneme labels etc.). The metadata and annotation structure of a corpus repository can be exported as an XML or JSON file; when these files are imported on another repository, *Praaline* recreates the corresponding database structures and NVL data.

2.3 Annotation

Annotations can be added to the corpus using one of the Manual Annotation editors: a spreadsheet-like editor that can combine multiple levels of annotation; a transcriber interface; an editor for sequences or for relations. The tabular editor is show in Figure 3.

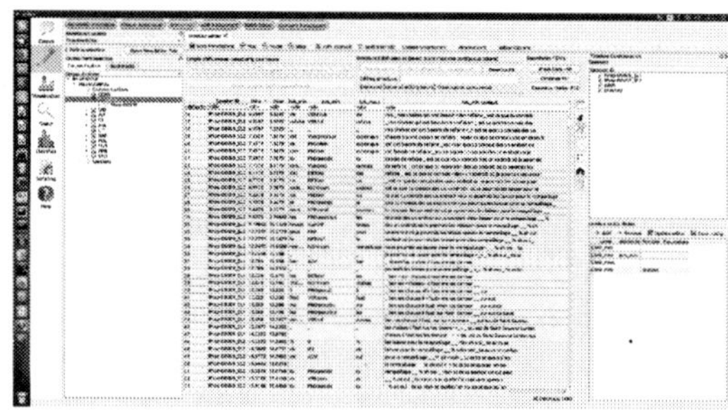

Figure 3: Manual Annotation Editor

The annotation tools offered attempt to cover the entire workflow of constructing a speech corpus: collecting recordings, transcribing them or re-using existing transcriptions, speech-text alignment, enrichment of the annotations with additional levels and feature extraction (before proceeding with analysing the data). The Transcriber module provides a user interface for quick manual transcription, especially in the presence of multiple speakers. The Long Sound Aligner module allows the user to reuse existing, possibly imperfect, transcriptions of the corpus materials. The Long Sound Aligner uses the output of a speech recognition engine and the transcription text to produce iteratively refined alignments of transcription utterances to the speech signal (similar to other long sound alignment tools, e.g. Katsamanis et al. (2011)). The Forced Alignment module allows the user to produce alignments at the phone, syllable and token level, based on a pronunciation dictionary or other system for phonetisation, and an ASR engine. The currently supported ASR engines in *Praaline* are HTK(Young et al., 2006), PocketSphinx (Walker et al., 2004) and Kaldi (Povey et al., 2011).

The annotation framework in *Praaline* is language independent: annotations are stored in Unicode format and no assumptions are made about language. However, several tasks require language-specific resources: tokenisation rules, pronunciation dictionaries, acoustic models and language models for the ASR engine. A collection of open resources is available, and the development of language resources for the back-end tools in the context of other open source projects can be harnessed.

Much of the functionality in *Praaline* comes from its automatic annotation plug-ins. The user can run a cascade of automatic annotation plugins, after setting the relevant parameters (each plugin defines its own set) on the entire corpus or on a subset of corpus items. The user interface for these operations is shown in Figure 4.

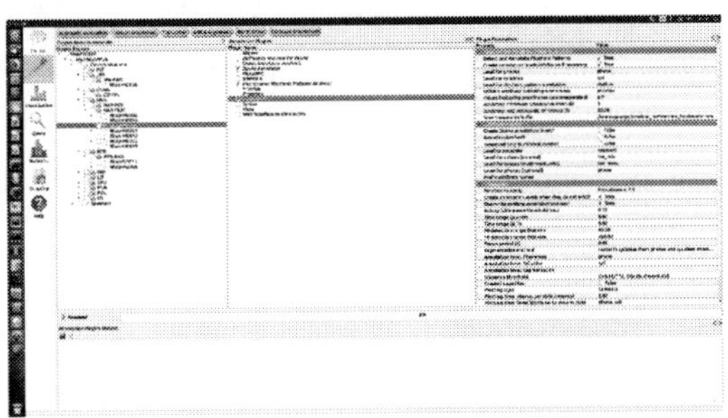

Figure 4: Automatic Annotation Plugins

Currently, plugins are available for the following tasks:

- Part-of-speech tagging and syntactical analysis of spoken language, in several languages,

using the *DisMo* plug-in (Christodoulides et al., 2014). Statistical models for many languages are provided, based on the work by the Universal Dependencies project (Nivre et al., 2016).

- Prosodic feature extraction and pitch stylisation, using either the Prosogram (Mertens, 2004) system, or the INTSINT/MoMel system (Hirst, 2007) for intonation annotation.

- Automatic detection and annotation of prosodic events, with language-specific statistical models extracted from manually annotated corpora.

2.4 Visualisation

The Visualisation module of *Praaline* reuses and extends the code of *Sonic Visualiser* (Cannam et al., 2010), which is also an open-source (GPL) project written in C++/Qt and used in the field of musicology. The user can create the visualisation that best suits their needs by combining panes and layers, containing: annotation tiers, points, curves, histograms, colour-coded regions, spectrograms etc. Extensions have been added for visualising intonation information, for studies in prosody. Visualisation templates can be saved in XMl and JSON formats; a collection of available visualisation templates is presented to the user. An example of a visualisation is show in Figure 5.

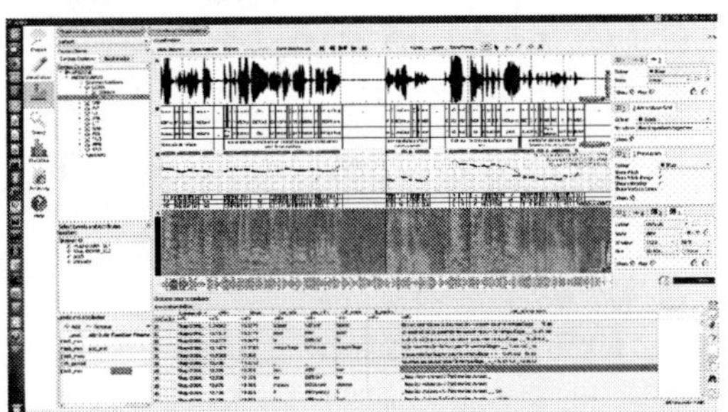

Figure 5: Visualisation

An annotation editor can be combined with the visualisation user interface, to facilitate use cases where the user codes a linguistic phenomenon with the aid of a visual representation. Visualisations can be exported in image formats for use in presentations and publications. A system of Bookmarks allows the user to save points of interest in the corpus: the identification data of the Communication, Recording and Annotation along with a time-code constitute a Bookmark that can be stored in collections of bookmarks for easy access. The results of a concordance search (see next section) can also be exported as bookmarks.

2.5 Queries and Concordances

The user can perform queries on any of the annotation levels or a combination of these levels. The results are displayed in keyword-in-context (KWIC) concordances and can be exported for further analysis. It is possible to search for sequences and patterns. The Concordancer results can be exported as Bookmarks for immediate access in the Annotation editors and in the Visualiser. The Concordancer is show in Figure 6.

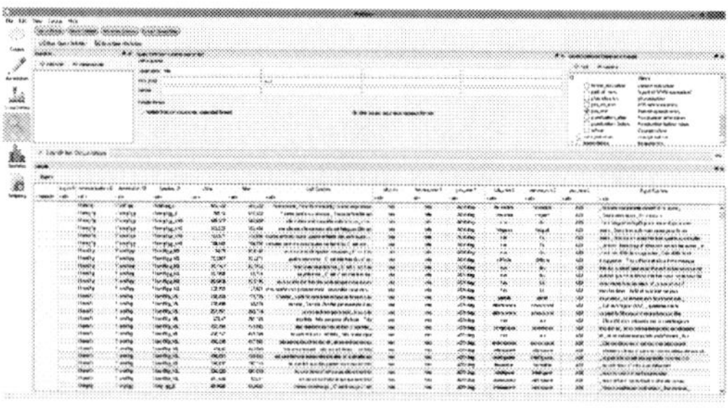

Figure 6: Concordancer

Furthermore, an interface is provided for creating datasets. Using a dataset, information from multiple annotation levels can be combined, a set of basic statistic operations can be applied and the results can be saved for further analysis. As an example, in a corpus annotated on four levels (phones, syllables, tokens, discourse units), the user may export a dataset containing: all the syllables in the corpus, their acoustic features (extracted from upstream plug-ins), the corresponding tokens and associated attributes (e.g. POS tags), the corresponding discourse units and associated attributes, and some metadata attributes. A dataset has a minimum unit (in the previous example, the syllable) and lower-level (grouped) or higher-level (associated) data.

2.6 Statistics

Praaline includes a set of statistical analysis plugins, covering a range of common analyses in speech research: basic counts; temporal analysis (pauses, speech rate, dialogue dynamics); prosodic and disfluency analysis; clustering corpus items using principal component analysis. The

results of the analysis can be exported, and the basic graphics can be immediately accessed from within *Praaline*. For more advanced statistical analysis of corpus data, users can use R scripts (R Core Team, 2018) that take advantage of the fact that the corpus data and annotations are stored in SQL format. An example of a PCA analysis is shown in Figure 7.

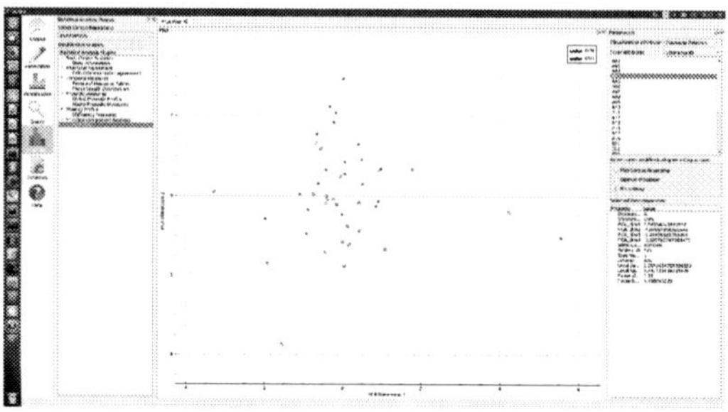

Figure 7: Statistics (PCA plot)

3 System Architecture and Extensibility

The system is following a modular design. A core library (Praaline Core) contains all the basic functionality needed to access and manage *Praaline* corpus metadata and annotations. The library can be reused in other software (see also next section). At the next level, a set of modules (Praaline Libraries) contain the functionality needed for automatic speech recognition, the application of machine learning algorithms, feature extraction etc. These libraries are often wrappers of existing and well-established open-source NLP tools, such as Sphinx, OpenSmile, HTK, CRF++ etc. An additional module contains the user interface elements (e.g. widgets for visualisation). All these modules are brought together in the main application.

An API for the Core library and for interfacing with the main application allows for the creation of plugins. Plugins add functionality to *Praaline* and include implementations of automatic annotation algorithms, statistical analysis plugins or new visualisation elements.

Examples of plug-in development are provided on the project's website: a skeleton C++ project is given, and Python scripts using the Praaline Core library, or other modules of the Praaline Libraries illustrate the use of these resources for common NLP tasks. The Praaline Core library can be used as a tool for input-output and interfacing with annotation information without using *Praaline*'s user interface.

4 Future Development

Praaline is under active development. The main priorities for adding features are as follows:

- A signal annotation editor strongly resembling Praat. We have found that researchers in some communities are strongly attached to this user interface, and this addition will facilitate the acceptance of a new system on their part.

- Stabilise the API of the Praaline Core library and provide Python and R bindings.

- Finalise the development of *PraalineWeb*, a system that allows the publication of corpora on the web, using Django.

- Add functionality for editing dependency relations.

The development of *Praaline* has been mainly driven by the expectations and needs of its users. It is hoped that this system demonstration will provide additional feedback.

References

Claude Barras, Edouard Geoffrois, Zhibiao Wu, and Mark Liberman. 1998. Transcriber: a free tool for segmenting, labeling and transcribing speech. In *LREC 1998 – 1ˢᵗ International Conference on Language Resources and Evaluation, 28–30 May, Granada, Spain Proceedings*, pages 1373–1376.

Paul Boersma and David Weenink. 2018. *Praat: doing phonetics by computer, ver. 6.0.37*.

Hennie Brugman and Albert Russel. 2004. Annotating multimedia and multi-modal resources with elan. In *LREC 2004 – 4ᵗʰ International Conference on Language Resources and Evaluation, May 26–28, Paris, France, Proceedings*, pages 2065–2068.

Chris Cannam, Christian Landone, and Sandler Mark. 2010. Sonic visualiser: An open source application for viewing, analysing, and annotating music audio files. In *Proceedings of the ACM Multimedia 2010 International Conference*, pages 1467–1468.

George Christodoulides. 2014. Praaline: Integrating tools for speech corpus research. In *LREC 2014 – 9ᵗʰ International Conference on Language Resources and Evaluation, May 26–31, Reykjavik, Iceland, Proceedings*, pages 31–34.

George Christodoulides, Mathieu Avanzi, and Jean Philippe Goldman. 2014. DisMo: A morphosyntactic, disfluency and multi-word unit annotator. In *LREC 2014 – 9ᵗʰ International Conference on Language Resources and Evaluation, May 26–31, Reykjavik, Iceland, Proceedings*, pages 3902–3907.

Daniel Hirst. 2007. A praat plugin for momel and intsint with improved algorithms for modelling and coding intonation.

Athanasios Katsamanis, Matthew P. Black, Panayiotis G. Georgiou, Louis Goldstein, and Shrikanth S. Narayanan. 2011. SailAlign: Robust long speech-text alignment. In *Proceedings of the Workshop on New Tools and Methods for Very-Large Scale Phonetics Research*.

Piet Mertens. 2004. The Prosogram: Semi-automatic transcription of prosody based on a tonal perception model. In *Proc. of Speech Prosody 2004, March 23–26, Nara, Japan*, pages 549–552.

Joakim Nivre, Marie-Catherine de Marneffe, Filip Ginter, Yoav Goldberg, Jan Hajic, Christopher D. Manning, Ryan McDonald, Slav Petrov, Sampo Pyysalo, Natalia Silveira, and et al. 2016. Universal dependencies v1: A multilingual treebank collection. In *Proceedings of the 10th International Conference on Language Resources and Evaluation (LREC 2016)*.

Daniel Povey, Arnab Ghoshal, Gilles Boulianne, Lukas Burget, Ondrej Glembek, Nagendra Goel, Mirko Hannemann, Petr Motlicek, Yanmin Qian, Petr Schwarz, Jan Silovsky, Georg Stemmer, and Karel Vesely. 2011. The kaldi speech recognition toolkit. In *IEEE 2011 Workshop on Automatic Speech Recognition and Understanding*. IEEE Signal Processing Society. IEEE Catalog No.: CFP11SRW-USB.

R Core Team. 2018. *R: A language and environment for statistical computing*. R Foundation for Statistical Computing, Vienna, Austria.

Thomas Schmidt and Kai Wörner. 2009. EXMARaLDA – creating, analysing and sharing spoken language corpora for pragmatic research. *Pragmatics*, 19(4):565–582.

Willie Walker, Paul Lamere, Philip Kwok, Bhiksha Raj, Rita Singh, Evandro Gouvea, Peter Wolf, and Joe Woelfel. 2004. Sphinx-4: A flexible open source framework for speech recognition. Technical report, Mountain View, CA, USA.

Steve J. Young, D. Kershaw, J. Odell, D. Ollason, V. Valtchev, and P. Woodland. 2006. *The HTK Book Version 3.4*. Cambridge University Press.

Marian: Fast Neural Machine Translation in C++

Marcin Junczys-Dowmunt[†] Roman Grundkiewicz[*‡] Tomasz Dwojak[*]
Hieu Hoang Kenneth Heafield[‡] Tom Neckermann[‡]
Frank Seide[†] Ulrich Germann[‡] Alham Fikri Aji[‡]
Nikolay Bogoychev[‡] André F. T. Martins[¶] Alexandra Birch[‡]

[†]Microsoft Translator [*]Adam Mickiewicz University in Poznań
[‡]University of Edinburgh [¶]Unbabel

Abstract

We present Marian, an efficient and self-contained Neural Machine Translation framework with an integrated automatic differentiation engine based on dynamic computation graphs. Marian is written entirely in C++. We describe the design of the encoder-decoder framework and demonstrate that a research-friendly toolkit can achieve high training and translation speed.

1 Introduction

In this paper, we present Marian,[1] an efficient Neural Machine Translation framework written in pure C++ with minimal dependencies. It has mainly been developed at the Adam Mickiewicz University in Poznań and at the University of Edinburgh. It is currently being deployed in multiple European projects and is the main translation and training engine behind the neural MT launch at the World Intellectual Property Organization.[2]

In the evolving eco-system of open-source NMT toolkits, Marian occupies its own niche best characterized by two aspects:

- It is written completely in C++11 and intentionally does not provide Python bindings; model code and meta-algorithms are meant to be implemented in efficient C++ code.
- It is self-contained with its own back end, which provides reverse-mode automatic differentiation based on dynamic graphs.

Marian has minimal dependencies (only Boost and CUDA or a BLAS library) and enables barrier-free optimization at all levels: meta-algorithms such as MPI-based multi-node training, efficient batched beam search, compact implementations of new models, custom operators, and custom GPU kernels. Intel has contributed and is optimizing a CPU backend.

Marian grew out of a C++ re-implementation of Nematus (Sennrich et al., 2017b), and still maintains binary-compatibility for common models. Hence, we will compare speed mostly against Nematus. OpenNMT (Klein et al., 2017), perhaps one of the most popular toolkits, has been reported to have training speed competitive to Nematus.

Marian is distributed under the MIT license and available from `https://marian-nmt.github.io` or the GitHub repository `https://github.com/marian-nmt/marian`.

2 Design Outline

We will very briefly discuss the design of Marian. Technical details of the implementations will be provided in later work.

2.1 Custom Auto-Differentiation Engine

The deep-learning back-end included in Marian is based on reverse-mode auto-differentiation with dynamic computation graphs and among the established machine learning platforms most similar in design to DyNet (Neubig et al., 2017). While the back-end could be used for other tasks than machine translation, we choose to optimize specifically for this and similar use cases. Optimization on this level include for instance efficient implementations of various fused RNN cells, attention mechanisms or an atomic layer-normalization (Ba et al., 2016) operator.

---

[1]Named after Marian Rejewski, a Polish mathematician and cryptologist who reconstructed the German military Enigma cipher machine sight-unseen in 1932. `https://en.wikipedia.org/wiki/Marian_Rejewski`.

[2]`https://slator.com/technology/neural-conquers-patent-translation-in-major-wipo-roll-out/`

Proceedings of the 56th Annual Meeting of the Association for Computational Linguistics-System Demonstrations, pages 116–121
Melbourne, Australia, July 15 - 20, 2018. ©2018 Association for Computational Linguistics

2.2 Extensible Encoder-Decoder Framework

Inspired by the stateful feature function framework in Moses (Koehn et al., 2007), we implement encoders and decoders as classes with the following (strongly simplified) interface:

```
class Encoder {
  EncoderState build(Batch);
};

class Decoder {
  DecoderState startState(EncoderState[]);
  DecoderState step(DecoderState, Batch);
};
```

A Bahdanau-style encoder-decoder model would implement the entire encoder inside `Encoder::build` based on the content of the batch and place the resulting encoder context inside the `EncoderState` object.

`Decoder::startState` receives a list of `EncoderState` (one in the case of the Bahdanau model, multiple for multi-source models, none for language models) and creates the initial `DecoderState`.

The `Decoder::step` function consumes the target part of a batch to produce the output logits of a model. The time dimension is either expanded by broadcasting of single tensors or by looping over the individual time-steps (for instance in the case of RNNs). Loops and other control structures are just the standard built-in C++ operations. The same function can then be used to expand over all given time steps at once during training and scoring or step-by-step during translation. Current hypotheses state (e.g. RNN vectors) and current logits are placed in the next `DecoderState` object.

Decoder states are used mostly during translation to select the next set of translation hypotheses. Complex encoder-decoder models can derive from `DecoderState` to implement non-standard selection behavior, for instance hard-attention models need to increase attention indices based on the top-scoring hypotheses.

This framework makes it possible to combine different encoders and decoders (e.g. RNN-based encoder with a Transformer decoder) and reduces implementation effort. In most cases it is enough to implement a single inference step in order to train, score and translate with a new model.

2.3 Efficient Meta-algorithms

On top of the auto-diff engine and encoder-decoder framework, we implemented many efficient meta-algorithms. These include multi-device (GPU or CPU) training, scoring and batched beam search, ensembling of heterogeneous models (e.g. Deep RNN models and Transformer or language models), multi-node training and more.

3 Case Studies

In this section we will illustrate how we used the Marian toolkit to facilitate our own research across several NLP problems. Each subsection is meant as a showcase for different components of the toolkit and demonstrates the maturity and flexibility of the toolkit. Unless stated otherwise, all mentioned features are included in the Marian toolkit.

3.1 Improving over WMT2017 systems

Sennrich et al. (2017a) proposed the highest scoring NMT system in terms of BLEU during the WMT 2017 shared task on English-German news translation (Bojar et al., 2017a), trained with the Nematus toolkit (Sennrich et al., 2017b). In this section, we demonstrate that we can replicate and slightly outperform these results with an identical model architecture implemented in Marian and improve on the recipe with a Transformer-style (Vaswani et al., 2017) model.

3.1.1 Deep Transition RNN Architecture

The model architecture in Sennrich et al. (2017a) is a sequence-to-sequence model with single-layer RNNs in both, the encoder and decoder. The RNN in the encoder is bi-directional. Depth is achieved by building stacked GRU-blocks resulting in very tall RNN cells for every recurrent step (deep transitions). The encoder consists of four GRU-blocks per cell, the decoder of eight GRU-blocks with an attention mechanism placed between the first and second block. As in Sennrich et al. (2017a), embeddings size is 512, RNN state size is 1024. We use layer-normalization (Ba et al., 2016) and variational drop-out with $p = 0.1$ (Gal and Ghahramani, 2016) inside GRU-blocks and attention.

3.1.2 Transformer Architecture

We very closely follow the architecture described in Vaswani et al. (2017) and their "base" model.

3.1.3 Training Recipe

Modeled after the description[3] from Sennrich et al. (2017a), we perform the following steps:

---

[3]The entire recipe is available in form of multiple scripts at `https://github.com/marian-nmt/marian-examples`.

System	test2016	test2017
UEdin WMT17 (single)	33.9	27.5
+Ensemble of 4	35.1	28.3
+R2L Reranking	36.2	28.3
Deep RNN (single)	34.3	27.7
+Ensemble of 4	35.3	28.2
+R2L Reranking	35.9	28.7
Transformer (single)	35.6	28.8
+Ensemble of 4	36.4	29.4
+R2L Reranking	36.8	29.5

Table 1: BLEU results for our replication of the UEdin WMT17 system for the en-de news translation task. We reproduced most steps and replaced the deep RNN model with a Transformer model.

- preprocessing of training data, tokenization, true-casing[4], vocabulary reduction to 36,000 joint BPE subword units (Sennrich et al., 2016) with a separate tool.[5]
- training of a shallow model for back-translation on parallel WMT17 data;
- translation of 10M German monolingual news sentences to English; concatenation of artificial training corpus with original data (times two) to produce new training data;
- training of four left-to-right (L2R) deep models (either RNN-based or Transformer-based);
- training of four additional deep models with right-to-left (R2L) orientation; [6]
- ensemble-decoding with four L2R models resulting in an n-best list of 12 hypotheses per input sentence;
- rescoring of n-best list with four R2L models, all model scores are weighted equally;
- evaluation on newstest-2016 (validation set) and newstest-2017 with sacreBLEU.[7]

We train the deep models with synchronous Adam on 8 NVIDIA Titan X Pascal GPUs with 12GB RAM for 7 epochs each. The back-translation model is trained with asynchronous Adam on 8 GPUs. We do not specify a batch size as Marian adjusts the batch based on available mem-

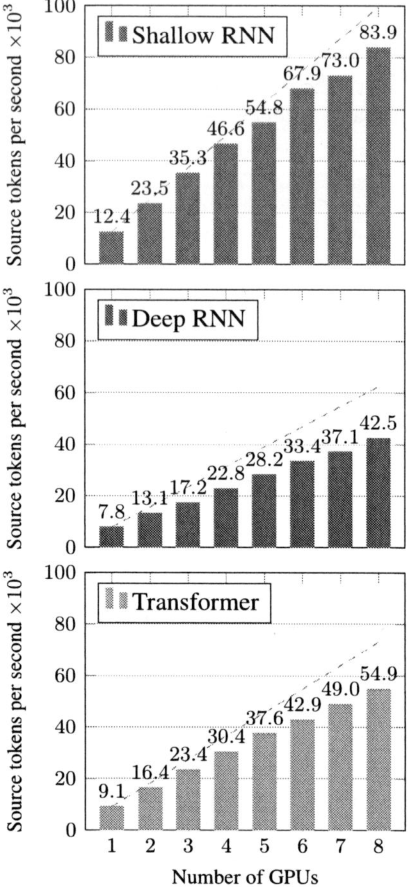

Figure 1: Training speed in thousands of source tokens per second for shallow RNN, deep RNN and Transformer model. Dashed line projects linear scale-up based on single-GPU performance.

ory to maximize speed and memory usage. This guarantees that a chosen memory budget will not be exceeded during training.

All models use tied embeddings between source, target and output embeddings (Press and Wolf, 2017). Contrary to Sennrich et al. (2017a) or Vaswani et al. (2017), we do not average checkpoints, but maintain a continuously updated exponentially averaged model over the entire training run. Following Vaswani et al. (2017), the learning rate is set to 0.0003 and decayed as the inverse square root of the number of updates after 16,000 updates. When training the transformer model, a linearly growing learning rate is used during the first 16,000 iterations, starting with 0 until the base learning rate is reached.

---

[4] Proprocessing was performed using scripts from Moses (Koehn et al., 2007).

[5] 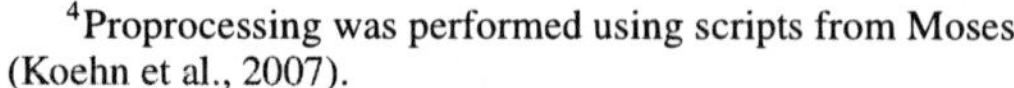https://github.com/rsennrich/subword-nmt

[6] R2L training, scoring or decoding does not require data processing, right-to-left inversion is built into Marian.

[7] https://github.com/mjpost/sacreBLEU

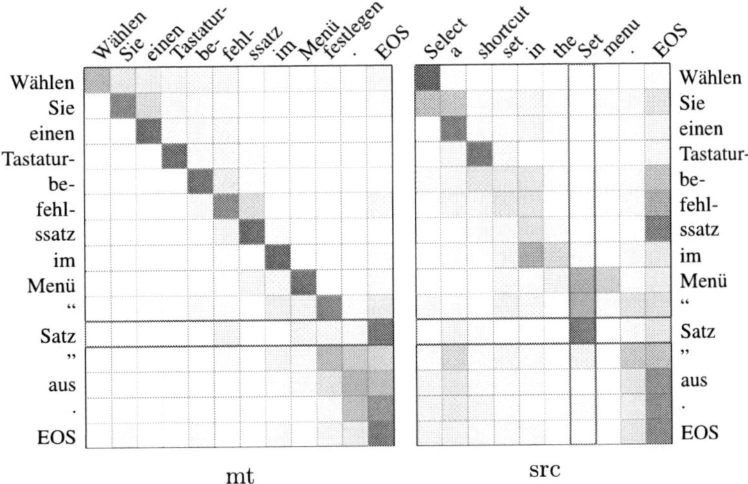

Figure 2: Example for error recovery based on dual attention. The missing word "Satz" could only be recovered based on the original source (marked in red) as it was dropped in the raw MT output.

Model	1	8	64
Shallow RNN	112.3	25.6	15.7
Deep Transition RNN	179.4	36.5	21.0
Transformer	362.7	98.5	71.3

Table 2: Translation time in seconds for newstest-2017 (3,004 sentences, 76,501 source BPE tokens) for different architectures and batch sizes.

3.1.4 Performance and Results

Quality. In terms of BLEU (Table 1), we match the original Nematus models from Sennrich et al. (2017a). Replacing the deep-transition RNN model with the transformer model results in a significant BLEU improvement of 1.2 BLEU on the WMT2017 test set.

Training speed. In Figure 1 we demonstrate the training speed as thousands of source tokens per second for the models trained in this recipe. All model types benefit from using more GPUs. Scaling is not linear (dashed lines), but close. The tokens-per-second rate (w/s) for Nematus on the same data on a single GPU is about 2800 w/s for the shallow model. Nematus does not have multi-GPU training. Marian achieves about 4 times faster training on a single GPU and about 30 times faster training on 8 GPUs for identical models.

Translation speed. The back-translation of 10M sentences with a shallow model takes about four hours on 8 GPUs at a speed of about 15,850 source tokens per second at a beam-size of 5 and a batch size of 64. Batches of sentences are translated in parallel on multiple GPUs.

In Table 2 we report the total number of seconds to translate newstest-2017 (3,004 sentences, 76,501 source BPE tokens) on a single GPU for different batch sizes. We omit model load time (usually below 10s). Beam size is 5.

3.2 State-of-the-art in Neural Automatic Post-Editing

In our submission to the Automatic Post-Editing shared task at WMT-2017 (Bojar et al., 2017b) and follow-up work (Junczys-Dowmunt and Grundkiewicz, 2017a,b), we explore multiple neural architectures adapted for the task of automatic post-editing of machine translation output as implementations in Marian. We focus on neural end-to-end models that combine both inputs mt (raw MT output) and src (source language input) in a single neural architecture, modeling $\{mt, src\} \rightarrow pe$ directly, where pe is post-edited corrected output.

These models are based on multi-source neural translation models introduced by Zoph and Knight (2016). Furthermore, we investigate the effect of hard-attention models or neural transductors (Aharoni and Goldberg, 2016) which seem to be well-suited for monolingual tasks, as well as combinations of both ideas. Dual-attention models that are combined with hard attention remain competitive despite applying fewer changes to the input.

The encoder-decoder framework described in section 2.2, allowed to integrate dual encoders and hard-attention without changes to beam-search or ensembling mechanisms. The dual-attention mechanism over two encoders allowed to recover missing words that would not be recognized based on raw MT output alone, see Figure 2.

Our final system for the APE shared task scored second-best according to automatic metrics and best based on human evaluation.

3.3 State-of-the-art in Neural Grammatical Error Correction

In Junczys-Dowmunt and Grundkiewicz (2018), we use Marian for research on transferring methods from low-resource NMT on the ground of automatic grammatical error correction (GEC). Previously, neural methods in GEC did not reach state-of-the-art results compared to phrase-based SMT baselines. We successfully adapt several low-resource MT methods for GEC.

We propose a set of model-independent methods for neural GEC that can be easily applied in most GEC settings. The combined effects of these methods result in better than state-of-the-art neural GEC models that outperform previously best neural GEC systems by more than 8% M^2 on the CoNLL-2014 benchmark and more than 4.5% on the JFLEG test set. Non-neural state-of-the-art systems are matched on the CoNLL-2014 benchmark and outperformed by 2% on JFLEG.

Figure 3 illustrates these results on the CoNLL-2014 test set. To produce this graph, 40 GEC models (four per entry) and 24 language models (one per GEC model with pre-training) have been trained. The language models follow the decoder architecture and can be used for transfer learning, weighted decode-time ensembling and re-ranking. This also includes a Transformer-style language model with self-attention layers.

Proposed methods include extensions to Marian, such as source-side noise, a GEC-specific weighted training-objective, usage of pre-trained embeddings, transfer learning with pre-trained language models, decode-time ensembling of independently trained GEC models and language models, and various deep architectures.

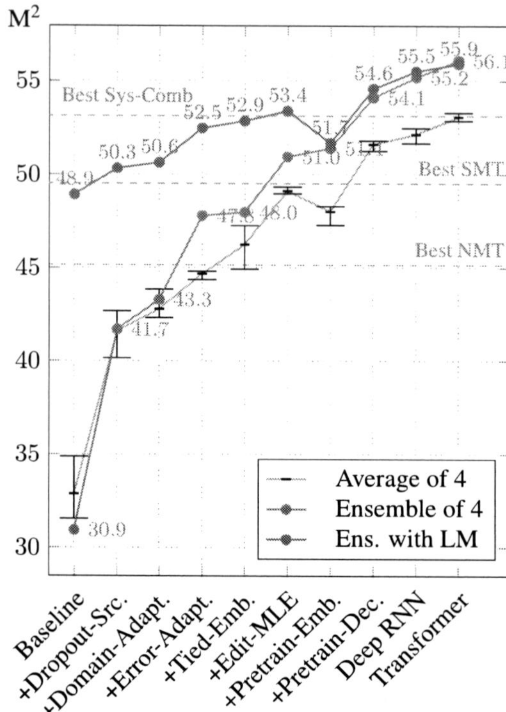

Figure 3: Comparison on the CoNLL-2014 test set for investigated methods.

4 Future Work and Conclusions

We introduced Marian, a self-contained neural machine translation toolkit written in C++ with focus on efficiency and research. Future work on Marian's back-end will look at faster CPU-bound computation, auto-batching mechanisms and automatic kernel fusion. On the front-end side we hope to keep up with future state-of-the-art models.

Acknowledgments

The development of Marian received funding from the European Union's Horizon 2020 Research and Innovation Programme under grant agreements 688139 (SUMMA; 2016-2019), 645487 (Modern MT; 2015-2017), 644333 (TraMOOC; 2015-2017), 644402 (HimL; 2015-2017), the Amazon Academic Research Awards program (to Marcin Junczys-Dowmunt and Adam Lopez), and the World Intellectual Property Organization. The CPU back-end was contributed by Intel under a partnership with the Alan Turing Institute.

This research is based upon work supported in part by the Office of the Director of National Intelligence (ODNI), Intelligence Advanced Research Projects Activity (IARPA), via contract #FA8650-17-C-9117. The views and conclusions contained herein are those of the authors and should not be interpreted as necessarily representing the official policies, either expressed or implied, of ODNI, IARPA, or the U.S. Government. The U.S. Government is authorized to reproduce and distribute reprints for governmental purposes notwithstanding any copyright annotation therein.

References

Roee Aharoni and Yoav Goldberg. 2016. Sequence to sequence transduction with hard monotonic attention. *arXiv preprint arXiv:1611.01487*.

Jimmy Lei Ba, Jamie Ryan Kiros, and Geoffrey E Hinton. 2016. Layer normalization. *arXiv preprint arXiv:1607.06450*.

Ondrej Bojar, Christian Buck, Rajen Chatterjee, Christian Federmann, Yvette Graham, Barry Haddow, Matthias Huck, Antonio Jimeno-Yepes, Philipp Koehn, and Julia Kreutzer, editors. 2017a. *Proc. of the 2nd Conference on Machine Translation, WMT 2017*. Association for Computational Linguistics.

Ondrej Bojar, Rajen Chatterjee, Christian Federmann, Yvette Graham, Barry Haddow, Shujian Huang, Matthias Huck, Philipp Koehn, Qun Liu, Varvara Logacheva, Christof Monz, Matteo Negri, Matt Post, Raphael Rubino, Lucia Specia, and Marco Turchi. 2017b. Findings of the 2017 Conference on Machine Translation (WMT17). In *Proceedings of the Second Conference on Machine Translation, Volume 2: Shared Task Papers*, pages 169–214, Copenhagen. Association for Computational Linguistics.

Yarin Gal and Zoubin Ghahramani. 2016. A theoretically grounded application of dropout in recurrent neural networks. In *Advances in neural information processing systems*, pages 1019–1027.

Marcin Junczys-Dowmunt and Roman Grundkiewicz. 2017a. The AMU-UEdin submission to the WMT 2017 shared task on automatic post-editing. In *Proceedings of the Second Conference on Machine Translation, Volume 2: Shared Task Papers*, pages 639–646, Copenhagen. Association for Computational Linguistics.

Marcin Junczys-Dowmunt and Roman Grundkiewicz. 2017b. An exploration of neural sequence-to-sequence architectures for automatic post-editing. In *Proceedings of the Eighth International Joint Conference on Natural Language Processing (Volume 1: Long Papers)*, pages 120–129. Asian Federation of Natural Language Processing.

Marcin Junczys-Dowmunt and Roman Grundkiewicz. 2018. Approaching neural grammatical error correction as a low-resource machine translation task. In *Proceedings of NAACL-HLT 2018*, New Orleans, USA. Association for Computational Linguistics. Accepted for publication.

Guillaume Klein, Yoon Kim, Yuntian Deng, Jean Senellart, and Alexander Rush. 2017. OpenNMT: Open-source toolkit for neural machine translation. In *Proceedings of ACL 2017, System Demonstrations*, pages 67–72.

Philipp Koehn, Hieu Hoang, Alexandra Birch, Chris Callison-Burch, Marcello Federico, Nicola Bertoldi, Brooke Cowan, Wade Shen, Christine Moran, Richard Zens, Chris Dyer, Ondrej Bojar, Alexandra Constantin, and Evan Herbst. 2007. Moses: Open source toolkit for statistical machine translation. In *ACL*. The Association for Computer Linguistics.

Graham Neubig, Chris Dyer, Yoav Goldberg, Austin Matthews, Waleed Ammar, Antonios Anastasopoulos, Miguel Ballesteros, David Chiang, Daniel Clothiaux, Trevor Cohn, Kevin Duh, Manaal Faruqui, Cynthia Gan, Dan Garrette, Yangfeng Ji, Lingpeng Kong, Adhiguna Kuncoro, Gaurav Kumar, Chaitanya Malaviya, Paul Michel, Yusuke Oda, Matthew Richardson, Naomi Saphra, Swabha Swayamdipta, and Pengcheng Yin. 2017. DyNet: the dynamic neural network toolkit. *arXiv preprint arXiv:1701.03980*.

Ofir Press and Lior Wolf. 2017. Using the output embedding to improve language models. In *Proceedings of the 15th Conference of the European Chapter of the Association for Computational Linguistics: Volume 2, Short Papers*, volume 2, pages 157–163.

Rico Sennrich, Alexandra Birch, Anna Currey, Ulrich Germann, Barry Haddow, Kenneth Heafield, Antonio Valerio Miceli Barone, and Philip Williams. 2017a. The University of Edinburgh's neural MT systems for WMT17. In (Bojar et al., 2017a), pages 389–399.

Rico Sennrich, Orhan Firat, Kyunghyun Cho, Alexandra Birch, Barry Haddow, Julian Hitschler, Marcin Junczys-Dowmunt, Samuel Läubli, Antonio Valerio Miceli Barone, Jozef Mokry, and Maria Nadejde. 2017b. Nematus: a toolkit for neural machine translation. In *Proceedings of the Software Demonstrations of the 15th Conference of the European Chapter of the Association for Computational Linguistics*, pages 65–68, Valencia, Spain. Association for Computational Linguistics.

Rico Sennrich, Barry Haddow, and Alexandra Birch. 2016. Neural machine translation of rare words with subword units. In *Proceedings of the 54th Annual Meeting of the Association for Computational Linguistics (Volume 1: Long Papers)*, pages 1715–1725, Berlin, Germany. Association for Computational Linguistics.

Ashish Vaswani, Noam Shazeer, Niki Parmar, Jakob Uszkoreit, Llion Jones, Aidan N Gomez, Ł ukasz Kaiser, and Illia Polosukhin. 2017. Attention is all you need. In I. Guyon, U. V. Luxburg, S. Bengio, H. Wallach, R. Fergus, S. Vishwanathan, and R. Garnett, editors, *Advances in Neural Information Processing Systems 30*, pages 5998–6008. Curran Associates, Inc.

Barret Zoph and Kevin Knight. 2016. Multi-source neural translation. In *Proceedings of the 2016 Conference of the North American Chapter of the Association for Computational Linguistics: Human Language Technologies*, pages 30–34, San Diego, California. Association for Computational Linguistics.

DeepPavlov: Open-Source Library for Dialogue Systems

Mikhail Burtsev, Alexander Seliverstov, Rafael Airapetyan, Mikhail Arkhipov,
Dilyara Baymurzina, Nickolay Bushkov, Olga Gureenkova, Taras Khakhulin,
Yuri Kuratov, Denis Kuznetsov, Alexey Litinsky, Varvara Logacheva,
Alexey Lymar, Valentin Malykh, Maxim Petrov, Vadim Polulyakh,
Leonid Pugachev, Alexey Sorokin, Maria Vikhreva, Marat Zaynutdinov

Moscow Institute of Physics and Technology /
9 Institutskiy per., Dolgoprudny, 141701, Russian Federation
`burtcev.ms@mipt.ru`

Abstract

Adoption of messaging communication and voice assistants has grown rapidly in the last years. This creates a demand for tools that speed up prototyping of feature-rich dialogue systems. An open-source library DeepPavlov is tailored for development of conversational agents. The library prioritises efficiency, modularity, and extensibility with the goal to make it easier to develop dialogue systems from scratch and with limited data available. It supports modular as well as end-to-end approaches to implementation of conversational agents. Conversational agent consists of skills and every skill can be decomposed into components. Components are usually models which solve typical NLP tasks such as intent classification, named entity recognition or pre-trained word vectors. Sequence-to-sequence chit-chat skill, question answering skill or task-oriented skill can be assembled from components provided in the library.

1 Introduction

Dialogue is the most natural way of interaction between humans. As many other human skills are already being mastered by machines, meaningful dialogue is still a grand challenge for artificial intelligence research. Conversational intelligence has multiple real-world applications. Dialogue systems can significantly ease mundane tasks in technical support, online shopping and consulting services.

However, at the moment the research and development in dialogue systems and chatbots are hampered by the scarcity of open-source baselines and impossibility to effectively reuse existing code in new solutions. Therefore, in order to improve upon state-of-the-art dialogue models one needs to implement such a system from scratch. This slows down the progress in the field. In order to overcome this limitation we create **DeepPavlov**[1] — an open-source library for fast development of dialogue systems. DeepPavlov is designed for:

- development of production-ready chatbots and complex conversational systems;
- research in dialogue systems and NLP in general.

Our goal is to enable AI application developers and researchers with:

- a set of pre-trained NLP models, pre-defined dialogue system components (ML/DL/Rule-based) and pipeline templates;
- a framework for implementing and testing their own dialogue models;
- tools for integration of applications with adjacent infrastructure (messengers, helpdesk software etc.);
- a benchmarking environment for conversational models and uniform access to relevant datasets.

The library has a wide range of state-of-the-art solutions for NLP tasks which are used in dialogue systems. These NLP functions address low-level tasks such as tokenisation and spell-checking as well as a more complex, e.g. recognition of user intents and entities. They are implemented as modules with unified structures and are easily combined into a pipeline. A user of library also has a set of pre-trained models for easy start. A

---

[1] `https://github.com/deepmipt/`
`DeepPavlov`

122

Proceedings of the 56th Annual Meeting of the Association for Computational Linguistics-System Demonstrations, pages 122–127
Melbourne, Australia, July 15 - 20, 2018. ©2018 Association for Computational Linguistics

model that suits user's task best can be adapted and fine-tuned to achieve required performance. Unlike many other frameworks, DeepPavlov allows combining trainable components with rule-based components and neural networks with non-neural ML methods. In addition to that, it allows end-to-end training for a pipeline of neural models.

The paper is organised as follows. In section 2 we review the existing NLP libraries and explain how they differ from our work. Section 3 describes architecture of DeepPavlov, and in section 4 we talk about features which are available for user of the library and ways of extending it. Section 5 presents some components of the library and benchmarks. Finally, in section 6 we conclude and outline directions for future work.

2   Related work

One of the closest analogues of DeepPavlov is **Rasa Stack** [2] tool. In terms of purpose it is similar to our library. It provides building blocks for creating dialogue agents: natural language understanding, dialogue state tracking and policy. Rasa's capabilities are mainly focused on task oriented dialogue, so unlike our library, it is not readily applicable for constructing agents with multiple skills including chit-chat. It is also important that Rasa Stack exports ML components from other libraries and DeepPavlov includes its' own models. That makes easier for developers to fit trainable parts of the system to the task at hand or add custom ML models. In addition to that, DeepPavlov is more general, and allows defining any NLP pipeline, not only the one related to task oriented dialogue.

Another framework for dialogue agents is **ParlAI** (Miller et al., 2017). ParlAI is in essence a collection of dialogue datasets and models. It defines standard interfaces for accessing the data, provides instruments for training models with any registered dataset and easy integration with Amazon Mechanical Turk. ParlAI does not have any restrictions on models which are implemented there. The only requirement is to support the standard interface. This enables efficient sharing, training and testing dialogue models. Alternatively, in DeepPavlov all agents, skills and models must have a standard structure to ensure reusability.

OpenDial[3] is a toolkit for developing spoken dialogue systems. It was designed to perform di-

	DeepPavlov	Rasa	ParlAI	spaCy	AllenNLP	Stanford NLP
Dialogue systems (DS) features						
Modular architecture of DS	X	X				
Framework for training and testing DS	X		X			
Collection of datasets and DSs			X			
Interactive data labeling and training		X		X		
Integration with messaging platforms	X		X			
Dialogue manager	X	X				
Slot filling	X	X				
NLP features						
Text pre-processing	X	X	X	X	X	X
Word embedding	X	X	X	X	X	X
Intent recognition	X	X		X		X
Entity recognition	X	X		X		X
POS tagging	X			X		X
Dependency parsing				X	X	X
Semantic role labelling					X	X
Sentence embedding			X		X	

Table 1: Comparison of DeepPavlov with other libraries and frameworks.

alogue management tasks, but then extended for building full-fledged dialogue systems, integrating speech recognition, language understanding, generation, speech synthesis, multimodal processing and situation awareness. OpenDial includes a number of advanced components but lacks recent deep learning models. Unfortunately ecosystem of deep learning models in Python is not easily accessible from OpenDial because it is Java-based.

AllenNLP (Gardner et al., 2017) is another example of a powerful NLP framework. It contains numerous solutions for NLP tasks, but does not include any dialogue models yet. Tailored for NLP research deep learning components of AllenNLP implemented in PyTorch (Paszke et al., 2017) library, which is more convenient for research, then for industrial applications. On the other hand, DeepPavlov by default uses TensorFlow[4] production grade machine learning framework. Another limitation of AllenNLP is the fact that it has only neural models, whereas in DeepPavlov it is possible to combine in a single pipeline heterogeneous components, such as rule-based modules, non-neural ML models and neural networks.

General NLP frameworks can be also used for development of dialogue systems, as they provide low-level operations such as tokenisation, lemmatisation, part-of-speech tagging and syntactic pars-

---

ing. The most notable examples of such frameworks are **Stanford CoreNLP** (Manning et al., 2014) and **spaCy**[5]. Both frameworks provide a set of pre-trained NLP models and functionality for training but have no specific tools and components related to the development of dialogue systems. Stanford tools are in Java, which complicates their integration with a trove of deep learning models in Python.

Table 1 gives comparison of DeepPavlov with other related frameworks.

3 Architecture

The high-level architecture of the library is shown in figure 1. It has several core concepts.

The smallest building block of the library is `Model`. `Model` stands for any kind of function in an NLP pipeline. It can be implemented as a neural network, a non-neural ML model or a rule-based system. Besides that, `Model` can have nested structure, i.e. a `Model` can include other `Model`(s). The library currently has models for intent classification, entity recognition, dialogue state tracking, spell-checking and ranking of texts by similarity.

Models can be joined into a `Skill`. `Skill` solves a larger NLP task compared to `Model`. However, in terms of implementation `Skills` are not different from `Models`. The only restriction for `Skills` is that their input and output should both be strings. Therefore, `Skills` are usually associated with dialogue tasks. There are currently three `Skills` implemented in the library, namely, modular and sequence-to-sequence goal-oriented skills as well as question answering module.

Finally, the core concept of the library is an `Agent`. `Agent` is supposed to be a multi-purpose dialogue system that comprises several `Skills` and can switch between them. It can be a dialogue system that contains a goal-oriented and chatbot skills and chooses which one to use for generating the answer depending on user input.

The choice of `Skill` relevant to the current dialogue state is managed by a `Skills Manager`. This is similar to architecture of Microsoft Cortana (Sarikaya et al., 2016) where *Experience providers* correspond to `Skills`, and selection between them is conducted by a separate module based on context and providers' responses. Systems with multiple skills and their

dynamic selection are state of the art in development of dialogue agents, but there is currently no available implementations of such technique.

`Models` are joined in a `Skill` via `Chainer`. `Chainer` takes configuration file in JSON format and sets parameters of `Models` and the order of their execution. Joining heterogeneous models is a striking feature of DeepPavlov library which distinguishes it from other frameworks. Unlike AllenNLP or Tensor2Tensor where all adjacent models need to be neural, in DeepPavlov the pipeline can include neural networks, other ML models, and rule-based models.

4 Usage

The DeepPavlov library is implemented in Python 3.6 and uses `Keras` and `TensorFlow` frameworks. It is open-source and available on GitHub under Apache 2.0 license.

A typical use scenario is the following. A developer takes a pre-build agent, for example, a modular task-oriented bot, and adapts it to the target task. Alternatively, an agent can be built from scratch. In this case skills or models are selected from available `Skills` and `Models`, or created by developer. The models which are included into the agent are trained according to a pipeline defined in a JSON file. DeepPavlov has a collection of pre-trained models, so training is not needed in many cases.

4.1 Training

DeepPavlov supports **end-to-end training**. `Models` implemented on top of `TensorFlow` can be stacked and trained jointly. This feature is sought after in many NLP tasks, in particular in goal-oriented dialogue systems. Usually task-oriented modular systems consist of independently trained building blocks, such as, natural language understanding module, user intent classification module, dialogue policy manager, etc. (Chen et al., 2017). There exist efforts of training such systems in the end-to-end mode (Li et al., 2018). However, such works are difficult to replicate and build upon because of lack of open implementations of end-to-end training. To the best of our knowledge, DeepPavlov is the only NLP framework which allows easy and configurable end-to-end training of dialogue agents created from interchangeable functional neural network blocks.

---

[5]https://spacy.io/

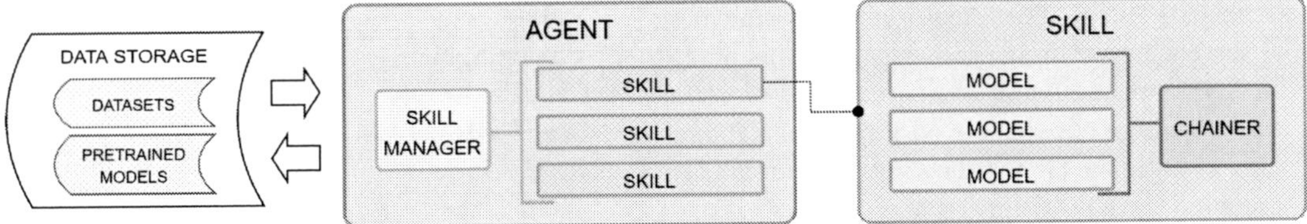

Figure 1: Conceptual architecture of DeepPavlov library.

4.2 Extension of the library

User can easily extend DeepPavlov library by registering a new `Model` or `Skill`. In order to include a new `Model`, a developer should implement a number of standard classes which are used to communicate with the environment:

- **dataset reader** — reads data and returns it in a specified format,
- **dataset iterator** — partitions data into training, validation and test sets, divides the data into batches,
- **vocabulary** — performs data indexing, e.g. converts words into indexes,
- **model** — performs training.

The library contains base classes which implement these functions (`DatasetReader`, `DatasetIterator`, `Vocab` classes). Developers can use them or write their own classes inherited from these base classes. Class for a model can be inherited from an abstract class `NNModel` if it is a neural network, or from a class `Estimator` if it is a non-neural ML model. In addition to that, a user should define a pipeline for the model.

5 Implemented Models and Skills

The library is currently being actively developed with a large set of `Models` and `Skills` already implemented. Some of them are available for interactive online testing.[6]

Skill: Goal-Oriented Dialogue System. The skill implements Hybrid Code Networks (HCNs) described in (Williams et al., 2017). It allows predicting responses in goal-oriented dialogue. The model is configurable: embeddings, slot filling component and intent classifier can be switched on and off on demand. Table 2 shows the performance of our goal-oriented bot on DSTC2 dataset (Henderson et al., 2014). The results demonstrate that our system is close to the state-of-the-art performance.

Model	Test accuracy
Bordes and Weston (2016)	41.1%
Perez and Liu (2016)	48.7%
Eric and Manning (2017)	48.0%
Williams et al. (2017)	55.6%
Deeppavlov[*]	55.0%

Table 2: Accuracy of predicting bot answers on DSTC2 dataset. *Figures cannot be compared directly, because DeepPavlov model used a different train/test data partition of the dataset.

Model: Entity Recognition. This model is based on BiLSTM-CRF architecture described in (Anh et al., 2017). It is also used for the slot-filling component of the library. Here fuzzy Levenshtein search is used on the recognition results, since the incoming utterances could be noisy. In addition to that, we provide pre-trained NER models for Russian and English. The performance of entity recognition on OntoNotes 5.0 dataset[7] is given in table 3. It shows that our implementation is on par with best-performing models.

Model	F_1-score
DeepPavlov	**87.07** $\pm$ 0.21
Strubell at al. (2017)	86.84 $\pm$ 0.19
Spacy	85.85
Chiu and Nichols (2015)	86.19 $\pm$ 0.25
Durrett and Klein (2014)	84.04

Table 3: Performance of DeepPavlov NER module on OntoNotes 5.0 dataset. Average F_1-score for 18 classes.

Model: Intent Classification. The model implements neural network architecture based on shallow-and-wide Convolutional Neural Network

---

[6]http://demo.ipavlov.ai

[7]https://catalog.ldc.upenn.edu/ldc2013t19

(Kim, 2014) and allows multi-label classification of sentences. We do benchmarking for this model on SNIPS dataset[8] and compare its performance with a number of available NLP services. The results given in the table 4 show that our intent classification model is comparable with other existing solutions.

Model	F_1-score
DeepPavlov	**99.10**
api.ai	98.68
IBM Watson	98.63
Microsoft LUIS	98.53
Wit.ai	97.97
Snips.ai	97.87
Recast.ai	97.64
Amazon Lex	97.59

Table 4: Performance of DeepPavlov intent recognition on SNIPS dataset. Average F_1-score for 7 categories. All scores except DeepPavlov are from Inten.to study[10].

Model: Spelling Correction. The component is based on work (Brill and Moore, 2000) and uses statistics-based error model, a static dictionary and an ARPA language model (Paul and Baker, 1992) to correct spelling errors. We tested it on the dataset released for SpellRuEval[11] — a competition on spelling correction for Russian. In table 5 we compare its performance with Yandex.Speller[12] service and open-source spell-checker GNU Aspell[13]. Our model is worse than Yandex.Speller, but it is better then Aspell which is the only freely available spelling correction tool. Even our baseline model outperforms Aspell by large margin, and use of a language model further boosts its performance.

Other Models. The library also contains a sequence-to-sequence goal-oriented bot, and a model for ranking texts by similarity. There are also models which are currently being developed and prepared for publication.

Method	Precision	Recall	F-score
Yandex.Speller	83.09	59.86	69.59
DeepPavlov	41.42	37.21	39.20
DeepPavlov + LM	51.92	53.94	52.91
GNU Aspell	27.85	34.07	30.65

Table 5: Performance of DeepPavlov spell-checker for Russian.

6 Conclusion

DeepPavlov is an open-source library for developing dialogue agents in Python. It allows assembling a dialogue system from building blocks that implement models for required NLP functionality. These blocks can be recombined and reused in agents for different dialogue tasks. Such modularity opens possibilities for fast prototyping and knowledge transfer. The library supports creation of multi-purpose agents with diverse `Skills`. This is important for real life application scenarios because skills can be added, upgraded or removed independently when a dialogue system is already deployed. New products and conversational solutions can utilise existing skills for faster development. The library currently contains a range of `Models` for solving various NLP tasks, as well as three `Skills`: two goal-oriented and a question-answering one. The library can be easily extended with new `Models` and `Skills`.

DeepPavlov is now being actively developed, and there are many directions for future work. Implementation of models for `Skill Manager` to enable developers assemble full-fledged dialogue agents with a possibility to switch between multiple `Skills` is one of the priorities. Other changes are in progress to improve the usability of the library. Users will be able to define the pipeline directly in the code bypassing a JSON config file. Furthermore, data loading and reading will be simplified, i.e. the majority of datasets will be loaded by a universal data reader.

Finally, we are working on publishing pre-trained models for Russian. This often involves not only training of a model on a Russian dataset, but sometimes changing the model itself.

We recognise that collaboration is an essential part of any scientific, technological and open-source project. DeepPavlov is open to comments, bug reports, feature requests and contributions to our GitHub repo.

---

[8]`https://github.com/snipsco/`
`nlu-benchmark/tree/master/`
`2017-06-custom-intent-engines/`
[11]`http://www.dialog-21.ru/en/`
`evaluation/2016/spelling_correction/`
[12]`https://tech.yandex.ru/speller/`
[13]`http://aspell.net/`

Acknowledgements

The work was supported by National Technology Initiative and PAO Sberbank project ID 0000000007417F630002.

References

Le Tanh Anh, Mikhail Y Arkhipov, and Mikhail S Burtsev. 2017. Application of a hybrid bi-lstm-crf model to the task of russian named entity recognition. *arXiv preprint arXiv:1709.09686* .

Antoine Bordes and Jason Weston. 2016. Learning end-to-end goal-oriented dialog. *CoRR* abs/1605.07683. http://arxiv.org/abs/1605.07683.

Eric Brill and Robert C Moore. 2000. An improved error model for noisy channel spelling correction. In *Proceedings of the 38th Annual Meeting on Association for Computational Linguistics*. Association for Computational Linguistics, pages 286–293.

Hongshen Chen, Xiaorui Liu, Dawei Yin, and Jiliang Tang. 2017. A survey on dialogue systems: Recent advances and new frontiers. *CoRR* abs/1711.01731. http://arxiv.org/abs/1711.01731.

Jason PC Chiu and Eric Nichols. 2015. Named entity recognition with bidirectional lstm-cnns. *arXiv preprint arXiv:1511.08308* .

Greg Durrett and Dan Klein. 2014. A joint model for entity analysis: Coreference, typing, and linking. *Transactions of the Association for Computational Linguistics* 2:477–490.

Mihail Eric and Christopher D. Manning. 2017. A copy-augmented sequence-to-sequence architecture gives good performance on task-oriented dialogue. *CoRR* abs/1701.04024. http://arxiv.org/abs/1701.04024.

M. Gardner, J Grus, M Neumann, O. Tafjord, P. Dasigi, N. Liu, M Peters, M. Schmitz, and L. Zettlemoyer. 2017. Allennlp: A deep semantic natural language processing platform Accessed: 2018-03-23.

Matthew Henderson, Blaise Thomson, and Jason D. Williams. 2014. The second dialog state tracking challenge. In *SIGDIAL Conference*.

Yoon Kim. 2014. Convolutional neural networks for sentence classification. *arXiv preprint arXiv:1408.5882* .

Lihong Li, Bhuwan Dhingra, Jianfeng Gao, Xiujun Li, Yun-Nung Chen, Li Deng, and Faisal Ahmed. 2018. End-to-end learning of dialogue agents for information access.

Christopher D. Manning, Mihai Surdeanu, John Bauer, Jenny Finkel, Steven J. Bethard, and David McClosky. 2014. The Stanford CoreNLP natural language processing toolkit. In *Association for Computational Linguistics (ACL) System Demonstrations*. pages 55–60. http://www.aclweb.org/anthology/P/P14/P14-5010.

A. H. Miller, W. Feng, A. Fisch, J. Lu, D. Batra, A. Bordes, D. Parikh, and J. Weston. 2017. Parlai: A dialog research software platform. *arXiv preprint arXiv:1705.06476* .

Adam Paszke, Sam Gross, Soumith Chintala, Gregory Chanan, Edward Yang, Zachary DeVito, Zeming Lin, Alban Desmaison, Luca Antiga, and Adam Lerer. 2017. Automatic differentiation in pytorch .

Douglas B Paul and Janet M Baker. 1992. The design for the wall street journal-based csr corpus. In *Proceedings of the workshop on Speech and Natural Language*. Association for Computational Linguistics, pages 357–362.

Julien Perez and Fei Liu. 2016. Gated end-to-end memory networks. *CoRR* abs/1610.04211. http://arxiv.org/abs/1610.04211.

R. Sarikaya, P. A. Crook, A. Marin, M. Jeong, J.P. Robichaud, A. Celikyilmaz, Y.B. Kim, A. Rochette, O. Z. Khan, X. Liu, D. Boies, T. Anastasakos, Z. Ramesh N. Feizollahi, H. Suzuki, R. Holenstein, and E. Radostev V. Krawczyk. 2016. An overview of end-to-end language understanding and dialog management for personal digital assistants. In *IEEE Workshop on Spoken Language Technology*.

Emma Strubell, Patrick Verga, David Belanger, and Andrew McCallum. 2017. Fast and accurate entity recognition with iterated dilated convolutions. In *Proceedings of the 2017 Conference on Empirical Methods in Natural Language Processing*. pages 2670–2680.

Jason D Williams, Kavosh Asadi, and Geoffrey Zweig. 2017. Hybrid code networks: practical and efficient end-to-end dialog control with supervised and reinforcement learning. *arXiv preprint arXiv:1702.03274* .

RETURNN as a Generic Flexible Neural Toolkit with Application to Translation and Speech Recognition

Albert Zeyer[1,2,3]**, Tamer Alkhouli**[1,2] **and Hermann Ney**[1,2]
[1]Human Language Technology and Pattern Recognition Group
RWTH Aachen University, Aachen, Germany,
[2]AppTek, USA, `http://www.apptek.com/`,
[3]NNAISENSE, Switzerland, `https://nnaisense.com/`
`surname@cs.rwth-aachen.de`

Abstract

We compare the fast training and decoding speed of RETURNN of attention models for translation, due to fast CUDA LSTM kernels, and a fast pure TensorFlow beam search decoder. We show that a layer-wise pretraining scheme for recurrent attention models gives over 1% BLEU improvement absolute and it allows to train deeper recurrent encoder networks. Promising preliminary results on max. expected BLEU training are presented. We obtain state-of-the-art models trained on the WMT 2017 German↔English translation task. We also present end-to-end model results for speech recognition on the Switchboard task. The flexibility of RETURNN allows a fast research feedback loop to experiment with alternative architectures, and its generality allows to use it on a wide range of applications.

1 Introduction

RETURNN, the RWTH extensible training framework for universal recurrent neural networks, was introduced in (Doetsch et al., 2017). The source code is fully open[1]. It can use Theano (Theano Development Team, 2016) or TensorFlow (TensorFlow Development Team, 2015) for its computation. Since it was introduced, it got extended by comprehensive TensorFlow support. A generic recurrent layer allows for a wide range of encoder-decoder-attention or other recurrent structures. An automatic optimization logic can optimize the computation graph depending on training, scheduled sampling, sequence training, or beam search decoding. The automatic optimization together with our fast native CUDA implemented LSTM kernels allows for very fast train-

ing and decoding. We will show in speed comparisons with Sockeye (Hieber et al., 2017) that we are at least as fast or usually faster in both training and decoding. Additionally, we show in experiments that we can train very competitive models for machine translation and speech recognition. This flexibility together with the speed is the biggest strength of RETURNN.

Our focus will be on recurrent attention models. We introduce a layer-wise pretraining scheme for attention models and show its significant effect on deep recurrent encoder models. We show promising preliminary results on expected maximum BLEU training. The configuration files of all the experiments are publicly available[2].

2 Related work

Multiple frameworks exist for training attention models, most of which are focused on machine translation.

- Sockeye (Hieber et al., 2017) is a generic framework based on MXNet (Chen et al., 2015) which is most compareable to RETURNN as it is generic although we argue that RETURNN is more flexible and faster.

- OpenNMT (Levin et al., 2017a,b) based on Lua (Ierusalimschy et al., 2006) which is discontinued in development. Separate PyTorch (PyTorch Development Team, 2018) and TensorFlow implementation exists, which are more recent. We will demonstrate that RETURNN is more flexible.

- Nematus (Sennrich et al., 2017) is based on Theano (Theano Development Team, 2016) which is going to be discontinued in development. We show that RETURNN is much faster in both training and decoding as can be concluded from our speed comparison to

---

[1]`https://github.com/rwth-i6/returnn`

[2]`https://github.com/rwth-i6/returnn-experiments/tree/master/2018-attention`

Proceedings of the 56th Annual Meeting of the Association for Computational Linguistics-System Demonstrations, pages 128–133
Melbourne, Australia, July 15 - 20, 2018. ©2018 Association for Computational Linguistics

Sockeye and the comparisons performed by the Sockeye authors (Hieber et al., 2017).

- Marian (Junczys-Dowmunt et al., 2016) is implemented directly in C++ for performance reasons. Again by our speed comparisons and the comparisons performed by the Sockeye authors (Hieber et al., 2017), one can conclude that RETURNN is very competitive in terms of speed, but is much more flexible.
- NeuralMonkey (Helcl and Libovický, 2017) is based on TensorFlow (TensorFlow Development Team, 2015). This framework is not as flexible as RETURNN. Also here we can conclude just as before that RETURNN is much faster in both training and decoding.
- Tensor2Tensor (Vaswani et al., 2018) is based on TensorFlow (TensorFlow Development Team, 2015). It comes with the reference implementation of the Transformer model (Vaswani et al., 2017), however, it lacks support for recurrent decoder models and overall is way less flexible than RETURNN.

3 Speed comparison

Various improved and fast CUDA LSTM kernels are available for the TensorFlow backend in RETURNN. A comparison of the speed of its own LSTM kernel vs. other TensorFlow LSTM kernels can be found on the website[3]. In addition, an automatic optimization path which moves out computation of the recurrent loop as much as possible improves the performance.

We want to compare different toolkits in training and decoding for a recurrent attention model in terms of speed on a GPU. Here, we try to maximize the batch size such that it still fits into the GPU memory of our reference GPU card, the Nvidia GTX 1080 Ti with 11 GB of memory. We keep the maximum sequence length in a batch the same, which is 60 words. We always use Adam (Kingma and Ba, 2014) for training. In Table 1, we see that RETURNN is the fastest, and also is most efficient in its memory consumption (implied by the larger batches). For these speed experiments, we did not tune any of the hyper parameters of RETURNN which explains its worse performance. The aim here is to match Sockeye's exact architecture for speed and memory comparison. During training, we observed that the learning rate scheduling settings of Sockeye are

---

[3] http://returnn.readthedocs.io/en/latest/tf_lstm_benchmark.html

toolkit	encoder n. layers	time [h]	batch size	BLEU [%] 2015	2017
RETURNN	4	**11.25**	8500	28.0	28.4
Sockeye		11.45	3000	**28.9**	**29.2**
RETURNN	6	**12.87**	7500	28.7	28.7
Sockeye		14.76	2500	**29.4**	**29.1**

Table 1: Training speed and memory consumption on WMT 2017 German→English. Train time is for seeing the full train dataset once. Batch size is in words, such that it almost maximizes the GPU memory consumption. The BLEU score is for the converged models, reported for newstest2015 (dev) and newstest2017. The encoder has one bidirectional LSTM layer and either 3 or 5 unidirectional LSTM layers.

more pessimistic, i.e. the decrease is slower and it sees the data more often until convergence. This greatly increases the total training time but in our experience also improves the model.

For decoding, we extend RETURNN with a fast pure TensorFlow beam search decoder, which supports batch decoding and can run on the GPU. A speed and memory consumption comparison is shown in Table 2. We see that RETURNN is the fastest. We report results for the batch size that yields the best speed. The slow speed of Sockeye is due to frequent cross-device communication.

toolkit	encoder n. layers	batch size [seqs]	time [secs] 2015	2017
RETURNN	4	50	**54**	**71**
Sockeye		5	398	581
RETURNN	6	50	**56**	**70**
Sockeye		5	403	585

Table 2: Decoding speed and memory consumption on WMT 2017 German→English. Time is for decoding the whole dataset, reported for newstest2015 (dev) and newstest2017, with beam size 12. Batch size is the number of sequences, such that it optimizes the decoding speed. This does not mean that it uses the whole GPU memory. These are the same models as in Table 1.

4 Performance comparison

We want to study what possible performance we can get with each framework on a specific task. We restrict this comparison here to recurrent attention models.

The first task is the WMT 2017 German to English translation task. We use the same 20K byte-pair encoding subword units in all toolkits (Sennrich et al., 2015). We also use Adam (Kingma and Ba, 2014) in all cases. The learning rate scheduling is also similar. In RETURNN, we use a 6 layer bidirectional encoder, trained with pre-training and label smoothing. It has bidirectional LSTMs in every layer of the encoder, unlike Sockeye, which only has the first layer bidirectional. We use a variant of attention weight / fertility feedback (Tu et al., 2016), which is inverse in our case, to use a multiplication instead of a division, for better numerical stability. Our model was derived from the model presented by (Bahar et al., 2017; Peter et al., 2017) and (Bahdanau et al., 2014).

We report the best performing Sockeye model we trained, which has 1 bidirectional and 3 unidirectional encoder layers, 1 pre-attention target recurrent layer, and 1 post-attention decoder layer. We trained with a max sequence length of 75, and used the 'coverage' RNN attention type. For Sockeye, the final model is an average of the 4 best runs according to the development perplexity. The results are collected in Table 3. We obtain the best results with Sockeye using a Transformer network model (Vaswani et al., 2017), where we achieve 32.0% BLEU on newstest2017. So far, RETURNN does not support this architecture; see Section 7 for details.

toolkit	BLEU [%]	
	2015	2017
RETURNN	**31.2**	**31.3**
Sockeye	29.7	30.2

Table 3: Comparison on German→English.

We compare RETURNN to other toolkits on the WMT 2017 English→German translation task in Table 4. We observe that our toolkit outperforms all other toolkits. The best result obtained by other toolkits is using Marian (25.5% BLEU). In comparison, RETURNN achieves 26.1%. We also compare RETURNN to the best performing single systems of WMT 2017. In comparison to the fine-tuned evaluation systems that also include back-translated data, our model performs worse by only 0.3 to 0.9 BLEU. We did not run experiments with back-translated data, which can potentially boost the performance by several BLEU points.

We also have preliminary results with recurrent attention models for speech recognition on the Switchboard task, which we trained on the 300h trainset. We report on both the Switchboard (SWB) and the CallHome (CH) part of Hub5'00 and Hub5'01. We also compare to a conventional frame-wise trained hybrid deep bidirec-

System	BLEU [%]
	newstest2017
RETURNN	**26.1**
OpenNMT-py	21.8
OpenNMT-lua	22.6
Marian	25.6
Nematus	23.5
Sockeye	25.3
WMT 2017 Single Systems + bt data	
LMU	26.4
+ reranking	27.0
Systran	26.5
Edinburgh	26.5

Table 4: Performance comparison on WMT 2017 English→German. The baseline systems (upper half) are trained on the parallel data of the WMT Enlgish→German 2017 task. We downloaded the hypotheses from here.[4] The WMT 2017 system hypotheses (lower half) are generated using systems having additional back- translation (bt) data. These hypotheses are downloaded from here.[5]

tional LSTM with 6 layers (Zeyer et al., 2017b), and a generalized full-sum sequence trained hybrid deep bidirectional LSTM with 5 layers (Zeyer et al., 2017a). The frame-wise trained hybrid model also uses focal loss (Lin et al., 2017). All the hybrid models use a phonetic lexicon and an external 4-gram language model which was trained on the transcripts of both the Switchboard and the Fisher corpus. The attention model does not use any external language model nor a phonetic lexicon. Its output labels are byte-pair encoded subword units (Sennrich et al., 2015). It has a 6 layer bidirectional encoder, which also applies max-pooling in the time dimension, i.e. it reduces the input sequence by factor 8. Pretraining as explained in Section 6 was applied. To our knowledge, this is the best reported result for an end-to-end system on Switchboard 300h without using a language model or the lexicon. For comparison, we also selected comparable results from the literature. From these, the Baidu DeepSpeech CTC model is modeled on characters and does not use the lexicon but it does use a language model. The results are collected in Table 5.

5 Maximum expected BLEU training

We implement expected risk minimization, i.e. expected BLEU maximization or expected WER

---

[4] https://github.com/awslabs/sockeye/tree/arxiv_1217/arxiv/output/rnn
[5] http://matrix.statmt.org/

model	training	WER [%]			
		Hub5'00			Hub5'01
		Σ	SWB	CH	
hybrid[1]	frame-wise		11.2		
hybrid[2]	LF-MMI	15.8	10.8		
CTC[3]	CTC	25.9	20.0	31.8	
hybrid	frame-wise	**14.4**	**9.8**	**19.0**	14.7
	full-sum	15.9	10.1	21.8	**14.5**
attention	frame-wise	20.3	13.5	27.1	19.9

Table 5: Performance comparison on Switchboard, trained on 300h. hybrid[1] is the IBM 2017 ResNet model (Saon et al., 2017). hybrid[2] trained with Lattice-free MMI (Hadian et al., 2018). CTC[3] is the Baidu 2014 DeepSpeech model (Hannun et al., 2014). Our attention model does not use any language model.

minimization, following (Prabhavalkar et al., 2017; Edunov et al., 2017). The results are still preliminary but promising. We do the approximation by beam search with beam size 4. For a 4 layer encoder network model, with forced alignment cross entropy training, we get 30.3% BLEU, and when we use maximum expected BLEU training, we get 31.1% BLEU.

6 Pretraining

RETURNN supports very generic and flexible pretraining which iteratively starts with a small model and adds new layers in the process. A similar pretraining scheme for deep bidirectional LSTMs acoustic speech models was presented earlier (Zeyer et al., 2017b). Here, we only study a layer-wise construction of the deep bidirectional LSTM encoder network of an encoder-decoder-attention model for translation on the WMT 2017 German→English task. Experimental results are presented in Table 6. The observations very clearly match our expectations, that we can both greatly improve the overall performance, and we are able to train deeper models. A minor benefit is faster training speed of the initial pretrain epochs.

encoder	BLEU [%]	
num. layers	no pretrain	with pretrain
2	29.3	-
3	29.9	-
4	29.1	30.3
5	-	30.3
6	-	30.6
7	-	**30.9**

Table 6: Pretraining comparison.

In preliminary recurrent attention experiments for speech recognition, pretraining seems very essential to get good performance.

Also, we use in all cases a learning rate scheduling scheme, which lowers the learning rate if the cross validation score does not improve enough. Without pretraining and a 2 layer encoder in the same setting as above, with a fixed learning rate, we get 28.4% BLEU, where-as with learning rate scheduling, we get 29.3% BLEU.

7 RETURNN features

Besides the fast speed, and the many features such as pretraining, scheduled sampling (Bengio et al., 2015), label smoothing (Szegedy et al., 2016), and the ability to train state-of-the-art models, one of the greatest strengths of RETURNN is its flexibility. The definition of the recurrent dependencies and the whole model architecture are provided in a very explicit way via a config file. Thus, e.g. trying out a new kind of attention scheme, adding a new latent variable to the search space, or drastically changing the whole architecture, is all supported already and does not need any more implementation in RETURNN. All that can be expressed by the neural network definition in the config. A (simplified) example of a network definition is given in Listing 1.

Each layer in this definition does some computation, specified via the `class` attribute, and gets its input from other layers via the `from` attribute, or from the input data, in case of layer `src`. The `output` layer defines a whole subnetwork, which can make use of recurrent dependencies via a `prev:` prefix. Depending on whether training or decoding is done, the `choice` layer class would return the true labels or the predicted labels. In case of scheduled sampling or max BLEU training, we can also use the predicted label during training. Depending on this configuration, during compilation of the computation graph, RETURNN figures out that certain calculations can be moved out of the recurrent loop. This automatic optimization also adds to the speedup. This flexibility and ease of trying out new architectures and models allow for a very efficient development / research feedback loop. Fast, consistent and robust feedback greatly helps the productivity and quality. This is very different to other toolkits which only support a predefined set of architectures.

To summarize the features of RETURNN:
- flexibility (see above),
- generality, wide range of models and appli-

```
network = {
# recurrent bidirectional encoder:
"src": {"class": "linear", "n_out": 620}, # embedding
"enc0_fw": {"class": "rec", "unit": "nativelstm2", "n_out": 1000, "direction": 1, "from": ["src"]},
"enc0_bw": {"class": "rec", "unit": "nativelstm2", "n_out": 1000, "direction": -1, "from": ["src"]},
# ... more encoder LSTM layers

"encoder": {"class": "copy", "from": ["enc5_fw", "enc5_bw"]},
"enc_ctx": {"class": "linear", "from": ["encoder"], "n_out": 1000},

# recurrent decoder:
"output": {"class": "rec", "from": [], "unit": {
  "output": {"class": "choice", "from": ["output_prob"]},
  "trg": {"class": "linear", "from": ["output"], "n_out": 620, "initial_output": 0},
  "weight_feedback": {"class": "linear", "from": ["prev:accum_a"], "n_out": 1000},
  "s_tr": {"class": "linear", "from": ["s"], "n_out": 1000},
  "e_in": {"class": "combine", "kind": "add", "from": ["base:enc_ctx", "weight_feedback", "s_tr"]},
  "e_tanh": {"class": "activation", "activation": "tanh", "from": ["e_in"]},
  "e": {"class": "linear", "from": ["e_tanh"], "n_out": 1},
  "a": {"class": "softmax_over_spatial", "from": ["e"]},
  "accum_a": {"class": "combine", "kind": "add", "from": ["prev:accum_a", "a"]},
  "att": {"class": "generic_attention", "weights": "a", "base": "base:encoder"},
  "s": {"class": "rnn_cell", "unit": "LSTMBlock", "from": ["prev:trg", "prev:att"], "n_out": 1000},
  "readout": {"class": "linear", "activation": "relu", "from": ["s", "prev:trg", "att"], "n_out": 1000},
  "output_prob": {"class": "softmax", "from": ["readout"], "dropout": 0.3, "loss": "ce",
                  "loss_opts": {"label_smoothing": 0.1}}
}},
"decision": {"class": "decide", "from": ["output"], "loss": "bleu"}
}
```

Listing 1: RETURNN config example for an attention model

cations, such as hybrid acoustic speech models, language models and attention models for translation and speech recognition,

- fast CUDA LSTM kernels,
- attention models, generic recurrent layer, fast beam search decoder,
- sequence training (min WER, max BLEU),
- label smoothing, scheduled sampling,
- TensorFlow backend and the old Theano backend, which has a separate fast attention implementation (Doetsch et al., 2016), fast CUDA MDLSTM kernels (Voigtlaender et al., 2016), as well as fast sequence training (Zeyer et al., 2017c).

One feature which is currently work-in-progress is the support for self-attention in the recurrent layer. The reason this needs some more work is because we currently only support access to the previous time step (`prev:`) but not to the whole past, which is needed for self-attention. That is why we did not present any Transformer (Vaswani et al., 2017) comparisons yet.

8 Conclusion

We have demonstrated many promising features of RETURNN and presented state-of-the-art systems in translation and speech recognition. We argue that it is a convenient testbed for research and applications. We introduced pretraining for recurrent attention models and showed its advantages while not having any disadvantages. Maximum expected BLEU training seems to be promising.

Acknowledgments

This research has received funding from the European Research Council (ERC) (under the European Union's Horizon 2020 research and innovation programme, grant agreement No 694537, project "SEQCLAS") and the Deutsche Forschungsgemeinschaft (DFG; grant agreement NE 572/8-1, project "CoreTec"). Tamer Alkhouli was partly funded by the 2016 Google PhD fellowship for North America, Europe and the Middle East. The work reflects only the authors' views and none of the funding parties is responsible for any use that may be made of the information it contains.

References

Parnia Bahar, Jan Rosendahl, Nick Rossenbach, and Hermann Ney. 2017. The RWTH Aachen machine translation systems for IWSLT 2017. In *IWSLT*, pages 29–34, Tokyo, Japan.

Dzmitry Bahdanau, Kyunghyun Cho, and Yoshua Bengio. 2014. Neural machine translation by jointly learning to align and translate. *arXiv preprint arXiv:1409.0473*.

Samy Bengio, Oriol Vinyals, Navdeep Jaitly, and Noam Shazeer. 2015. Scheduled sampling for sequence prediction with recurrent neural networks. In *NIPS*, pages 1171–1179.

Tianqi Chen, Mu Li, Yutian Li, Min Lin, Naiyan Wang, Minjie Wang, Tianjun Xiao, Bing Xu, Chiyuan Zhang, and Zheng Zhang. 2015. Mxnet: A flexible and efficient machine learning library for heterogeneous distributed systems. *arXiv preprint arXiv:1512.01274*.

Patrick Doetsch, Albert Zeyer, and Hermann Ney. 2016. Bidirectional decoder networks for attention-based end-to-end offline handwriting recognition. In *ICFHR*, pages 361–366, Shenzhen, China.

Patrick Doetsch, Albert Zeyer, Paul Voigtlaender, Ilia Kulikov, Ralf Schlüter, and Hermann Ney. 2017. RE-TURNN: the RWTH extensible training framework for universal recurrent neural networks. In *ICASSP*, pages 5345–5349, New Orleans, LA, USA.

Sergey Edunov, Myle Ott, Michael Auli, David Grangier, and Marc'Aurelio Ranzato. 2017. Classical structured prediction losses for sequence to sequence learning. *arXiv preprint arXiv:1711.04956*.

Hossein Hadian, Hossein Sameti, Daniel Povey, and Sanjeev Khudanpur. 2018. Towards discriminatively-trained HMM-based end-to-end model for automatic speech recognition. Submitted to ICASSP 2018.

Awni Hannun, Carl Case, Jared Casper, Bryan Catanzaro, Greg Diamos, Erich Elsen, Ryan Prenger, Sanjeev Satheesh, Shubho Sengupta, Adam Coates, et al. 2014. DeepSpeech: Scaling up end-to-end speech recognition. *arXiv preprint arXiv:1412.5567*.

Jindřich Helcl and Jindřich Libovický. 2017. Neural monkey: An open-source tool for sequence learning. *The Prague Bulletin of Mathematical Linguistics*, 107(1):5–17.

Felix Hieber, Tobias Domhan, Michael Denkowski, David Vilar, Artem Sokolov, Ann Clifton, and Matt Post. 2017. Sockeye: A toolkit for neural machine translation. *arXiv preprint arXiv:1712.05690*.

Roberto Ierusalimschy, Luiz Henrique de Figueiredo, and Waldemar Celes. 2006. *Lua 5.1 Reference Manual*. Lua.Org.

Marcin Junczys-Dowmunt, Tomasz Dwojak, and Hieu Hoang. 2016. Is neural machine translation ready for deployment? a case study on 30 translation directions. *arXiv preprint arXiv:1610.01108*.

Diederik P Kingma and Jimmy Ba. 2014. Adam: A method for stochastic optimization. *arXiv preprint arXiv:1412.6980*.

Pavel Levin, Nishikant Dhanuka, Talaat Khalil, Fedor Kovalev, and Maxim Khalilov. 2017a. Toward a full-scale neural machine translation in production: the booking. com use case. *MT Summit, arXiv preprint arXiv:1709.05820*.

Pavel Levin, Nishikant Dhanuka, and Maxim Khalilov. 2017b. Machine translation at booking. com: Journey and lessons learned. *arXiv preprint arXiv:1707.07911*.

Tsung-Yi Lin, Priya Goyal, Ross Girshick, Kaiming He, and Piotr Dollár. 2017. Focal loss for dense object detection. *arXiv preprint arXiv:1708.02002*.

Jan-Thorsten Peter, Andreas Guta, Tamer Alkhouli, Parnia Bahar, Jan Rosendahl, Nick Rossenbach, Miguel Graça, and Ney Hermann. 2017. The RWTH Aachen university english-german and german-english machine translation system for WMT 2017. In *EMNLP*, Copenhagen, Denmark.

Rohit Prabhavalkar, Tara N Sainath, Yonghui Wu, Patrick Nguyen, Zhifeng Chen, Chung-Cheng Chiu, and Anjuli Kannan. 2017. Minimum word error rate training for attention-based sequence-to-sequence models. *arXiv preprint arXiv:1712.01818*.

PyTorch Development Team. 2018. PyTorch. Software available from pytorch.org.

George Saon, Gakuto Kurata, Tom Sercu, Kartik Audhkhasi, Samuel Thomas, Dimitrios Dimitriadis, Xiaodong Cui, Bhuvana Ramabhadran, Michael Picheny, Lynn-Li Lim, et al. 2017. English conversational telephone speech recognition by humans and machines. *arXiv preprint arXiv:1703.02136*.

Rico Sennrich, Orhan Firat, Kyunghyun Cho, Alexandra Birch, Barry Haddow, Julian Hitschler, Marcin Junczys-Dowmunt, Samuel Läubli, Antonio Valerio Miceli Barone, Jozef Mokry, et al. 2017. Nematus: a toolkit for neural machine translation. *EACL Demo, arXiv preprint arXiv:1703.04357*.

Rico Sennrich, Barry Haddow, and Alexandra Birch. 2015. Neural machine translation of rare words with subword units. *arXiv preprint arXiv:1508.07909*.

Christian Szegedy, Vincent Vanhoucke, Sergey Ioffe, Jon Shlens, and Zbigniew Wojna. 2016. Rethinking the inception architecture for computer vision. In *IC-CVPR*, pages 2818–2826.

TensorFlow Development Team. 2015. TensorFlow: Large-scale machine learning on heterogeneous systems. Software available from tensorflow.org.

Theano Development Team. 2016. Theano: A Python framework for fast computation of mathematical expressions. *arXiv e-prints*, abs/1605.02688.

Zhaopeng Tu, Zhengdong Lu, Yang Liu, Xiaohua Liu, and Hang Li. 2016. Modeling coverage for neural machine translation. In *ACL*.

Ashish Vaswani, Samy Bengio, Eugene Brevdo, Francois Chollet, Aidan N Gomez, Stephan Gouws, Llion Jones, Łukasz Kaiser, Nal Kalchbrenner, Niki Parmar, et al. 2018. Tensor2tensor for neural machine translation. *arXiv preprint arXiv:1803.07416*.

Ashish Vaswani, Noam Shazeer, Niki Parmar, Jakob Uszkoreit, Llion Jones, Aidan N Gomez, Łukasz Kaiser, and Illia Polosukhin. 2017. Attention is all you need. In *NIPS*, pages 6000–6010.

Paul Voigtlaender, Patrick Doetsch, and Hermann Ney. 2016. Handwriting recognition with large multidimensional long short-term memory recurrent neural networks. In *ICFHR*, pages 228–233, Shenzhen, China. IAPR Best Student Paper Award.

Albert Zeyer, Eugen Beck, Ralf Schlüter, and Hermann Ney. 2017a. CTC in the context of generalized full-sum HMM training. In *Interspeech*, pages 944–948, Stockholm, Sweden.

Albert Zeyer, Patrick Doetsch, Paul Voigtlaender, Ralf Schlüter, and Hermann Ney. 2017b. A comprehensive study of deep bidirectional LSTM RNNs for acoustic modeling in speech recognition. In *ICASSP*, pages 2462–2466, New Orleans, LA, USA.

Albert Zeyer, Ilia Kulikov, Ralf Schlüter, and Hermann Ney. 2017c. Faster sequence training. In *ICASSP*, pages 5285–5289, New Orleans, LA, USA.

A Flexible, Efficient and Accurate Framework for Community Question Answering Pipelines

Salvatore Romeo, Giovanni Da San Martino, Alberto Barrón-Cedeño,
Qatar Computing Research Institute, HBKU, Doha, Qatar
`{sromeo,gmartino,albarron}@hbku.edu.qa`

Alessandro Moschitti[*]
Amazon, Manhattan Beach, CA, USA
`amosch@amazon.com`

Abstract

Although deep neural networks have been proving to be excellent tools to deliver state-of-the-art results, when data is scarce and the tackled tasks involve complex semantic inference, deep linguistic processing and traditional structure-based approaches, such as tree kernel methods, are an alternative solution. Community Question Answering is a research area that benefits from deep linguistic analysis to improve the experience of the community of forum users. In this paper, we present a UIMA framework to distribute the computation of cQA tasks over computer clusters such that traditional systems can scale to large datasets and deliver fast processing.

1 Introduction

Web forums have been developed to help users to share their information. Given the natural use of questions and answers in the human communication process, traditional automated Question Answering (QA) techniques have been recently applied to improve the forum user experience.

Community Question Answering (cQA) deals with difficult tasks, including comment re-ranking and question re-ranking. The former task is defined as follows: given a thread of comments related to a user question, re-rank the comments in order of relevance with respect to the question. The latter task comes into play when a user wants to ask a new question. In this case an automatic system can be used to retrieve semantically similar questions, together with their threads of comments, already posted in the forum, and sort them according to their relevance against the freshly-posted question. Solving these tasks is beneficial both for the user, who avoids to manually look for such information, and the forum, since related information is not spread into multiple threads.

Previous cQA challenges, e.g., (Nakov et al., 2015, 2016, 2017) have shown that, to build accurate rankers, structural information and linguistic processing are required. Indeed, the results of the challenges have shown that (i) neural approaches are not enough to deliver the state of the art and (ii) kernel methods applied to syntactic structures often achieve top performance (Barrón-Cedeño et al., 2016; Filice et al., 2016).

Unfortunately, the models above are rather inefficient, as they require among others the syntactic parsing of long texts and kernel machine processing. The latter can be computationally expensive as the classification step requires quadratic time in the number of support vectors. Thus, approaches to speed up computation are very appealing. The classical method in these cases is to distribute and parallelize the computation. However, as the cQA processing pipelines can be very complex, an engineering approach to distributed computing is required.

In this paper, we propose a UIMA framework to manage the computation distribution of the complicated processing pipelines involved in cQA systems. In particular, we make the computation of standard linguistic processing components, feature/structure extractors and classification or learning phases scalable. This way, we both attain (i) the state-of-the-art accuracy of tree kernel-based rerankers and (ii) fast response. This makes our models useful for practical applications. We highlight the fact that our framework is rather flexible and extensible as new linguistic or machine learning components can be easily added. Indeed, we built two different cQA systems for English

---

[*]This work was carried out when the author was principal scientist at QCRI.

Proceedings of the 56th Annual Meeting of the Association for Computational Linguistics-System Demonstrations, pages 134–139
Melbourne, Australia, July 15 - 20, 2018. ©2018 Association for Computational Linguistics

and Arabic (Barrón-Cedeño et al., 2016) by simply adding basic linguistic modules, e.g., the syntactic parsers, for both languages.

We make our software framework, based on UIMA technology, freely available to the research and industrial community by also providing our toolkit with tutorials and usage options for different degrees of user expertise.

2 Related Work

One of the first approaches to answer ranking relied on metadata (Jeon et al., 2006) (e.g., click counts). Agichtein et al. (2008) explored a graph-based model of contributors relationships together with both content- and usage-based features. Some of the most recent proposals aim at classifying whole threads of answers (Joty et al., 2015; Zhou et al., 2015) rather than each answer in isolation.

Regarding question ranking, Duan et al. (2008) searched for equivalent questions by considering the question's focus. Zhou et al. (2011) used a (monolingual) phrase-based translation model and Wang et al. (2009) computed similarities on syntactic-trees. A different approach using topic modeling for question retrieval was introduced by Ji et al. (2012) and Zhang et al. (2014). dos Santos et al. (2015) applied convolutional neural networks.

The three editions of the SemEval Task 3 on cQA (Nakov et al., 2015, 2016, 2017) have triggered a manifold of approaches. The challenges of 2016 and 2017 included Task 3-A on comment re-ranking and Task 3-B on question re-ranking. For task 3-A, Tran et al. (2015) applied machine translation, topic models, embeddings, and similarities. Hou et al. (2015) and Nicosia et al. (2015) applied supervised models with lexical, syntactic and meta-data features.

For task 3-B The top-three participants applied SVMs as learning models (Franco-Salvador et al., 2016; Barrón-Cedeño et al., 2016; Filice et al., 2016). Franco-Salvador et al. (2016) relied heavily on distributed representations and semantic information sources, such as Babelnet and Framenet. Both Barrón-Cedeño et al. (2016) and Filice et al. (2016) use lexical similarities and tree kernels on parse trees. No statistically-significant differences were observed in the performance of these three systems.

In summary, the results for both tasks show that SVM systems based on a combination of vectorial features and tree kernels perform consistently well on the different editions of the competition (Barrón-Cedeño et al., 2016; Filice et al., 2016, 2017): the systems described in those papers won Task 3-A both years, placed second and first on Task 3-B in years 2016 and 2017, respectively.

The most related demonstration papers to ours are (Uryupina et al., 2016; Rücklé and Gurevych, 2017). As ours, the system of Uryupina et al. (2016) is a UIMA-based pipeline. Yet in their case the input is a single text and the output is the result of different levels of textual annotation (e.g., tokens, syntactic information, or wikification). Rücklé and Gurevych (2017) developed an architecture to perform question and answer re-ranking in cQA based on deep learning. Their main focus is the analysis of attention models in these tasks.

3 Structural Linguistic Models for cQA

In this section, we describe the components of the two learning systems.

The ranking function for both tasks can be implemented by the scoring function of an SVM, $r : X \times X \to \mathbb{R}$, where X is either a set of comments (Task 3-A) or a set of questions (Task 3-B). For example, r can be a linear function, $r(x, x') = \vec{w} \cdot \phi(x, x')$, where $\vec{w}$ is the model and $\phi()$ provides a feature vector representation of the pair, (x, x'). The vectors ϕ used by Barrón-Cedeño et al. (2016); Filice et al. (2016) are a combination of tree kernel similarity functions and features derived from similarity measures between the two comments/questions constituting one learning example, as well as features extracting information from the forum threads the comments/questions belong to.

3.1 Tree Kernel

We use the kernel function defined by Filice et al. (2015):

$$K((x_1, x_1'), (x_2, x_2')) = \text{TK}\big(t_{x_1'}(x_1), t_{x_2'}(x_2)\big) \\ + \text{TK}\big(t_{x_1}(x_1'), t_{x_2}(x_2')\big)$$

where TK is the Partial Tree Kernel by Moschitti (2006) and $t_y(x)$ is a function which enriches the tree x with information derived from its structural similarity with the tree y (see (Severyn and Moschitti, 2012; Filice et al., 2016) for details).

3.2 Feature Vectors

Various sets of features have been developed in
(Barrón-Cedeño et al., 2016; Filice et al., 2016).
A number of features which include similarities
between the two texts constituting one learning example are computed. Such features include greedy
string tiling, longest common subsequence, Jac-
card coefficient, word containment, and cosine
similarity, which can be computed on n-grams or
bag-of-word representations. Another similarity
can be obtained by comparing syntactic trees with
the Partial Tree Kernel, i.e., $\mathrm{TK}\big(t_{x_1}(x_1'), t_{x_1'}(x_1)\big)$.
Note that, different from the model in Section 3.1,
the Partial Tree Kernel here is applied to the members of the same pair and thus only produces
one feature. In the case of question re-ranking,
the SemEval datasets include information about
the ranking of the question, as generated by the
Google search engine. Such information is ex-
ploited in two ways: "as-is", by using directly the
position, pos, as a feature of the question, or its
inverse, pos^{-1}.

4 Distributed Framework using UIMA

4.1 UIMA introduction

The Unstructured Information Management Architecture (UIMA) is a software framework for
creating, combining, and deploying an arbitrary
number of language analytics. UIMA Asynchronous Scaleout (UIMA-AS) is a set of functionalities integrated in UIMA to enable scalability using a distributed environment. In UIMA,
each document is contained in a Common Analysis Structure (CAS), annotated by processing units
called *Analysis Engines*, or *Annotators*.

In UIMA-AS, there are basically three actors:
(i) client applications, (ii) brokers, and (iii) UIMA
pipelines. The latter is connected to the broker
and listens for requests on a queue managed by the
broker. The annotation steps are as follows: (a) the
client sends the CAS to the broker; (b) the broker,
in turn, sends it to the pipeline, which is listening
to a specific queue; (c) the pipeline annotates the
CAS and send it back to the broker; and finally,
(d) the broker send the annotated CAS back to the
client. Our pipeline is designed and developed in
this framework.

4.2 Our Pipeline

There are three main modules: (i) feature extraction, (ii) learning, and (iii) classification. Each
module is designed to be replicated in multiple instances to achieve scalability. Each of these modules is a pipeline deployed as UIMA-AS service
that listens to a queue of processing requests (registered on the broker). Each module can interact
with others by means of the broker if necessary.
For instance, both learning and classification use
the feature extraction to extract the features for the
input instances.

The entire framework offers two levels of scalability. The first one deploys the same pipeline
in different UIMA-AS services but listens to the
same queue. In this case, the broker distributes
the processing requests to the different CPUs. The
second one replicates the pipeline a number of
times internally to a UIMA-AS service. In this
case, UIMA-AS internally handles the parallel
processing of multiple requests.

In UIMA each annotator and pipeline is described and configured with XML descriptors.
The descriptors of an annotator include information related to the implementation class, configuration parameters and binding of resources (if
any). The descriptor of a pipeline includes information regarding the annotators it is composed
of and their order. Furthermore, the deployment
descriptors for the pipelines include information
about the location of the broker and the queue's
name, where the pipeline listen to the processing
requests. This configuration process is fully automated in our pipeline and all the required descriptors are generated automatically. Finally, the
pipeline can also be deployed on a single machine
for either local or parallel computation.

Feature Extraction. Each CAS received by this
module contains an instance of one of the aforementioned tasks, i.e., a question along with a set
of comments or a set of other questions. The first
step of the feature extraction is a sequence of standard preprocessing steps, e.g., segmentation, POS-
tagging, lemmatization, syntactic parsing. The
questions and comments of each instance of the
specific task can be processed in parallel. The input CASes are hence split in a way that each of
the output CASes contains either a single question
or a single comment and it is asynchronously processed in the *Preprocessing sub-pipeline*. The pre-
processed CASes are then aggregated back to form
the input task instances. In its current status, our
pipeline is meant to work with pairs. Therefore,
the aggregated CASes are split in order to form

question–comment (for comment re-ranking) or question–question (for question re-ranking) pairs. These are instances to be used in the learning or classification phase.

The output CASes are fed into the *Feature Computation sub-pipeline*. This sub-component computes a set of features for each CAS using the annotation previously created. It is composed of a sequence of *Vectorial Features Annotators* and each of them makes use of a *Feature Computer* (FC) to compute each feature. A FC is implemented as a resource that, given a CAS representing a pair, computes a feature based on the first, the second, or both members of the pair. This allows for sharing FC among different annotators. After the computation of all features is completed, it is possible to add additional information and/or representations of the CAS contents, e.g., syntactic parse trees. This is done by means of the *Decoration sub-pipeline* that is a sequence of *Decorators*. Finally, a *Representation Extractor* (RE) produces the features' representation that the learner and the classifier expect to process. The RE uses a *serializer*, which is a resource in charge of serializing the generic pair in the target representation format. The serializer is plugged into the RE at deployment time to allow the integration of any learning and classification component.

Learning. The learning module is composed of a single annotator that makes use of a *Learner*. A learner is a resource plugged at deployment time. This allows to plug any algorithm by wrapping it in a learner. Furthermore, a single instance can be shared among multiple instances of the learning module. Note that all representation instances are collected before the learning process can start. The resulting trained model is stored and the local file path is sent back to the client in an output CAS. At publication time, the pipeline implements SVM-based models, but it can be extended with others.

Classification. This module is composed by a single annotator that makes use of a resource plugged at deployment time as well. In this case, the resource is a *Classifier* that uses one of the trained models stored by the learning module. Again, implementing the classifier as a resource allows to plug any type of classification algorithm and to share it among multiple instances of the classification module. Every time the classification annotator receives a new instance, it computes the prediction, updates the input CAS adding the corresponding information and gives it as output.

5 Software Package

Our cQA pipeline is available for download [1] and is distributed under the terms of the Apache 2.0 License. By taking advantage of the Apache Maven project management tool, most dependencies are automatically handled. The only exception is the UIMA framework toolkit. Still, its installation is straightforward. The pipeline is able to process natural language texts and metadata information associated with them and offers three main functionalities:

Feature and **representation extraction** allows to compute features, such as the ones described in Section 3.2. Moreover, the pipeline allows to compute parse trees by using any third-party UIMA parser. Currently we integrated the DKPro (Eckart de Castilho and Gurevych, 2014) wrapper of the Stanford parser.

Learning and **classification** allow to apply a variety of learning algorithms on vectorial or structured data. Currently KeLP (Filice et al., 2018) [2] is integrated in the pipeline. KeLP allows to apply a growing number of kernel-based algorithms and kernel functions to perform unsupervised, online and batch supervised kernel methods. We opt for integrating KeLP because the kernel-based cQA systems relying on it perform at state-of-the-art level (see Section 2). Our pipeline is able to reproduce the state-of-the-art models for SemEval cQA tasks 3-A and 3-B.

Besides the functionalities just described, the pipeline has a modular structure. It allows to easily plug in new components, such as alternative natural language preprocessing components (lemmatizers, POS taggers, parsers), features, representations, and learning algorithms. The pipeline can either be run on a stand-alone machine or deployed on a cluster to distribute the computation load. In either case, simple classes are provided to run the pipeline from the command line.

Since this is an ongoing effort, we provide updated information on the wiki page of the GitHub project. The wiki provides instructions on the installation and tutorials to illustrate how to use the three main functionalities: (i) create representations, (ii) learn models, and (iii) classify data.

---

[1] `https://github.com/QAML/S3QACoreFramework`
[2] `http://www.kelp-ml.org`

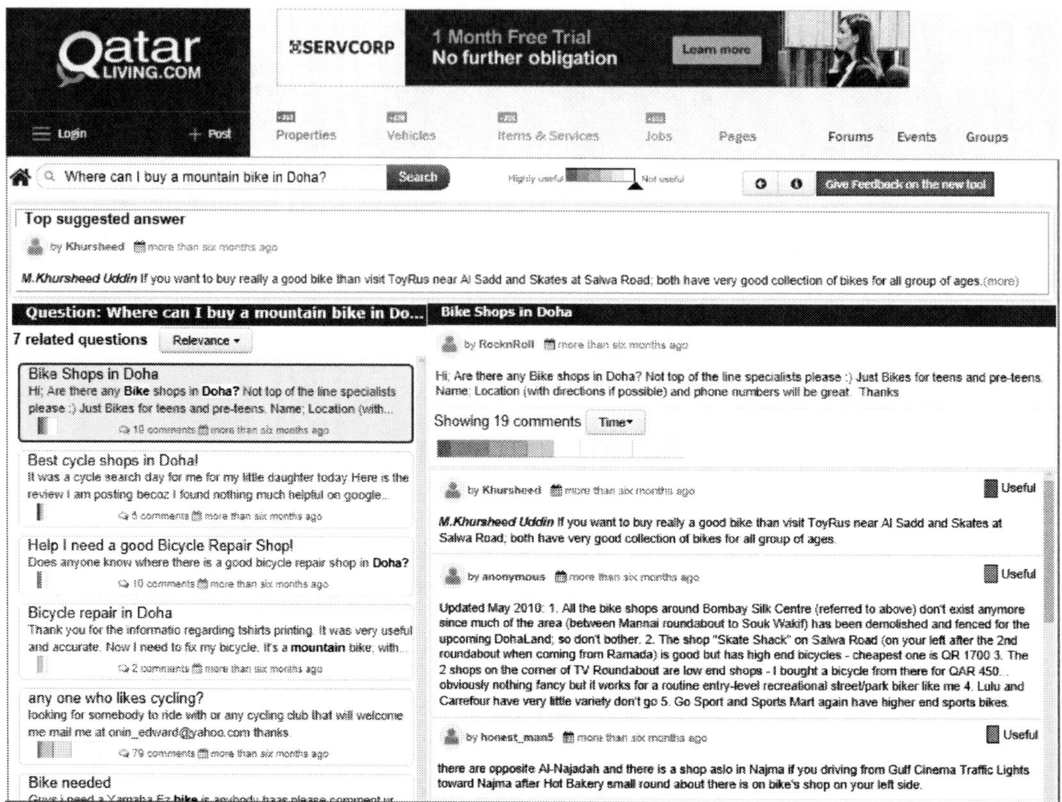

Figure 1: A prototype of the UIMA pipeline applied to a real-world forum.

Our pipeline has been used in a number of prototypes. Qatarliving.com is a forum where expats in Qatar may ask questions on a variety of different topics and comment on them. We implemented the technology described in Section 3 both for question and comment re-ranking [3]. Fig. 1 shows an example of usage: the user asks the question "Where can I buy a bike in Doha?", the systems returns similar questions in the forum together with the best overall comment. By clicking on a question, the right panel shows the corresponding thread of comments with their relevance.

A second example is a cQA demo[4] in Arabic, which retrieves data from multiple medical forums from middle-east. In this case physicians answer to patients' questions: the left panel shows a question from a user and the right panel similar questions with the answers from the expert. In general there is only one (good) answer from the doctor, so this is mostly a question re-ranking task.

---

[3] http://www.qatarliving.com/betasearch
[4] http://cqa.iyas.qcri.org/cQA-Arabic-Demo

6 Conclusions

We presented a UIMA framework to distribute the computation of community question answering tasks. As a result, we can scale deep linguistic analysis and kernel technology to large datasets and deliver fast processing. Our toolkit is rather flexible and can be extended with new linguistic components as well as new machine learning components and algorithms. In addition to support state-of-the-art community question answering frameworks, an interesting consequence of the properties above is the fact that our framework also enables multilingual and potentially cross-language pipelines.

References

E. Agichtein, A. Gionis, C. Castillo, G. Mishne, and D. Donato. 2008. Finding High-quality Content in Social Media with an Application to Community-based Question Answering. In *Proceedings of WSDM*.

A. Barrón-Cedeño, G. Da San Martino, S. Joty, A. Moschitti, F. Al-Obaidli, S. Romeo, K. Tymoshenko, and A. Uva. 2016. ConvKN at SemEval-2016 Task 3: Answer and Question Selection for Question Answering on Arabic and English Fora. In *Proceedings of SemEval-2016*.

C. dos Santos, L. Barbosa, D. Bogdanova, and B. Zadrozny. 2015. Learning Hybrid Representations to Retrieve Semantically Equivalent Questions. In *Proceedings of ACL-IJCNLP*.

H. Duan, Y. Cao, C.-Y. Lin, and Y. Yu. 2008. Searching Questions by Identifying Question Topic and Question Focus. In *Proceedings of ACL*.

Richard Eckart de Castilho and Iryna Gurevych. 2014. A Broad-coverage Collection of Portable NLP Components for Building Shareable Analysis Pipelines. In *Proceedings of OIAF4HLT*.

S. Filice, D. Croce, A. Moschitti, and R. Basili. 2016. KeLP at SemEval-2016 Task 3: Learning Semantic Relations between Questions and Answers. In *Proceedings of SemEval-2016*.

S. Filice, G. Da San Martino, and A. Moschitti. 2015. Structural Representations for Learning Relations between Pairs of Texts. In *Proceedings of ACL-IJCNLP*.

S. Filice, G. Da San Martino, and A. Moschitti. 2017. KeLP at SemEval-2017 Task 3: Learning Pairwise Patterns in Community Question Answering. In *Proceedings of SemEval-2017*.

Simone Filice, Giuseppe Castellucci, Giovanni Da San Martino, Danilo Croce, Alessandro Moschitti, and Roberto Basili. 2018. KeLP: A Kernel-based Learning Platform. *To appear in the Journal of Machine Learning Research* .

M. Franco-Salvador, S Kar, T. Solorio, and P. Rosso. 2016. UH-PRHLT at SemEval-2016 Task 3: Combining Lexical and Semantic-based Features for Community Question Answering. In *Proceedings of SemEval-2016*.

Y. Hou, C. Tan, X. Wang, Y. Zhang, J. Xu, and Q. Chen. 2015. HITSZ-ICRC: Exploiting Classification Approach for Answer Selection in Community Question Answering. In *Proceedings of SemEval-2015*.

J. Jeon, W. B. Croft, J. H. Lee, and S. Park. 2006. A Framework to Predict the Quality of Answers with Non-textual Features. In *Proceedings of SIGIR*.

Z. Ji, F. Xu, B. Wang, and B. He. 2012. Question-answer Topic Model for Question Retrieval in Community Question Answering. In *Proceedings of CIKM*.

S. Joty, A. Barrón-Cedeño, G. Da San Martino, S. Filice, L. Màrquez, A. Moschitti, and P. Nakov. 2015. Global Thread-level Inference for Comment Classification in Community Question Answering. In *Proceedings of EMNLP*.

A. Moschitti. 2006. Efficient Convolution Kernels for Dependency and Constituent Syntactic Trees. In *Proceedings of ECML*.

P. Nakov, D. Hoogeveen, L. Màrquez, A. Moschitti, H. Mubarak, T. Baldwin, and K. Verspoor. 2017. SemEval-2017 Task 3: Community Question Answering. In *Proceedings of SemEval-2017*.

P. Nakov, L. Màrquez, W. Magdy, A. Moschitti, J. Glass, and B. Randeree. 2015. SemEval-2015 Task 3: Answer Selection in Community Question Answering. In *Proceedings of SemEval-2015*.

P. Nakov, L. Màrquez, A. Moschitti, W. Magdy, H. Mubarak, A. Freihat, J. Glass, and B. Randeree. 2016. SemEval-2016 Task 3: Community Question Answering. In *Proceedings of SemEval-2016*.

M. Nicosia, S. Filice, A. Barrón-Cedeño, I. Saleh, H. Mubarak, W. Gao, P. Nakov, G. Da San Martino, A. Moschitti, K. Darwish, L. Màrquez, S. Joty, and W. Magdy. 2015. QCRI: Answer Selection for Community Question Answering - Experiments for Arabic and English. In *Proc. of SemEval-2015*.

A. Rücklé and I. Gurevych. 2017. End-to-End Non-Factoid Question Answering with an Interactive Visualization of Neural Attention Weights. In *Proceedings of ACL (System Demonstrations)*.

Aliaksei Severyn and Alessandro Moschitti. 2012. Structural Relationships for Large-scale Learning of Answer Re-ranking. In *Proceedings of SIGIR*.

Q. H. Tran, V. Tran, T. Vu, M. Nguyen, and S. Bao Pham. 2015. JAIST: Combining Multiple Features for Answer Selection in Community Question Answering. In *Proceedings SemEval-2015*.

O. Uryupina, B. Plank, G. Barlacchi, F. J. Valverde-Albacete, M. Tsagkias, Antonio Uva, and Alessandro Moschitti. 2016. LiMoSINe Pipeline: Multilingual UIMA-based NLP Platform. In *Proceedings of ACL (System Demonstrations)*.

K. Wang, Z. Ming, and T. Chua. 2009. A Syntactic Tree Matching Approach to Finding Similar Questions in Community-based QA Services. In *Proceedings of SIGIR*.

K. Zhang, W. Wu, H. Wu, Z. Li, and M. Zhou. 2014. Question Retrieval with High Quality Answers in Community Question Answering. In *Proceedings of CIKM*.

G. Zhou, L. Cai, J. Zhao, and K. Liu. 2011. Phrase-based Translation Model for Question Retrieval in Community Question Answer Archives. In *Proceedings of ACL*.

G. Zhou, T. He, J. Zhao, and P. Hu. 2015. Learning Continuous Word Embedding with Metadata for Question Retrieval in Community Question Answering. In *Proceedings of ACL-IJCNLP*.

Moon IME: Neural-based Chinese Pinyin Aided Input Method with Customizable Association

Yafang Huang[1,2,*], Zuchao Li[1,2,*], Zhuosheng Zhang[1,2], Hai Zhao[1,2,†]
[1]Department of Computer Science and Engineering, Shanghai Jiao Tong University
[2]Key Laboratory of Shanghai Education Commission for Intelligent Interaction
and Cognitive Engineering, Shanghai Jiao Tong University, Shanghai, 200240, China
{huangyafang, charlee, zhangzs}@sjtu.edu.cn, zhaohai@cs.sjtu.edu.cn

Abstract

Chinese pinyin input method engine (IME) lets user conveniently input Chinese into a computer by typing pinyin through the common keyboard. In addition to offering high conversion quality, modern pinyin IME is supposed to aid user input with extended association function. However, existing solutions for such functions are roughly based on oversimplified matching algorithms at word-level, whose resulting products provide limited extension associated with user inputs. This work presents the Moon IME, a pinyin IME that integrates the attention-based neural machine translation (NMT) model and Information Retrieval (IR) to offer amusive and customizable association ability. The released IME is implemented on Windows via text services framework.

1 Introduction

Pinyin is the official romanization representation for Chinese and pinyin-to-character (P2C) which concerts the inputted pinyin sequence to Chinese character sequence is the core module of all pinyin based IMEs. Previous works in kinds of literature only focus on pinyin to the character itself, paying less attention to user experience with associative advances, let along predictive typing or automatic completion. However, more agile associa-tion outputs from IME predication may undoubtedly lead to incomparable user typing experience, which motivates this work.

Modern IMEs are supposed to extend P2C with association functions that additionally predict the next series of characters that the user is attempting to enter. Such IME extended capacity can be generally fallen into two categories: auto-completion and follow-up prediction. The former will look up all possible phrases that might match the user input even though the input is incomplete. For example, when receiving a pinyin syllable "bei", auto-completion module will predict "北京" (beijing, Beijing) or "背景" (beijing, Background) as a word-level candidate. The second scenario is when a user completes entering a set of words, in which case the IME will present appropriate collocations for the user to choose. For example, after the user selects "北京" (Beijing) from the candidate list in the above example, the IME will show a list of collocations that follows the word Beijing, such as "市" (city), "奥运会" (Olympics).

This paper presents the Moon IME, a pinyin IME engine with an association cloud platform, which integrates the attention-based neural machine translation (NMT) model with diverse associations to enable customizable and amusive user typing experience.

Compared to its existing counterparts, Moon IME has extraordinarily offered the following promising advantages:

• It is the first attempt that adopts attentive NMT method to achieve P2C conversion in both IME research and engineering.

• It provides a general association cloud platform which contains follow-up-prediction and machine translation module for typing assistance.

• With an information retrieval based module, it realizes fast and effective auto-completion which can help users type sentences in a more convenient

---

*These authors contribute equally. † Corresponding author. This paper was partially supported by National Key Research and Development Program of China (No. 2017YFB0304100), National Natural Science Foundation of China (No. 61672343 and No. 61733011), Key Project of National Society Science Foundation of China (No. 15-ZDA041), The Art and Science Interdisciplinary Funds of Shanghai Jiao Tong University (No. 14JCRZ04).

Proceedings of the 56th Annual Meeting of the Association for Computational Linguistics-System Demonstrations, pages 140–145
Melbourne, Australia, July 15 - 20, 2018. ©2018 Association for Computational Linguistics

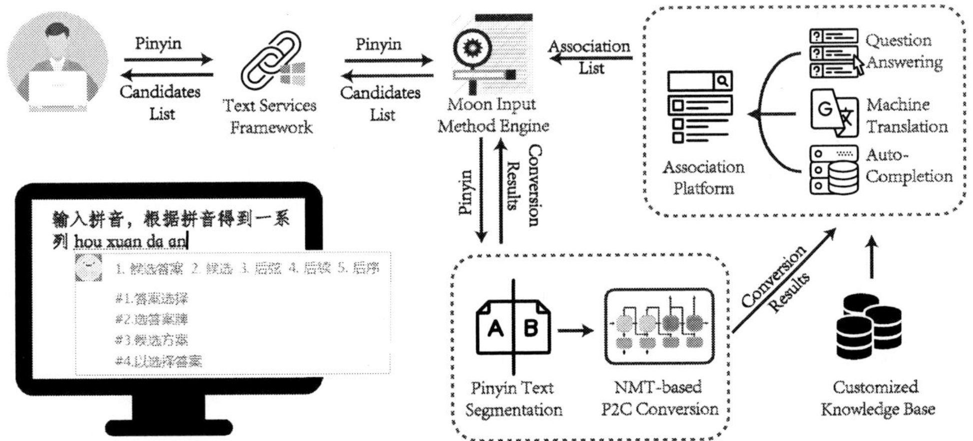

Figure 1: Architecture of the proposed Moon IME.

and efficient manner.

• With a powerful customizable design, the association cloud platform can be adapted to any specific domains such as the fields of law and medicine which contain complex specialized terms.

The rest of the paper is organized as follows: Section 2 demonstrates the details of our system. Section 3 presents the feature functions of our realized IME. Some related works are introduced in Section 4. Section 5 concludes this paper.

2 System Details

Figure **1** illustrates the architecture of Moon IME. The Moon IME is based on Windows Text Services Framework (TSF) [1]. Our Moon IME extends the Open-source projects PIME[2] with three main components: a) pinyin text segmentation, b) P2C conversion module, c) IR-based association module. The nub of our work is realizing an engine to stably convert pinyin to Chinese as well as giving reasonable association lists.

2.1 Input Method Engine

Pinyin Segmentation For a convenient reference, hereafter a *character* in pinyin also refers to an independent syllable in the case without causing confusion, and *word* means a pinyin syllable sequence with respect to a true Chinese word.

As (Zhang et al., 2017) proves that P2C conversion of IME may benefit from decoding longer pinyin sequence for more efficient inputting. When a given pinyin sequence becomes longer, the list of the corresponding legal character sequences will significantly reduce. Thus, we train our P2C model with segmented corpora. We used baseSeg (Zhao et al., 2006) to segment all text, and finish the training in both word-level and character-level.

NMT-based P2C module Our P2C module is implemented through OpenNMT Toolkit[3] as we formulize P2C as a translation between pinyin and character sequences. Given a pinyin sequence X and a Chinese character sequence Y, the encoder of the P2C model encodes pinyin representation in word-level, and the decoder is to generate the target Chinese sequence which maximizes $P(Y|X)$ using maximum likelihood training.

The encoder is a bi-directional long short-term memory (LSTM) network (Hochreiter and Schmidhuber, 1997). The vectorized inputs are fed to forward LSTM and backward LSTM to obtain the internal features of two directions. The output for each input is the concatenation of the two vectors from both directions: $\overleftrightarrow{\mathbf{h}_t} = \overrightarrow{\mathbf{h}_t} \parallel \overleftarrow{\mathbf{h}_t}$.

Our decoder is based on the global attentional model proposed by (Luong et al., 2015) which takes the hidden states of the encoder into consideration when deriving the context vector. The probability is conditioned on a distinct context vector for each target word. The context vec-

---

[1]TSF is a system service available as a redistributable for Windows 2000 and later versions of Windows operation system. A TSF text service provides multilingual support and delivers text services such as keyboard processors, handwriting recognition, and speech recognition.

[2]https://github.com/EasyIME/PIME

[3]http://opennmt.net

tor is computed as a weighted sum of previously hidden states. The probability of each candidate word as being the recommended one is predicted using a softmax layer over the inner-product between source and candidate target characters.

Our model is initially trained on two datasets, namely the People's Daily (PD) corpus and Douban (DC) corpus. The former is extracted from the People's Daily from 1992 to 1998 that has word segmentation annotations by Peking University. The DC corpus is created by (Wu et al., 2017) from Chinese open domain conversations. One sentence of the DC corpus contains one complete utterance in a continuous dialogue situation. The statistics of two datasets is shown in Table 1. With character text available, the needed parallel corpus between pinyin and character texts is automatically created following the approach proposed by (Yang et al., 2012).

		Chinese	Pinyin
PD	# MIUs	5.04M	
	# Vocab	54.3K	41.1K
DC	# MIUs	1.00M	
	# Vocab	50.0K	20.3K

Table 1: MIUs count and vocab size statistics of our training data. PD refers to the People's Daily, TP is TouchPal corpus.

Here is the hyperparameters we used: (a) deep LSTM models, 3 layers, 500 cells, (c) 13 epoch training with plain SGD and a simple learning rate schedule - start with a learning rate of 1.0; after 9 epochs, halve the learning rate every epoch, (d) mini-batches are of size 64 and shuffled, (e) dropout is 0.3. The pre-trained pinyin embeddings and Chinese word embeddings are trained by word2vec (Mikolov et al., 2013) toolkit on Wikipedia[4] and unseen words are assigned unique random vectors.

2.2 IR-based association module

We use IR-based association module to help user type long sentences which can predict the whole expected inputs according to the similarity between user's incomplete input and the candidates in a corpus containing massive sentences. In this work, we use Term Frequency-Inverse Document Frequency (TF-IDF) to calculate the similarity measurement, which has been usually used in

text classification and information retrieval. The TF (term-frequency) term is simply a count of the number of times a word appearing in a given context, while the IDF (invert document frequency) term puts a penalty on how often the word appears elsewhere in the corpus. The final TF-IDF score is calculated by the product of these two terms, which is formulated as:

$$\text{TF-IDF}(w, d, D) = f(w, d) \times \log \frac{N}{|\{d \in D : w \in d\}|}$$

where $f(w, d)$ indicates the number of times word w appearing in context d, N is the total number of dialogues, and the denominator represents the number of dialogues in which the word w appears.

In the IME scenario, the TF-IDF vectors are first calculated for the input context and each of the candidate responses from the corpus. Given a set of candidate response vectors, the one with the highest cosine similarity to the context vector is selected as the output. For Recall @ k, the top k candidates are returned. In this work, we only make use of the top 1 matched one.

3 User Experience Advantages

3.1 High Quality of P2C

We utilize Maximum Input Unit (MIU) Accuracy (Zhang et al., 2017) to evaluate the quality of our P2C module by measuring the conversion accuracy of MIU, whose definition is the longest uninterrupted Chinese character sequence inside a sentence. As the P2C conversion aims to output a ranked list of corresponding character sequences candidates, the top-K MIU accuracy means the possibility of hitting the target in the first K predicted items. We will follow the definition of (Zhang et al., 2017) about top-K accuracy.

Our model is compared to other models in Table 2. So far, (Huang et al., 2015) and (Zhang et al., 2017) reported the state-of-the-art results among statistical models. We list the top-5 accuracy contrast to all baselines with top-10 results, and the comparison indicates the noticeable advancement of our P2C model. To our surprise, the top-5 result on PD of our P2C module approaches the top-10 accuracy of Google IME. On DC corpus, the P2C module with the best setting achieves 90.17% accuracy, surpassing all the baselines. The comparison shows the high quality of our P2C conversion.

3.2 Association Cloud Platform

Follow-up Prediction An accurate P2C conversion is only the fundamental requirement to build

---

[4]https://dumps.wikimedia.org/zhwiki/20180201/zhwiki-20180201-pages-articles-multistream.xml.bz2

	DC			PD		
	Top-1	Top-5	Top-10	Top-1	Top-5	Top-10
(Huang et al., 2015)	59.15	71.85	76.78	61.42	73.08	78.33
(Zhang et al., 2017)	57.14	72.32	80.21	64.42	72.91	77.93
Google IME	62.13	72.17	74.72	**70.93**	80.32	**82.23**
P2C of Moon	**71.31**	**89.12**	**90.17**	70.51	**79.83**	80.12

Table 2: Comparison with previous state-of-the-art P2C models.

an intelligent IME which is not only supposed to give accurate P2C conversion, but to help users type sentences in a more convenient and efficient manner. To this end, follow-up prediction is quite necessary for input acceleration. Given an unfinished input, Moon IME now enables the follow-up prediction to help the user complete the typing. For example, given "快速傅里" (Fast Fourier), the IME engine will provide the candidate "快速傅里叶变换" (fast Fourier transform). Specifically, we extract each sentence in the Wikipedia corpus and use the IR-based association module to retrieve the index continuously and give the best-matched sentence as the prediction.

Pinyin-to-English Translation Our Moon IME is also equipped with a multi-lingual typing ability. For users of different language backgrounds, a satisfying conversation can benefit from the direct translation in IME engine. For example, if a Chinese user is using our IME chatting with a native English speaker, but get confused with how to say "Input Method Engine", simply typing the words "输入法" in mother tongue, the IME will give the translated expression. This is also achieved by training a Seq2Seq model from OpenNMT using WMT17 Chinese-English dataset[5].

Factoid Question Answering As an instance of IR-based association module, we make use of question answering (QA) corpus for automatic question completion. Intuitively, if a user wants to raise a question, our IME will retrieve the most matched question in the corpus along with the corresponding answer for typing reference. We use the WebQA dataset (Li et al., 2016) as our QA corpus, which contains more than 42K factoid question-answer pairs. For example, if a user input "吉他有" or "吉他弦" (guitar strings), the candidate "吉他有几根弦" (How many strings are there in the guitar?).

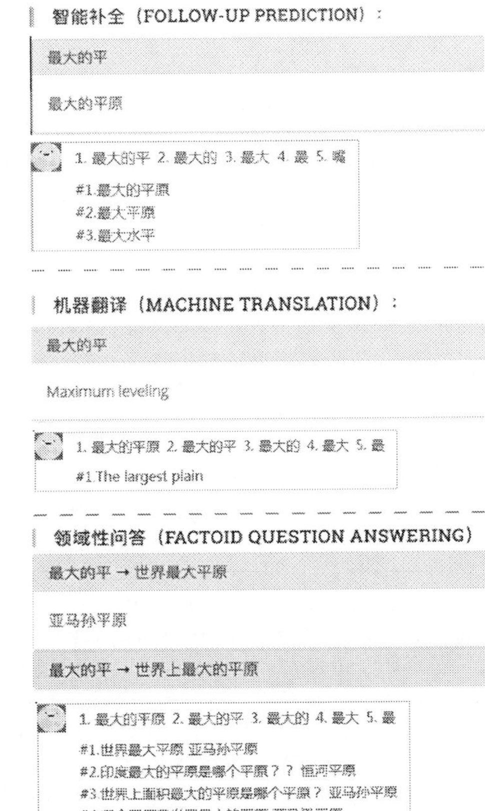

Figure 2: A case study of Association Cloud Platform.

Figure 2 shows a typical result returned by the platform when a user gives incomplete input. When user input pinyin sequence such as "zui da de ping", the P2C module returns "最大的平" as one candidate of the generated list and sends it to association platform. Then associative prediction is given according to the input mode that user current selections. Since the demands of the users are quite diverse, our platform to support such demands can be adapted to any specific domains with complex specialized terms. We provide a

---

[5]http://www.statmt.org/wmt17/translation-task.html

143

Demo homepage[6] for better reference, in which we display the main feature function of our platform and provide a download link.

4 Related Work

There are variable referential natural language processing studies(Cai et al., 2018; Li et al., 2018b; He et al., 2018; Li et al., 2018a; Zhang et al., 2018a; Cai et al., 2017a,b) for IME development to refer to. Most of the engineering practice mainly focus on the matching correspondence between the Pinyin and Chinese characters, namely, pinyin-to-character converting with the highest accuracy. (Chen, 2003) introduced a conditional maximum entropy model with syllabification for grapheme-to-phoneme conversion. (Zhang et al., 2006) presented a rule-based error correction approach to improving preferable conversion rate. (Lin and Zhang, 2008) present a statistical model that associates a word with supporting context to offer a better solution to Chinese input. (Jiang et al., 2007) put forward a PTC framework based on support vector machine. (Okuno and Mori, 2012) introduced an ensemble model of word-based and character-based models for Japanese and Chinese IMEs. (Yang et al., 2012; Wang et al., 2018, 2016; Pang et al., 2016; Jia and Zhao, 2013, 2014) regarded the P2C conversion as a transformation between two languages and solved it by statistical machine translation framework. (Chen et al., 2015) firstly use natural machine thanslation method to translate pinyin to Chinese. (Zhang et al., 2017) introduced an online algorithm to construct an appropriate dictionary for IME.

The recent trend on state-of-the-art techniques for Chinese input methods can be put into two lines. Speech-to-text input as iFly IM[7] (Zhang et al., 2015; Saon et al., 2014; Lu et al., 2016) and the aided input methods which are capable of generating candidate sentences for users to choose to complete input tasks, means that users can yield coherent text with fewer keystrokes. The challenge is that the input pinyin sequences are too imperfect to support sufficient training. Most existing commercial input methods offer auto-completion to users as well as extended association functions, to aid users input. However, the performance of association function of existing commercial IMEs are unsatisfactory to relevant user requirement for oversimplified modeling.

It is worth mentioning that we delivery Moon IME as a type of IME service rather than a simple IME software because it can be adjusted to adapt to diverse domains with the Association Cloud Platform (Zhang et al., 2018b,c; Zhang and Zhao, 2018), which helps user type long sentences and predicts the whole expected inputs based on customized knowledge bases.

5 Conclusion

This work makes the first attempt at establishing a general cloud platform to provide customizable association services for Chinese pinyin IME as to our best knowledge. We present Moon IME, a pinyin IME that contains a high-quality P2C module and an extended information retrieval based module. The former is based on an attention-based NMT model and the latter contains follow-up-prediction and machine translation module for typing assistance. With a powerful customizable design, the association cloud platform can be adapted to any specific domains including complex specialized terms. Usability analysis shows that core engine achieves comparable conversion quality with the state-of-the-art research models and the association function is stable and can be well adopted by a broad range of users. It is more convenient for predicting complete, extra and even corrected character outputs especially when user input is incomplete or incorrect.

References

Deng Cai, Hai Zhao, Yang Xin, Yuzhu Wang, and Zhongye Jia. 2017a. A hybrid model for Chinese spelling check. In *ACM Transactions on Asian Low-Resource Language Information Process*.

Deng Cai, Hai Zhao, Zhisong Zhang, Yang Xin, Yongjian Wu, and Feiyue Huang. 2017b. Fast and accurate neural word segmentation for Chinese. In *ACL*, pages 608–615.

Jiaxun Cai, Shexia He, Zuchao Li, and Hai Zhao. 2018. A full end-to-end semantic role labeler, syntax-agnostic or syntax-aware? In *COLING*.

Shenyuan Chen, Rui Wang, and Hai Zhao. 2015. Neural network language model for Chinese pinyin input method engine. In *PACLIC-29*, pages 455–461.

Stanley F. Chen. 2003. Conditional and joint models for grapheme-to-phoneme conversion. In *INTERSPEECH*, pages 2033–2036.

Shexia He, Zuchao Li, Hai Zhao, Hongxiao Bai, and Gongshen Liu. 2018. Syntax for semantic role labeling, to be, or not to be. In *ACL*.

Sepp Hochreiter and Jurgen Schmidhuber. 1997. Long short-term memory. *Neural Computation*, 9(8):1735–1780.

Guoping Huang, Jiajun Zhang, Yu Zhou, and Chengqing Zong. 2015. A new input method for human translators: integrating machine translation effectively and imperceptibly. In *IJCAI*, pages 1163–1169.

Zhongye Jia and Hai Zhao. 2013. Kyss 1.0: a framework for automatic evaluation of Chinese input method engines. In *IJCNLP*, pages 1195–1201.

Zhongye Jia and Hai Zhao. 2014. A joint graph model for pinyin-to-Chinese conversion with typo correction. In *ACL*, pages 1512–1523.

Wei Jiang, Yi Guan, Xiao Long Wang, and Bing Quan Liu. 2007. Pinyin to character conversion model based on support vector machines. *Journal of Chinese Information Processing*, 21(2):100–105.

Haonan Li, Zhisong Zhang, yuqi Ju, and Hai Zhao. 2018a. Neural character-level dependency parsing for Chinese. In *AAAI*.

Peng Li, Wei Li, Zhengyan He, Xuguang Wang, Ying Cao, Jie Zhou, and Wei Xu. 2016. Dataset and neural recurrent sequence labeling model for open-domain factoid question answering. *arXiv preprint arXiv:1607.06275v2*.

Zuchao Li, Shexia He, and Hai Zhao. 2018b. Seq2seq dependency parsing. In *COLING*.

Bo Lin and Jun Zhang. 2008. A novel statistical Chinese language model and its application in pinyin-to-character conversion. In *ACM Conference on Information and Knowledge Management*, pages 1433–1434.

Liang Lu, Kong Lingpeng, Chris Dyer, Noah A. Smith, and Steve Renals. 2016. Unfolded recurrent neural networks for speech recognition. In *INTERSPEECH*, pages 385–389.

Minh Thang Luong, Hieu Pham, and Christopher D Manning. 2015. Effective approaches to attention-based neural machine translation. In *EMNLP*, pages 1412–1421.

Tomas Mikolov, Kai Chen, Greg Corrado, and Jeffrey Dean. 2013. Efficient estimation of word representations in vector space. *arXiv preprint arXiv:1301.3781*.

Yoh Okuno and Shinsuke Mori. 2012. An ensemble model of word-based and character-based models for Japanese and Chinese input method. In *CoLING*, pages 15–28.

Chenxi Pang, Hai Zhao, and Zhongyi Li. 2016. I can guess what you mean: A monolingual query enhancement for machine translation. In *CCL*, pages 50–63.

George Saon, Hagen Soltau, Ahmad Emami, and Michael Picheny. 2014. Unfolded recurrent neural networks for speech recognition. In *INTERSPEECH*, pages 343–347.

Rui Wang, Hai Zhao, Bao-Liang Lu, Masao Utiyama, and Eiichiro Sumita. 2016. Connecting phrase based statistical machine translation adaptation. In *CoLING*, pages 3135–3145.

Rui Wang, Hai Zhao, Sabine Ploux, Bao-Liang Lu, Masao Utiyama, and Eiichiro Sumita. 2018. Graph-based bilingual word embedding for statistical machine translation. In *ACM Transaciton on Asian and Low-Resource Language Information Processing*, volume 17.

Yu Wu, Wei Wu, Chen Xing, Zhoujun Li, and Ming Zhou. 2017. Sequential matching network: A new architecture for multi-turn response selection in retrieval-based chatbots. In *ACL*, pages 496–505.

Shaohua Yang, Hai Zhao, and Bao-liang Lu. 2012. A machine translation approach for Chinese whole-sentence pinyin-to-character conversion. In *PACLIC-26*, pages 333–342.

Shiliang Zhang, Cong Liu, Hui Jiang, Si Wei, Lirong Dai, and Yu Hu. 2015. Feedforward sequential memory networks: A new structure to learn long-term dependency. *arXiv preprint arXiv:1512.08301*.

Xihu Zhang, Chu Wei, and Hai Zhao. 2017. Tracing a loose wordhood for Chinese input method engine. *arXiv preprint arXiv:1712.04158*.

Yan Zhang, Bo Xu, and Chengqing Zong. 2006. Rule-based post-processing of pin to Chinese characters conversion system. In *International Symposium on Chinese Spoken Language Processing*, pages 1–4.

Zhuosheng Zhang, Jiangtong Li, Hai Zhao, and Bingjie Tang. 2018a. Sjtu-nlp at semeval-2018 task 9: Neural hypernym discovery with term embeddings. In *SemEval-2018, Workshop of NAACL-HLT*.

Zhuosheng Zhang, Jiangtong Li, Pengfei Zhu, and Hai Zhao. 2018b. Modeling multi-turn conversation with deep utterance aggregation. In *CoLING*.

Zhuosheng Zhang, Huang Yafang, and Hai Zhao. 2018c. Subword-augmented embedding for cloze reading comprehension. In *CoLING*.

Zhuosheng Zhang and Hai Zhao. 2018. One-shot learning for question-answering in gaokao history challenge. In *CoLING*.

Hai Zhao, Chang-Ning Huang, Mu Li, and Taku Kudo. 2006. An improved Chinese word segmentation system with conditional random field. In *Sighan*, pages 162–165.

Author Index

Association for Computational Linguistics
209 N. Eighth Street
Stroudsburg, Pennsylvania 18360